Guided Comprehension

IN ACTION

LESSONS FOR GRADES 3–8

Maureen McLaughlin
East Stroudsburg University of Pennsylvania
East Stroudsburg, Pennsylvania, USA

Mary Beth Allen
East Stroudsburg University of Pennsylvania
East Stroudsburg, Pennsylvania, USA

INTERNATIONAL
Reading
Association

800 Barksdale Road, PO Box 8139
Newark, Delaware 19714-8139, USA
www.reading.org

The International Reading Association attempts, through its publications, to provide a forum for a wide spectrum of opinions on reading. This policy permits divergent viewpoints without implying the endorsement of the Association.

Director of Publications Joan M. Irwin
Editorial Director, Books and Special Projects Matthew W. Baker
Senior Editor, Books and Special Projects Tori Mello Bachman
Permissions Editor Janet S. Parrack
Production Editor Shannon Benner
Assistant Editor Corinne M. Mooney
Editorial Assistant Tyanna L. Collins
Publications Manager Beth Doughty
Production Department Manager Iona Sauscermen
Supervisor, Electronic Publishing Anette Schütz
Senior Electronic Publishing Specialist Cheryl J. Strum
Electronic Publishing Specialist R. Lynn Harrison
Proofreader Charlene M. Nichols

Project Editors Matthew W. Baker and Shannon Benner

Art Credits Cover Design, Linda Steere
Cover Photo, PhotoDisc

Library of Congress Cataloging-in-Publication Data
McLaughlin, Maureen.
   Guided comprehension in action : lessons for grades 3-8 / Maureen McLaughlin, Mary Beth Allen.
     p.   cm.
Designed to complement authors' Guided comprehension.
Includes bibliographical references and index.
   ISBN 0-87207-343-2
1. Reading comprehension--Study and teaching (Elementary)--United States.
  2. Reading (Elementary)--United States--Curricula. I. Allen, Mary Beth, 1957- II. McLaughlin, Maureen. Guided comprehension. III. Title.
LB1573.7 .M37 2002
372.47--dc21

                                         2002001514

Sixth Printing, July 2006   Printed in Canada

CONTENTS

PREFACE

As literacy professionals we know that readers use a repertoire of strategies to comprehend text. One of our persistent challenges is teaching these strategies to our students. Guided Comprehension, a context in which students learn comprehension strategies in a variety of settings using multiple levels and types of text, provides a viable teaching framework. This three-stage process focuses on direct instruction, application (teacher-guided small groups, comprehension centers, and comprehension routines), and reflection.

In *Guided Comprehension: A Teaching Model for Grades 3–8* (McLaughlin & Allen, 2002), we presented the research-based Guided Comprehension Model and discussed its implementation. We also provided all the resources necessary to implement Guided Comprehension: teaching ideas, forms to facilitate organization and management, literature response prompts, leveled book resources, and informal assessments. We have designed *Guided Comprehension in Action: Lessons for Grades 3–8* as a complement to that volume.

In this book we extend the application of Guided Comprehension in grades 3–8 by situating it within theme-based curriculums. Each of the theme-based chapters features an overview as well as teacher-designed, classroom-tested Guided Comprehension plans and lessons. The Guided Comprehension plans provide outlines of the lessons, while the narratives recount the actual teaching experiences. A number of grade 3–8 teachers who use Guided Comprehension in their classrooms, including those who participated in our original research study, contributed to the design and implementation of the lessons. The teacher-authored narratives describe what actually transpired as the lessons took place.

We have divided this book into eight chapters. Chapter 1 provides an overview of Guided Comprehension and describes its application within theme-based curriculums. In Chapters 2 through 7 we situate Guided Comprehension in a variety of themes: multiple perspectives, mysteries, favorite authors, poetry, biography and autobiography, and fantasy. Each of the theme-based chapters includes the following components:

- theme description
- theme-based plan for Guided Comprehension
- four Guided Comprehension planning forms
- four Guided Comprehension lessons
- teacher-authored lesson commentaries
- samples of student work
- theme-based resources including related texts, websites, performance extensions across the curriculum, and culminating activities

In Chapter 8, we suggest additional themes and resources that can be used when planning and teaching Guided Comprehension. We also provide practical forms for planning themes and lessons based on the Guided Comprehension Model.

Descriptions of those teaching ideas that are not delineated in *Guided Comprehension: A Teaching Model for Grades 3–8* and blackline masters to support strategy applications in the theme-based lessons are presented in the Appendix.

We have developed this book as a resource for teaching comprehension strategies. It contains a wide variety of theme-based plans, lessons, and resources to facilitate implementing the Guided Comprehension Model in grade 3–8 classrooms.

ACKNOWLEDGMENTS

As always, there are many people to thank for making this book possible. We express our appreciation to all who contributed to the manuscript's development as well as all who enhanced the quality of our lives during the research and writing process. We thank them for their insight, their understanding, and their support.

We are particularly grateful to the following people:

- all the teachers who participated in our research study and contributed to this book—especially Susan Sillivan, Katie Moran, Liz Sisco, Betsy Paugh, Mary Ellen Rock, Julie Mignosi, Mary Galayda, Cynthia Jordan, Wayne Koberlein, Karen Metzger, Amy Homeyer, Jennifer Sassaman, Kathleen Andreas, Deborah Butchkoski, Dorothy Conway, Lou DeLauro, Sharon Gilroy, Howard Gregory, Heather Gress, Christine Heath, Julia Klein, Barbara Lynch, Judith Mesko, Stacey Olewine, Jennifer Pullis, Linda Dickinson, Maryann Calpin, Colleen Connors, Elizabeth Boyer, Kristine Maziarz, Sara Nero, Amy Pinkerton, and Valerie Shaffer—and their students

- our graduate assistants, Katie Moran, Judy Mesko, Jean Sandberg, and Amanda Sandt

- our colleagues and our students

- our families and friends

- Shannon Benner, Production Editor, International Reading Association

- Matt Baker, Editorial Director, International Reading Association

Finally, we thank you, our readers, for joining us in our search for effective ways to teach reading comprehension strategies. We hope that you find this book to be a valuable companion to *Guided Comprehension: A Teaching Model for Grades 3–8* and that both volumes help you to enhance your students' understanding of text.

MM and MBA

CHAPTER 1

Situating Guided Comprehension in Theme-Based Curriculums

A quality context is an integral facet of meaningful literacy instruction. Lipson and Wixson (1997) describe context as a broad concept that encompasses instructional settings, resources, approaches, and tasks. Duke (2001) suggests we expand our perception of context to include curriculum, activity, classroom environment, teaching, talk, text, and society. Researchers and practitioners agree that both teaching and learning are greatly influenced by the contextual choices we make.

The current view of reading comprehension instruction is based on the understanding that comprehension strategies can be taught. Duffy (2001) suggests that direct explanation of strategies includes teacher think-alouds. Pearson (2001), while noting the importance of direct instruction, also suggests that teachers release responsibility quickly and encourage active responding on the part of the students. Other influential factors include reader engagement, exposure and access, discussion, writing, and a strong base in decoding, monitoring, and fluency (Duke, 2001). All of these components are represented in the Guided Comprehension Model.

In this chapter we describe Guided Comprehension, a context for meaningful comprehension instruction, and discuss how to situate it within a variety of themes. We begin by defining Guided Comprehension and briefly delineating its theoretical underpinnings. Then we provide background information about curriculum integration and thematic teaching. Finally, we demonstrate how to link the two concepts, and we provide a graphic organizer to facilitate this process.

WHAT IS GUIDED COMPREHENSION?

The ultimate goal of reading instruction is to help students use a repertoire of strategies to comprehend text. In order to achieve this goal, we need to teach students comprehension strategies and a variety of ways to use them while reading. To facilitate this process, we developed the Guided Comprehension Model (see Figure 1). Guided Comprehension is "a context in which students learn comprehension strategies in a variety of settings using multiple levels and types of text" (McLaughlin & Allen, 2002, p. 3). It is a three-stage process (see Figure 2). Teacher-directed whole-group

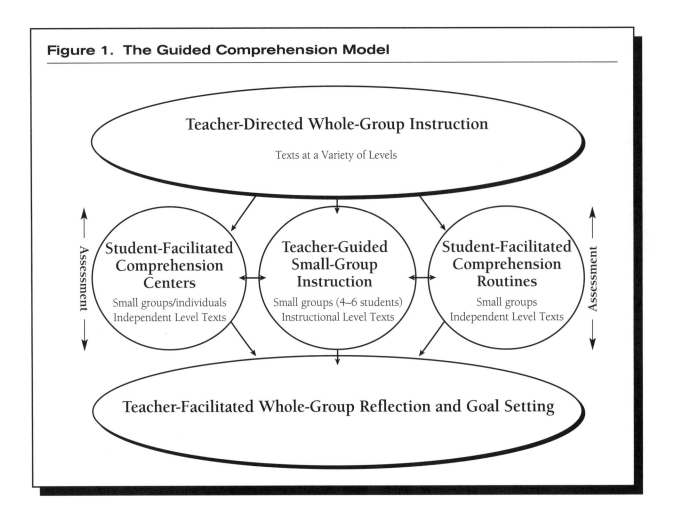

Figure 1. The Guided Comprehension Model

Teacher-Directed Whole-Group Instruction

Texts at a Variety of Levels

Assessment

Student-Facilitated Comprehension Centers

Small groups/individuals
Independent Level Texts

Teacher-Guided Small-Group Instruction

Small groups (4–6 students)
Instructional Level Texts

Student-Facilitated Comprehension Routines

Small groups
Independent Level Texts

Assessment

Teacher-Facilitated Whole-Group Reflection and Goal Setting

instruction is the focus of Stage One. In this phase, the teacher engages in direct explanation of the comprehension strategies and related teaching ideas. Because the teacher reads the text in this stage, it can be at an easy, just right, or challenging level. Teacher-guided small-group instruction, comprehension centers, and comprehension routines characterize Stage Two. The teacher uses texts at students' instructional levels to guide students to apply the comprehension strategies. Students use texts at their independent levels when they apply the strategies in comprehension centers and routines. Teacher-facilitated whole-group reflection and goal setting occurs in Stage Three.

Guided Comprehension is based on the following research-based tenets (McLaughlin & Allen, 2002, p. 6):

- Comprehension is a social constructivist process.
- Balanced literacy is a curriculum framework that fosters comprehension.
- Excellent reading teachers influence students' learning.
- Good readers are strategic and take active roles in the reading process.
- Reading should occur in meaningful contexts.
- Students benefit from transacting with a variety of texts at multiple levels.

Figure 2. Overview of Guided Comprehension Instruction

STAGE ONE

Teacher-Directed Whole-Group Instruction—Teaching a comprehension strategy using easy, instructional, or challenging text.

> **Explain** the strategy of the day and how it relates to the class goal.
>
> **Demonstrate** the strategy using a think-aloud and a read-aloud.
>
> **Guide** student practice by reading additional sections of text aloud and having students apply the strategy with support. Monitor students' applications.
>
> **Practice** by having students apply the strategy to another section of text you have read, providing minimal support. Applications can occur in small groups or pairs.
>
> **Reflect** by having students think about how they can use this strategy with texts they are reading on their own.

STAGE TWO

Students apply the comprehension strategies in teacher-guided small groups and student-facilitated comprehension centers and routines. In these settings, students work with varying levels of support and use appropriate instructional and independent level texts.

Teacher-Guided Small-Group Instruction—Applying comprehension strategies with teacher guidance using instructional level texts and dynamic grouping (4 to 6 students).

> **Review** previously taught strategies and focus on the strategy of the day.
>
> **Guide** the students to apply the strategy of the day as well as previously taught strategies as they read a section of the instructional level text. Prompt the students to construct personal meanings. Scaffold as necessary, gradually releasing support as students become more proficient. Encourage discussion and repeat with other sections of text.
>
> **Practice** by having students work in pairs or individually to apply the strategy. Have students record their applications in their Guided Comprehension Journals and share them during reflection in either small group or whole group.
>
> **Reflect and extend** by having students share ways in which the strategy helped them to understand the text. Talk about ways in which students can apply the strategy in the comprehension centers and routines.

Student-Facilitated Comprehension Centers and Routines—Applying comprehension strategies individually, in pairs, or in small groups with independent level texts.

> **Comprehension centers** are independent activities to practice strategy application and extend understandings.
>
> **Comprehension routines** are procedures that foster habits of thinking that promote comprehension of text.

STAGE THREE

Teacher-Facilitated Whole-Group Reflection and Goal Setting—Reflecting on performance, sharing experiences, and setting new goals.

ASSESSMENT OPTIONS

Use authentic measures in all stages.

- Vocabulary development and instruction affect reading comprehension.
- Engagement is a key factor in the comprehension process.
- Comprehension strategies and skills can be taught.
- Dynamic assessment informs comprehension instruction.

Guided Comprehension provides a framework for teaching that focuses on the following eight strategies (McLaughlin & Allen, 2002, pp. 13–14):

- previewing—activating background knowledge, predicting, and setting a purpose
- self-questioning—generating questions to guide reading
- making connections—relating reading to self, text, and world
- visualizing—creating mental pictures of the text while reading
- knowing how words work—understanding words through strategic vocabulary development, including the use of the graphophonic, syntactic, and semantic cueing systems to figure out unknown words
- monitoring—asking "Does this make sense?" and clarifying by adapting strategic processes to accommodate the response
- summarizing—synthesizing important ideas
- evaluating—making judgments

A variety of skills—including generating questions, sequencing, distinguishing between important and less important ideas, and making generalizations—underpin these strategies. To help students understand what each strategy is, how it functions, and when it might be used, we engage in direct and guided instruction using an assortment of teaching ideas and multiple types of text at varied levels.

In Guided Comprehension, teachers and students are active participants in the reading process. Teachers direct instruction in a whole-group setting, guide instruction in small-group settings, and facilitate reflection and goal setting. Students take an active role in each of these settings and also independently apply the strategies in comprehension centers and routines. Students share their independent applications and engage in self-assessment in the reflection and goal-setting stage. (For more detailed information about Guided Comprehension, including descriptions of each stage of the Model and a wide variety of teaching resources, see *Guided Comprehension: A Teaching Model for Grades 3–8*.)

CURRICULUM INTEGRATION AND THEME-BASED INSTRUCTION

Curriculum integration is a way of thinking that focuses on larger concepts and issues rather than isolated facts and fragmented information. It views learning as the continuous integration of knowledge and experience and promotes the active construction of personal meaning. The goal of this curricular framework is not the abandonment of discipline-specific knowledge, but rather the construction of an integrated knowledge base (Beane, 1995; Lipson, Valencia, Wixson, & Peters 1993; Shanahan, 1997).

Although there are a variety of ways to integrate curriculums, the thematic approach is the one used most frequently (Lipson et al., 1993). According to Meinbach, Rothlein, and Fredericks (2000), "A thematic approach to learning offers students a realistic arena in which they can pursue learning using a host of contexts and a panorama of literature" (p. 10). These authors suggest the following ideas are characteristic of the thematic approach:

- It combines structured, sequential, and well-organized strategies, activities, literature, and materials to expand a particular concept.
- It is multidisciplinary and multidimensional.
- It is responsive to the interests, abilities, and needs of children and is respectful of their developing aptitudes and attitudes.

Theme-based learning benefits both teachers and students. Instructional advantages include developing natural connections between and among subjects, integrating language arts across the curriculum, exploring concepts in depth, promoting problem solving and critical thinking, and developing a community of learners. Advantages for students include a process-oriented, student-centered curriculum, deeper understanding, opportunities for risk-taking, an integrated knowledge base, and sustained time for inquiry, performance, and reflection (Lipson et al., 1993; Meinbach et al., 2000).

Meaningful themes need to be well conceived and well organized. The following steps facilitate the development of themes that engage students and enhance their knowledge (Lipson et al., 1993; Meinbach et al., 2000; Shanahan, 1997; Shanahan, Robinson, & Schneider, 1995):

- Base themes on ideas that express a position or perspective.
- Integrate the subjects that naturally relate to the theme.
- Develop clearly stated goals.
- Provide instruction throughout the theme.
- Focus on themes, not activities.
- Work toward developing an integrated knowledge base.
- Use your knowledge of your students and good professional judgment.

INTEGRATING GUIDED COMPREHENSION AND THEMATIC INSTRUCTION

One of the important aspects of theme-based instruction is the opportunity for students to experience teaching, guidance, and practice within the theme (Shanahan, 1997). Guided Comprehension readily accommodates this. It provides a viable means for integrating both direct and guided strategy-based reading instruction. It also uses multiple types of theme-related texts written at a variety of levels and provides multiple opportunities for students to practice in a variety of settings. Guided Comprehension enhances theme-based teaching by providing a framework for strategy integration.

SITUATING GUIDED COMPREHENSION IN THEME-BASED CURRICULUMS

In Chapters 2 through 7, we situate Guided Comprehension within a variety of themes. Figure 3 presents an overview of the themes, including the comprehension strategies and teaching ideas that are embedded in each lesson.

To facilitate this view of theme-based instruction, we have provided a planning graphic (see Figure 4). The organizer is based on the concept of backward design (Wiggins & McTighe, 1998), which espouses beginning the planning process by identifying the desired results. We have expressed our desired results as the theme's goals and resulting connections to state standards. The second step in backward design is determining acceptable evidences. The final step is planning teaching and learning experiences, including appropriate texts and resources. Samples of the following components are included in the theme-based planning organizers that appear at the start of each chapter:

Figure 3. Overview of Strategies and Teaching Ideas in Chapters 2–7

Lesson	1	2	3	4
Chapter				
2	Making Connections: Double-Entry Journals	Monitoring: Mind Portraits	Evaluating: Contrast Charts	Evaluating: Thinking Hats
3	Previewing: Probable Passages	Monitoring: Say Something	Summarizing: Lyric Summaries	Summarizing: Mystery Cubes
4	Making Connections: Save the Last Word for Me	Knowing How Words Work: Context Clues	Summarizing: Comic Strip Summaries	Evaluating: Evaluative Questioning
5	Previewing: That Was Then... This Is Now	Visualizing: Photographs of the Mind	Knowing How Words Work: Diamantes	Knowing How Words Work: Text Transformations
6	Self-Questioning: Thick and Thin Questions	Making Connections: Biography/ Autobiography Organizer	Summarizing: Bio-Cubes	Summarizing: Bio-Pyramids
7	Previewing: Story Impressions	Self-Questioning: "I Wonder" Statements	Visualizing: Drawing Visualizations	Summarizing: Narrative Pyramids

Figure 4. Sample Theme-Based Plan for Guided Comprehension

Goals and Connections to State Standards

Assessment
The following measures can be used for a variety of purposes, including diagnostic, formative, and summative assessment:

Comprehension Strategies	Teaching Ideas

Text	Title	Theme	Level

Comprehension Centers
Students will apply the comprehension strategies and related teaching ideas in the following comprehension centers:

Technology Resources

Comprehension Routines
Students will apply the comprehension strategies and related teaching ideas in the following comprehension routines:

- goals and connections to state standards
- assessments
- texts (themes and levels)
- technology resources
- comprehension strategies and teaching ideas
- comprehension centers
- comprehension routines

The following six chapters illustrate the Guided Comprehension–thematic teaching connection. Integration of the arts, multiple modes of response, critical and creative thinking, and multiple literacies characterize the strategy-based lessons in which both teachers and students take active roles. The final chapter provides resources for situating Guided Comprehension in a variety of other themes.

CHAPTER 2

Multiple Perspectives: Alternative Voices, Alternative Visions

xpressing ideas from a variety of perspectives challenges us to expand our thinking and discover diverse beliefs, positions, and understandings. Appreciation for and exploration of these alternative perceptions fosters and facilitates our viewing situations from a critical stance.

Questions we ponder when thinking critically about text include the following (G. DeVoogd, personal communication, November 16, 2001; C. Harrison, personal communication, September 13, 2001; Hobbs, 1996; McLaughlin & Bean, 2001):

- What is the author or photographer trying to make us think about the situation?
- What meanings do different people see in the words or images?
- How does language shape the meaning of the images?
- What might have been the effects if the information had been communicated differently?
- Whose voices are missing, silenced, or discounted?
- What would an alternative narrative or visual be?

As Harrison (2001) has noted,

> Such analyses lead to students gaining a thoughtful, critical and better-informed personal understanding not only of the events that occurred, but also of the ways in which it is impossible to represent "reality" without an editorial bias—and then to more informed understanding of how meaning is made for us in our world.

In this chapter, we explore multiple viewpoints through a variety of genres including letters, diaries, books, photos, and hypertext. Our goal is to use strategies, texts, and in-depth thinking to discover and acknowledge voices and visions that have been missing, silenced, or discounted. The situations we explore range from fairy tales to wars.

The Sample Theme-Based Plan for Guided Comprehension: Multiple Perspectives (see Figure 5) presents a sampling of goals, state standards, assessments, texts, technology resources, comprehension strategies, teaching ideas, comprehension centers, and comprehension routines. The plan begins by delineating examples of student goals and related state standards. The student goals for this theme include the following:

- using appropriate comprehension strategies
- analyzing, evaluating, and critiquing a variety of information sources
- communicating effectively

These goals support the following state standards:

- learning to read independently
- researching
- reading critically in the content areas
- reading, analyzing, and interpreting literature
- types and quality of writing
- speaking and listening

Observation, a variety of strategy applications, and student self-assessments are examples of the dynamic assessments used during Guided Comprehension. The following are the comprehension strategies and related teaching ideas on which the lessons are based:

- Making Connections: Double-Entry Journals
- Monitoring: Mind Portraits
- Evaluating: Contrast Charts
- Evaluating: Thinking Hats

The texts used in teacher-directed whole-group instruction include *If a Bus Could Talk: The Story of Rosa Parks*, *War Letters: Extraordinary Correspondence From American Wars*, *The True Story of the 3 Little Pigs!*, and *Bull Run*. Numerous additional theme-related texts, including those used in teacher-guided small-group instruction and the student-facilitated comprehension centers and routines, are featured in the Theme Resources at the end of the chapter.

Comprehension centers used in the Guided Comprehension lessons include art, multiple perspectives, music, research and technology, and writing. Descriptions of strategy applications in these and other centers are delineated in the lesson plan narratives. Comprehension routines, which provide another setting in which students can apply the strategies, include Literature Circles, Questioning the Author, and Reciprocal Teaching.

Figure 5. Sample Theme-Based Plan for Guided Comprehension: Multiple Perspectives

Goals and Connections to State Standards | Students will

- use appropriate comprehension strategies. Standard: learning to read independently
- analyze, evaluate, and critique a variety of information sources. Standards: researching; reading critically in content areas; reading, analyzing, and interpreting literature
- communicate effectively. Standards: types and quality of writing; speaking and listening

Assessment

The following measures can be used for a variety of purposes, including diagnostic, formative, and summative assessment:

Observation   *We Were There* trifold
Mind Portraits   Contrast Charts
Mind Posters   Student Self-Assessments
Double-Entry Journals

Text	Title	Theme	Level
1.	*If a Bus Could Talk: The Story of Rosa Parks*	MP	3
2.	*War Letters: Extraordinary Correspondence From American Wars*	MP	7
3.	*The True Story of the 3 Little Pigs!*	MP	3
4.	*Bull Run*	MP	6

Technology Resources

EyeWitness: History Through the Eyes of Those Who Lived It
    www.ibiscom.com
Media Literacy Clearinghouse
    www.med.sc.edu/medialit
Women Were There
    userpages.aug.com/captbarb/femvets2.html

Comprehension Strategies

1. Making Connections
2. Monitoring
3. Evaluating
4. Evaluating

Teaching Ideas

Double-Entry Journals
Mind Portraits
Contrast Charts
Thinking Hats

Comprehension Centers

Students will apply the comprehension strategies and related teaching ideas in the following comprehension centers:

Art Center   Research and Technology Center
Multiple Perspectives Center   Writing Center
Music Center

Comprehension Routines

Students will apply the comprehension strategies and related teaching ideas in the following comprehension routines:

Literature Circles
Questioning the Author
Reciprocal Teaching

GUIDED COMPREHENSION LESSONS

Guided Comprehension Strategy: Making Connections
Teaching Idea: Double-Entry Journals

STAGE ONE: Teacher-Guided Whole-Group Instruction

Text: *If a Bus Could Talk: The Story of Rosa Parks* (Ringgold, 1999)

Explain: I began by engaging in direct explanation of making connections, noting that the connections we make are usually text-self, text-text, and text-world. Then I delineated the multiple purposes of Double-Entry Journals and explained that we would be using them to make connections before and during reading.

Demonstrate: I used an overhead to share a Double-Entry Journal planning form (see Appendix A, *Guided Comprehension: A Teaching Model for Grades 3–8*), noting the two-column structure and the labels we would be using for each. The left column was "Ideas From the Text" and the right was "My Connections." Next, I used a think-aloud to share my connections to *If a Bus Could Talk: The Story of Rosa Parks*. I began by thinking aloud about the cover, the title, the dedication, and the first two pages of the story. I thought aloud about several ideas from the text, which I recorded in the left column of the Double-Entry Journal (see Figure 6). As I spoke, I noted my connections in the right column and labeled each text-self, text-text, or text-world. I began with the title, noting my personal connection that when I have ridden in buses they haven't been able to talk. I also shared my thinking about the bus's appearance, the young girl and woman on the cover, and the two print references to Rosa Parks. Then I read the dedication about the Civil Rights movement and made text-self, text-text, and text-world connections. These included my memories of living through that time period as a child, my knowledge of Martin Luther King, Jr., and books such as *Martin's Big Words*, *Martin Luther King*, *The Century for Young People*, and *The African-American Century*. The dedication talked about acts of courage, so I made a text-self connection and thought aloud about what courage means to me. I continued to record ideas and connections on the journal form.

Guide: Students joined in at this point, offering their personal definitions of courage. This resulted in an interesting discussion. Their definitions included bravery, valor, and heroism. They offered examples from their own lives as well as historical events. I explained that they were making text-self and text-world connections and that they should continue to make those and text-text connections as I continued to read. I added a few of their ideas to our Double-Entry Journal. Then I read aloud the section of the book that describes Rosa Parks's childhood and guided students to work in pairs to jot their personal connections to ideas from the text that I had provided. When I finished reading, we discussed the ideas and their connections. Then I asked the pairs of students to choose another important idea from the text and make connections. They focused on ideas such as "one-room schoolhouse," and we discussed their connections.

Practice: Students practiced by recording ideas and connections as I read aloud the rest of the story. The ideas from the text that students recorded included Rosa Parks's arrest and subsequent struggles, the death of Martin Luther King, and the celebration of Rosa's birthday. Connections

GUIDED COMPREHENSION: MULTIPLE PERSPECTIVES
MAKING CONNECTIONS: DOUBLE-ENTRY JOURNALS

Teacher-Directed Whole-Group Instruction

- **Explain** making connections and using Double-Entry Journals. Note that this is just one of the purposes for which Double-Entry Journals can be used.
- **Demonstrate** how to use a Double-Entry Journal to record ideas from the text in one column and personal connections in another. Use a think-aloud, read-aloud, and an overhead projector or chalkboard.
- **Guide** pairs of students to use Double-Entry Journals. Provide copies of Double-Entry Journal pages to students. Continue to read aloud and invite students to contribute. Discuss.
- **Practice** by having students complete Double-Entry Journals. Finish reading the story and have students record two ideas and the personal connections they made. Discuss.
- **Reflect** on how making connections helped us comprehend and how we can use Double-Entry Journals in other settings.

Student-Facilitated Comprehension Routines

- **Literature Circles:** Work with a partner to create Double-Entry Journals by selecting quotations from the chapter and making personal connections. Use as the basis of discussion.
- **Questioning the Author:** Record your questions for the author in a Triple-Entry Journal and make personal and author connections.
- **Reciprocal Teaching:** Use a Double-Entry Journal format in the monitoring phase by recording ideas from the story and making connections. Discuss your choices and reasoning with your group.

Teacher-Guided Small-Group Instruction

- **Review** the comprehension strategies that good readers use and focus on making connections by using Double-Entry Journals.
- **Guide** students to begin reading *Witness*, stopping to record ideas and personal connections on the journal form. Discuss.
- **Practice** by having students finish reading the rest of the chapter and create Double-Entry Journals containing text ideas and personal connections. Discuss.
- **Reflect** on how Double-Entry Journals helped us make connections and how we can use them with other texts we read.

Student-Facilitated Comprehension Centers

- **Multiple Perspectives Center:** With a partner, select and read a first person account. Use the information to create a trifold for our If We Had Been There... Gallery.
- **Art Center:** Read first person accounts from texts provided. Complete Double-Entry Journals and use as the basis for creating double-sided mobiles. On side one, include information from reading; on side two, tell what you would have done if you had lived at that time in history.

Teacher-Facilitated Whole-Group Reflection and Goal Setting

- **Share** completed journal entries and assess ability to use them to make connections.
- **Reflect** on how Double-Entry Journals helped us make connections.
- **Set new goals** or extend existing ones.

Guided Comprehension in Action: Lessons for Grades 3–8 by Maureen McLaughlin and Mary Beth Allen ©2002. Newark, DE: International Reading Association. May be copied for classroom use.

Figure 6. Double-Entry Journal

Ideas From the Text	My Connections
Title and cover illustration: *If a Bus Could Talk: The Story of Rosa Parks*	The buses I have ridden on have not been able to talk. They also have not had painted faces as the one on the cover does. Type of Connection: Text-self (mine) I know Rosa Parks did something courageous and it happened on a bus. Type of Connection: Text-world (mine)
The dedication is about the Civil Rights movement.	I remember seeing Martin Luther King and news about the Civil Rights movement on television when I was a child. Type of Connection: Text-self (mine) I have read books related to this topic such as *Martin's Big Words, The Century for Young People,* and *The African-American Century.* Type of Connection: Text-text (mine)
The dedication talks about courage.	Courage to me means doing what you believe in, no matter what happens. Type of Connection: Text-self (mine) Courage is bravery, valor, and heroism. Type of Connection: Text-self (students') Many courageous people helped on 9/11/01. Type of Connection: Text-world (students')
Rosa Parks's childhood: Ku Klux Klan Differences in schools	The Ku Klux Klan did scary things like burning churches and houses. Type of Connection: Text-world (students') Black children's schools were more crowded and farther away than ours. Type of Connection: Text-self (students')
One-room schoolhouse	Our great grandparents went to school in one-room schoolhouses. Type of Connection: Text-self (students') It's like the school in the Little House on the Prairie stories. Type of Connection: Text-text (students')

they made ranged from sadness over her arrest and King's death to their knowledge of arrests from current news reports and their personal experiences with birthdays.

Reflect: We reflected both on the life of Rosa Parks and on how making connections helped us to understand what we read. The students liked that the book told about Parks as a child as well as an adult. They thought that making connections helped them to understand that their perspective was valuable. Finally, we talked about how we would make connections using Double-Entry Journals with other types of books in other settings. Students enjoyed making connections and did a good job creating their journal entries. An excerpt from our group Double-Entry Journal is featured in Figure 6.

STAGE TWO: Teacher-Guided Small-Group Instruction

Text: *Witness* (Hesse, 2001) (Texts varied according to students' abilities.)

Review: I reminded students about the comprehension strategies good readers use and focused on using Double-Entry Journals to make connections. We discussed text-self, text-text, and text-world connections, noting student-created examples from Stage One of Guided Comprehension.

Guide: I introduced *Witness*, a novel that presents multiple perspectives of the Ku Klux Klan in a small town. Students immediately noted connections to the legal meaning of the title. They also made connections to the photographs on the cover, the setting, the introduction of the characters, and the format of the book. They recorded these ideas and connections, which included text-text connections between the topic of this book and an illustration of the Ku Klux Klan in *If a Bus Could Talk* on their Double-Entry Journal forms. We discussed these entries. Next, I explained to the students that we were going to read aloud because the book is formatted in the style of a play. We chose roles, and we took a few minutes to review the section of the text we would be reading. Then we began reading. As we read, we noted at least two ideas from the text and recorded our connections. Then we discussed our additional entries and connections.

Practice: Students practiced by completing their Double-Entry Journals as we finished reading that section of the book. They seemed to enjoy doing this, and we discussed the journal entries when they were completed.

Reflect: We reflected on how Double-Entry Journals helped us to make connections and talked about how we could use this technique with narrative and expository texts.

Student-Facilitated Comprehension Centers

Multiple Perspectives Center: Students created *We Were There* trifolds. They worked with partners to read self-selected entries from *We Were There, Too: Young People in American History*. They completed Double-Entry Journals and used that information for the trifold projects. In the center section of the trifold, they recorded the information about the person they had read about, including name, situation, major accomplishment, and illustration. On the left and right sections of the trifold, each of the partners wrote what he or she would have done if in that situation. These sections were also illustrated. The trifolds were then discussed with another pair and hung in our If We Had Been There... Gallery.

Art Center: Students read self-selected first person accounts from *The Century for Young People*, *We Were There, Too*, or other texts. They completed Double-Entry Journals as they read and then used these to create double-sided mobiles. On side one, they listed major points of information about the person they read about. On side two, they listed major points of information about what they would have done if they had been in that situation. They shared their completed mobiles with another student and then hung them in our If We Had Been There... Gallery. The information from both sides of Delia's mobile is featured in Figure 7.

Student-Facilitated Comprehension Routines

Literature Circles: Students recorded selected quotations from the books they were reading on the left side of their Double-Entry Journals and their connections on the right side. They used these as the basis of their group discussion.

Questioning the Author: Students used Triple-Entry Journals (see Appendix, page 164) by recording their author queries in the left column and their reason for raising those questions in the center. As they discussed the completed portions of the journal entries, they reasoned through ideas the author may have used to respond to their queries. They recorded these in the right column.

Reciprocal Teaching: Students used Double-Entry Journals to record ideas from the text and their connections as they were reading. Then they shared and discussed this information during the clarifying and summarizing phases of Reciprocal Teaching.

Figure 7. Delia's Double-Sided Mobile

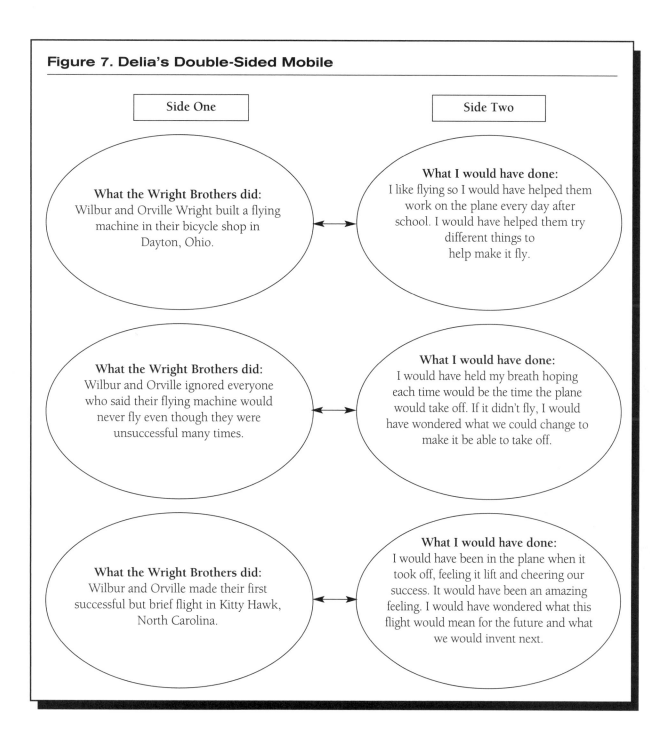

| Side One | Side Two |

What the Wright Brothers did:
Wilbur and Orville Wright built a flying machine in their bicycle shop in Dayton, Ohio.

What I would have done:
I like flying so I would have helped them work on the plane every day after school. I would have helped them try different things to help make it fly.

What the Wright Brothers did:
Wilbur and Orville ignored everyone who said their flying machine would never fly even though they were unsuccessful many times.

What I would have done:
I would have held my breath hoping each time would be the time the plane would take off. If it didn't fly, I would have wondered what we could change to make it be able to take off.

What the Wright Brothers did:
Wilbur and Orville made their first successful but brief flight in Kitty Hawk, North Carolina.

What I would have done:
I would have been in the plane when it took off, feeling it lift and cheering our success. It would have been an amazing feeling. I would have wondered what this flight would mean for the future and what we would invent next.

STAGE THREE: Teacher-Facilitated Whole-Group Reflection and Goal Setting

Share: We began by sharing Double-Entry Journal applications from Stage Two. Students especially enjoyed journeying through our If We Had Been There... Gallery. They made connections to the exhibits and discussed them with a partner. Next we talked about our abilities to make connections using the Double-Entry Journal technique. All the students seemed confident in their abilities, and their applications from Stage Two supported their thinking.

Reflect: Then we reflected on how Double-Entry Journals helped us to make the three different kinds of connections and how that helped us understand what we read. Students also talked about how we could use Double-Entry Journals with all kinds of text including poetry, plays, song lyrics, newspaper articles, and hypertext.

Set New Goals: Feeling confident with our ability to use Double-Entry Journals, we decided to extend our goal about making connections to another technique.

Assessment Options

Observation and review of students' Double-Entry Journal entries, trifolds, and mobiles informed my understanding of students' abilities to use this strategy.

Guided Comprehension Strategy: Monitoring
Teaching Idea: Mind Portraits

STAGE ONE: Teacher-Directed Whole-Group Instruction

Text: *War Letters: Extraordinary Correspondence From American Wars* (Carroll, 2001)

Explain: I began by explaining how monitoring works as a comprehension strategy and how creating Mind Portraits and Alternative Mind Portraits (see Appendix, page 159) helps us monitor our reading.

Demonstrate: I demonstrated by reading aloud a Civil War soldier's letter to his father from *War Letters: Extraordinary Correspondence from American Wars* using a think-aloud and an overhead projector. Because the students were familiar with letters as an information source, I offered just a brief introduction to the 1862 letter. Then I read the letter aloud and thought aloud about the letter's message and what it was telling us about the author. When I finished reading, I sketched an outline of the soldier's head and jotted phrases describing his thinking inside the outline to complete the Mind Portrait. Then I modeled how to create an Alternative Mind Portrait, which presents the situation from a different perspective. I chose to do the Alternative Mind Portrait about the soldier's father. I sketched an outline of a head and wrote phrases describing the father's thinking inside. Then the students and I discussed what we learned from the perspectives of the soldier and his father, and brainstormed other perspectives from which the soldier's letter could be viewed.

Guide: I guided students to complete a Mind Portrait by reading aloud another soldier's letter. As I read, students jotted ideas to include in the portrait. When I finished reading, we discussed the thoughts they had recorded. Then I wrote their ideas inside a portrait outline. Next, I guided students to construct Alternative Mind Portraits. We began by choosing perspectives on which to focus. Students chose a variety of people: fathers, mothers, sisters, brothers, grandparents, and friends. Two of the students chose to use the perspective of soldiers fighting for the opposition. We labeled the Alternative Mind Portraits and described the perspective by jotting phrases inside the portrait outline. Then students shared their portraits, commenting on the perspective and why they chose it.

Practice: I read another soldier's letter, and students practiced by working in pairs to create Mind and Alternative Mind Portraits using outline forms I had provided (see Appendix, page 165). Kevin and Karen created a Mind Portrait of the soldier and an Alternative Mind Portrait of the soldier's brother who was at home because he was too young to fight in the war (see Figure 8). Students shared their portraits and discussed their efforts.

Reflect: We concluded Stage One by reflecting on how examining multiple perspectives helped us to monitor our understanding. Then we talked about how we could use portraits in other settings.

STAGE TWO: Teacher-Guided Small-Group Instruction

Text: *Dear Mr. Blueberry* (James, 1991) (Texts varied according to students' abilities.)

Review: I began by reviewing the comprehension strategies good readers use and focused on monitoring by using Mind Portraits.

Guide: I guided students to create Mind Portraits based on *Dear Mr. Blueberry*. I guided their reading of the text and invited them to focus on the character Emily to create their portraits. We shared and discussed the completed portraits.

GUIDED COMPREHENSION: MULTIPLE PERSPECTIVES

MONITORING: MIND PORTRAITS

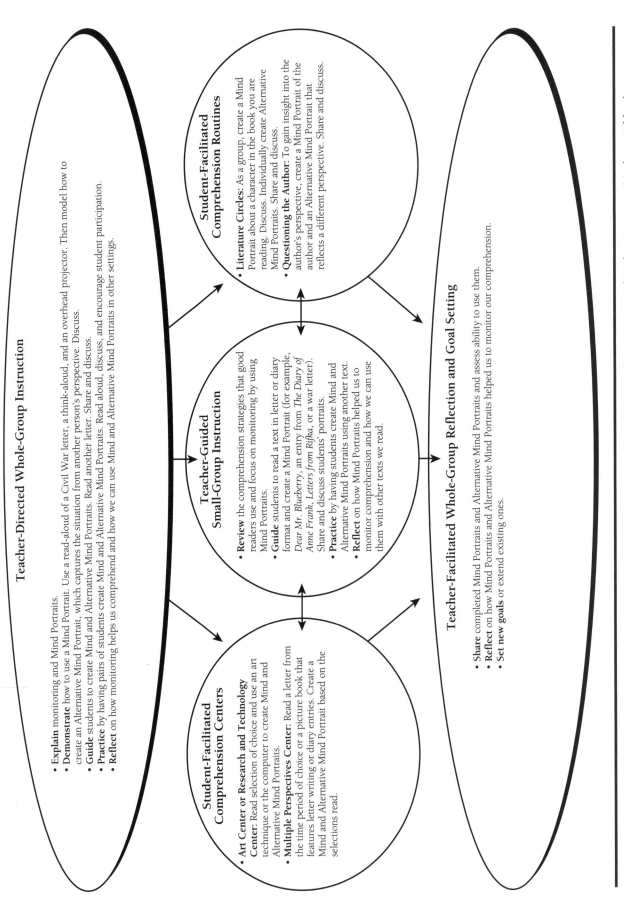

Teacher-Directed Whole-Group Instruction

- **Explain** monitoring and Mind Portraits.
- **Demonstrate** how to use a Mind Portrait. Use a read-aloud of a Civil War letter, a think-aloud, and an overhead projector. Then model how to create an Alternative Mind Portrait, which captures the situation from another person's perspective. Discuss.
- **Guide** students to create Mind and Alternative Mind Portraits. Read another letter. Share and discuss.
- **Practice** by having pairs of students create Mind and Alternative Mind Portraits. Read aloud, discuss, and encourage student participation.
- **Reflect** on how monitoring helps us comprehend and how we can use Mind and Alternative Mind Portraits in other settings.

Student-Facilitated Comprehension Centers

- **Art Center or Research and Technology Center:** Read selection of choice and use an art technique or the computer to create Mind and Alternative Mind Portraits.
- **Multiple Perspectives Center:** Read a letter from the time period of choice or a picture book that features letter writing or diary entries. Create a Mind and Alternative Mind Portrait based on the selections read.

Teacher-Guided Small-Group Instruction

- **Review** the comprehension strategies that good readers use and focus on monitoring by using Mind Portraits.
- **Guide** students to read a text in letter or diary format and create a Mind Portrait (for example, *Dear Mr. Blueberry*, an entry from *The Diary of Anne Frank*, *Letters from Rifka*, or a war letter). Share and discuss students' portraits.
- **Practice** by having students create Mind and Alternative Mind Portraits using another text.
- **Reflect** on how Mind Portraits helped us to monitor comprehension and how we can use them with other texts we read.

Student-Facilitated Comprehension Routines

- **Literature Circles:** As a group, create a Mind Portrait about a character in the book you are reading. Discuss. Individually create Alternative Mind Portraits. Share and discuss.
- **Questioning the Author:** To gain insight into the author's perspective, create a Mind Portrait of the author and an Alternative Mind Portrait that reflects a different perspective. Share and discuss.

Teacher-Facilitated Whole-Group Reflection and Goal Setting

- **Share** completed Mind Portraits and Alternative Mind Portraits and assess ability to use them.
- **Reflect** on how Mind Portraits and Alternative Mind Portraits helped us to monitor our comprehension.
- **Set new goals** or extend existing ones.

Guided Comprehension in Action: Lessons for Grades 3–8 by Maureen McLaughlin and Mary Beth Allen ©2002. Newark, DE: International Reading Association. May be copied for classroom use.

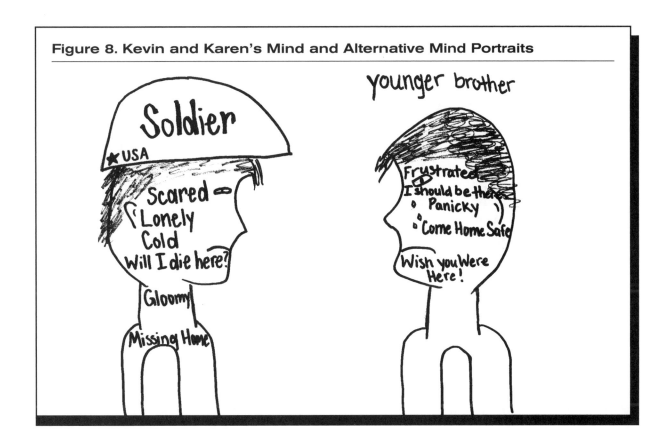

Figure 8. Kevin and Karen's Mind and Alternative Mind Portraits

Practice: Then students practiced by creating an Alternative Mind Portrait. Several students used Mr. Blueberry as their focus. I also encouraged them to choose a perspective other than Mr. Blueberry's if they wished. Kanisha's Mind and Alternative Mind Portraits were about Emily and Arthur the whale (see Figure 9).

Reflect: We reflected on using Mind and Alternative Mind Portraits to help us monitor our comprehension and how we could use the portraits in other settings. One of the students noted that the portraits "are all about the thinking, not the drawing."

Student-Facilitated Comprehension Centers

Art Center or Research and Technology Center: Students self-selected an article or trade book to read and created Mind and Alternative Mind Portraits based on their reading. Instead of writing phrases to describe what the people were thinking and feeling, students expressed the ideas using sketches, collage, or clip art. Figure 10 shows Susan's clip art portraits of Anne Frank and Miep Gies from *The Diary of Anne Frank*.

Multiple Perspectives Center: Some of the students read soldiers' letters from other time periods or picture books or chapter books that featured letter writing or diary entries. They used their reading to create Mind and Alternative Mind Portraits.

Student-Facilitated Comprehension Routines

Literature Circles: In their group, students created a Mind Portrait of the main character in the book they were reading and discussed the completed portrait. Then students separated and

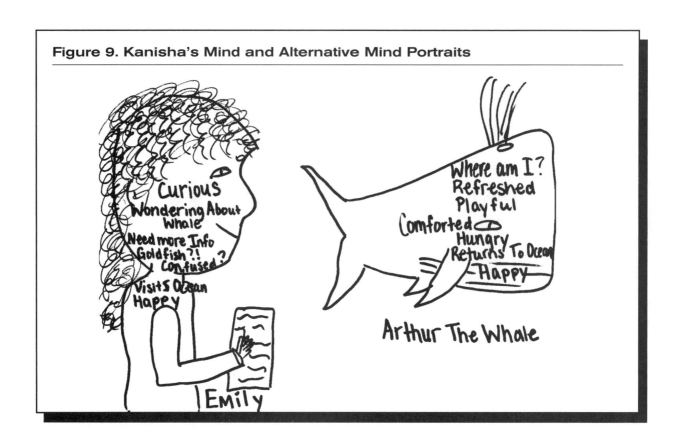

Figure 9. Kanisha's Mind and Alternative Mind Portraits

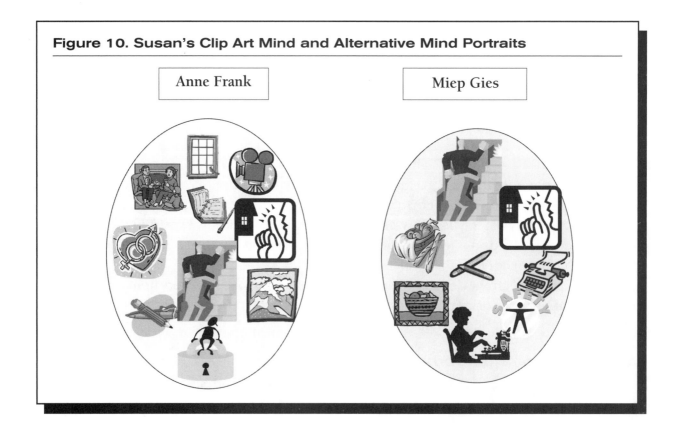

Figure 10. Susan's Clip Art Mind and Alternative Mind Portraits

individually created Alternative Mind Portraits to represent other perspectives of their choice. Finally, they returned to their group to share their portraits and discuss their reasoning.

Questioning the Author: Students created a Mind Portrait of the author and an Alternative Mind Portrait that reflected a different perspective of the story. They shared portraits, discussed their thinking, and questioned the author's thinking.

STAGE THREE: Teacher-Facilitated Whole-Group Reflection and Goal Setting

Share: The students shared their applications of Mind and Alternative Mind Portraits from Stage Two in small groups. Then a representative from each group shared with the class.

Reflect: In whole group we reflected on what we had learned about multiple perspectives and how they helped us to expand our views. That led to a discussion of how being attentive to multiple perspectives and using ideas like Mind and Alternative Mind Portraits helped us comprehend. One of the students observed that she had to be very focused to think about the views the author had not expressed. Another noted that since we had started this theme he found himself thinking about multiple perspectives—not just when reading, but when watching television, listening to music, and during conversations. This started quite an engaging discussion in which students shared their ideas about multiple perspectives in everyday situations.

Set New Goals: We discussed our ability to use Mind and Alternative Mind Portraits. The students indicated they felt quite confident and their applications from Stage Two supported their assessment of their abilities. We decided to extend our goal and learn how to use another technique that promotes comprehension monitoring.

Assessment Options

I observed students during all stages of Guided Comprehension. I also used the Mind and Alternative Mind Portraits as assessment sources.

Guided Comprehension Strategy: Evaluating
Teaching Idea: Contrast Charts

STAGE ONE: Teacher-Directed Whole-Group Instruction

Text: *The True Story of the 3 Little Pigs!* (Scieszka, 1989)

Explain: I reminded students about our goal of evaluating text and introduced Contrast Charts (adapted from Tompkins, 2001; see Appendix, page 159) as an idea that helps us make judgments about text. I explained to my students that stories are based on the author's perspective and pictures are based on the photographer's point of view. As an example, I used the idea that there are at least two sides to every story. I wanted the students to realize that the author's interpretation influences the reader's thinking and that the reader's thinking could change if the story were told from a different perspective. I used a classroom example of a student explaining he was late for school, saying it was not his fault because his parents forgot to wake him on time. I asked the students how the teacher might have perceived this. I explained that we could use a contrast chart to illustrate this, using the student's explanation and, in contrast, the teacher's. We discussed these different perspectives of the same occurrence and how the person sharing the information influenced our thinking.

Demonstrate: I wanted to further activate the students' prior knowledge about perspectives, so I asked for volunteers to briefly retell the original story of the Three Little Pigs. Then I demonstrated how to create Contrast Charts (see Appendix, page 166). I read aloud a portion of *The True Story of the 3 Little Pigs!* and used a think-aloud to express my ideas about the perspective from which the story was told. I thought aloud about how this story being told from the wolf's perspective was different from or contrasted the original story being told from the pigs' perspective. As I was thinking aloud, I began creating a Contrast Chart for the two stories (see Figure 11). I labeled the left column "*The Three Little Pigs*" and the right column "*The True Story of the 3 Little Pigs!*" As I thought aloud about the stories being told from different perspectives, I recorded those contrasts on the chart. I was careful to note that each issue and its contrast should be recorded directly opposite from each other in the appropriate columns. I discussed the Contrast Chart that I had begun with the students to assure they understood the process.

Guide: Then I read the next few pages of *The True Story of the 3 Little Pigs!* and guided students in pairs to add two more contrasts on the chart. These included the idea of the wolf baking a cake for his grandmother and going to the pigs' houses to borrow sugar.

Practice: I finished reading the story and had students work in pairs to complete the Contrast Charts. Information included the contrasting ways in which the stories ended. We used the completed charts as the basis of discussion.

Reflect: To conclude this whole-group lesson, we discussed how making Contrast Charts helped us to understand situations from more than one perspective. We reflected on how Contrast Charts helped us to evaluate or make judgments about texts, and we shared ideas about how we could use them in other settings.

STAGE TWO: Teacher Guided Small-Group Instruction

Text: *I Never Knew Your Name* (Garland, 1994) (Texts varied according to students' abilities.)

GUIDED COMPREHENSION: MULTIPLE PERSPECTIVES
EVALUATING: CONTRAST CHARTS

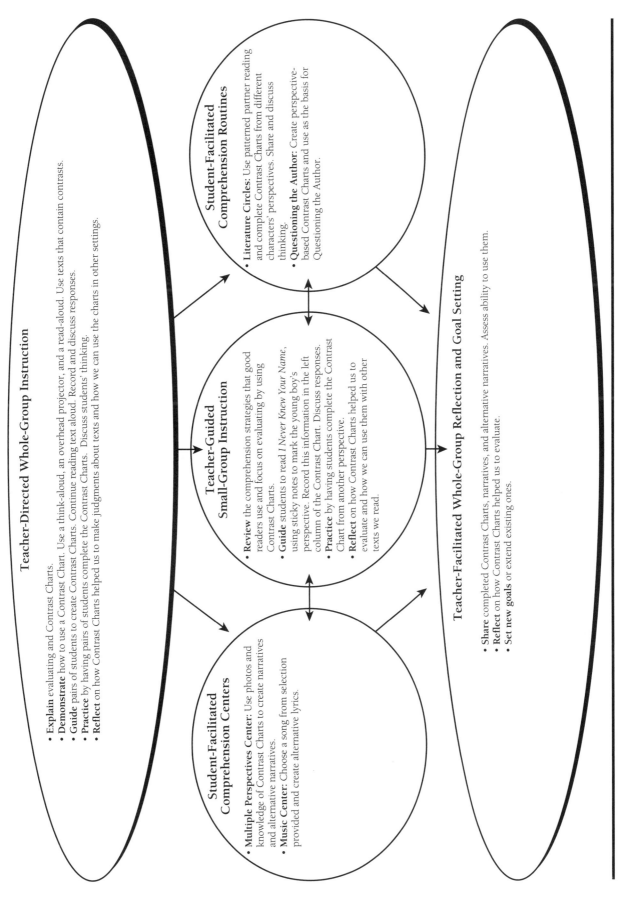

Teacher-Directed Whole-Group Instruction

- **Explain** evaluating and Contrast Charts.
- **Demonstrate** how to use a Contrast Chart. Use a think-aloud, an overhead projector, and a read-aloud. Use texts that contain contrasts.
- **Guide** pairs of students to create Contrast Charts. Continue reading text aloud. Record and discuss responses.
- **Practice** by having pairs of students complete the Contrast Charts. Discuss students' thinking.
- **Reflect** on how Contrast Charts helped us to make judgments about texts and how we can use the charts in other settings.

Student-Facilitated Comprehension Routines

- **Literature Circles:** Use patterned partner reading and complete Contrast Charts from different characters' perspectives. Share and discuss thinking.
- **Questioning the Author:** Create perspective-based Contrast Charts and use as the basis for Questioning the Author.

Teacher-Guided Small-Group Instruction

- **Review** the comprehension strategies that good readers use and focus on evaluating by using Contrast Charts.
- **Guide** students to read *I Never Knew Your Name*, using sticky notes to mark the young boy's perspective. Record this information in the left column of the Contrast Chart. Discuss responses.
- **Practice** by having students complete the Contrast Chart from another perspective.
- **Reflect** on how Contrast Charts helped us to evaluate and how we can use them with other texts we read.

Student-Facilitated Comprehension Centers

- **Multiple Perspectives Center:** Use photos and knowledge of Contrast Charts to create narratives and alternative narratives.
- **Music Center:** Choose a song from selection provided and create alternative lyrics.

Teacher-Facilitated Whole-Group Reflection and Goal Setting

- **Share** completed Contrast Charts, narratives, and alternative narratives. Assess ability to use them.
- **Reflect** on how Contrast Charts helped us to evaluate.
- **Set new goals** or extend existing ones.

Figure 11. Contrast Chart

The Three Little Pigs	*The True Story of the 3 Little Pigs!*
1. Pigs' perspective	1. Wolf's perspective
2. The wolf went to pigs' houses to eat the pigs.	2. The wolf went to pigs' houses to borrow a cup of sugar to bake a cake for his grandmother.
3. The wolf blew houses down.	3. The wolf sneezed and the houses fell down.
4. The pig was alive and ran to the next house after his house was blown down.	4. The pig was dead after the wolf sneezed and the house fell on him.
5. The wolf frightened the pigs.	5. The third pig angered the wolf by talking about the wolf's grandmother.
6. The wolf landed in a pot of boiling soup when he went down the chimney.	6. The wolf was arrested and went to jail for trying to break the door down out of anger.

Review: First I discussed comprehension strategies that active readers use, and then I focused on evaluating using Contrast Charts. I asked students to write down certain things they learned about this story from the narrator's perspective.

Guide: I was working with young adults, so I guided students to read *I Never Knew Your Name* about a young boy who notices that his teenage neighbor spends a lot of time alone. He never befriends the neighbor and regrets this when the neighbor commits suicide. I encouraged the students to use sticky notes to mark places in the text that reflected the young boy's perspective. Then they recorded these in one column of their Contrast Chart.

Practice: After they finished reading the story, we discussed the points they had listed. Then I asked them to think about the story of the teenage boy from another perspective; the boy's parents, a close friend, and his teacher were some of the ideas they generated. The students completed their Contrast Charts from their chosen perspective. My students became very involved with this topic and wanted to use their Contrast Charts to rewrite the story. They shared the results in Stage Three. (Note: I also use texts such as *The Diary of Anne Frank* and students create Contrast Charts for Anne's perspective and the German soldiers who captured the Franks.)

Reflect: We ended our session by reflecting on how we could use the completed Contrast Charts to tell and write stories from different perspectives. We also discussed how Contrast Charts helped us evaluate the texts we read and how they could be used with other texts.

Student-Facilitated Comprehension Centers

Multiple Perspectives Center: Students used photographs provided and their knowledge of Contrast Charts to develop narratives and alternative narratives. Their narratives focused on what they saw happening in the photo; the alternative narrative addressed another perspective that could have been photographed. After students completed the narratives, they sketched their vision of the alternative photograph. The photographs focused on a number of different topics, including the tragedies of September 11, 2001, and environmental issues such as ocean pollution, rain forest destruction, and global warming. The following is an example of a narrative and alternative narrative developed by Jesse:

> **Narrative:** The news photograph showed a beach area that was closed because the water was polluted and trash had been left all over the beach after high tide. The garbage was mostly used needles and other medical trash.

> **Alternative Narrative:** As I was looking at the photograph of the polluted beach area I thought about the beach my family and I visit every summer. I decided that the voice that was missing belonged to the ocean. I thought at first I would write about the people who use the beach, but at least they could see the trash and the warning signs. The ocean had no one to protect it. The picture looks as if some garbage truck was emptied along the shore. There must have been a lot of garbage dumped in the ocean for that much to have made it to shore. The ocean is a natural resource. It's a lot more than a place to vacation. It gives a home to a lot of ocean animals and it gives us a lot of food. Polluting it hurts everyone.

Music Center: Students listened to one of the songs provided and created alternative lyrics to the same tune. For example, Katie used "Cat's in the Cradle" by Harry Chapin. The original lyrics of this song tell about a son who has no time to visit his father. In her alternative lyrics, Katie wrote about the father's memories of making time to be with his son when he was growing up. What follows is a segment from Katie's lyrics:

> Son you arrived just the other day,
> I was so excited I didn't know what to say.
> Learning to walk you were on your way,
> Before I knew it you were ready to play.
> We went fishing, swimming, traveling together too.
> You'd say, "I'm gonna be like you, Dad.
> You know I'm gonna be like you."
>
> And the cat's in the cradle and the silver spoon,
> Little boy blue and the man in the moon.
> "What are we going to do, Dad? I know it'll be fun."
> You'll quickly get your work done,
> To spend time with your number one son.

Student-Facilitated Comprehension Routines

Literature Circles: Students read a chapter of their book, using partner reading and the read-pause-discuss pattern (see Appendix A, *Guided Comprehension: A Teaching Model for Grades 3–8*). The pairs used the results of their discussion to create a Contrast Chart that focused on two characters' contrasting perceptions of the same situation. This led to group sharing and discussion.

Questioning the Author: Students used QtA to generate queries about a chapter in a book they had selected to read. They recorded the narrator's perspectives on a Contrast Chart and examined them from another perspective. For example, some of the students were reading *Speak* by Laurie Halse Anderson. In the chapter titled "Clash of the Titans," the 13-year-old girl, Melinda, tells the reader a lot about what she is thinking, but she does not communicate this information to her peers or the adults involved. The chapter focuses on a parent-teacher conference being held at her school. Students who read this chapter created a Contrast Chart by listing what Melinda revealed to the reader and what they thought Melinda might say to the group of adults who were involved in the conference at school or to a group of friends. They then queried why the author had made the choices she had concerning the sharing of this information and discussed what they would have done if they had been in Melinda's situation.

STAGE THREE: Teacher-Facilitated Whole-Group Reflection and Goal Setting

Share: The students shared the Contrast Charts, narratives and alternative narratives, photographs and alternative photographs, and alternative lyrics they had created in Stage Two. We had quite a variety. Some of the students sang the alternative lyrics they had written. Students also shared the versions of *I Never Knew Your Name* that they had written from different perspectives.

Reflect: We reflected on how evaluating helped us understand text and why it was important to know a variety of ways to evaluate. Students noted that they really needed to know a lot about the text or photo before they could evaluate it and that using Contrast Charts helped them to organize their thinking when examining differences in texts. This seemed to give them a sense of ownership of the process.

Set New Goals: We assessed how well we thought we could evaluate text and decided to extend this goal by learning how to use Discussion Webs (Alvermann, 1991), which require readers to draw a conclusion after examining two sides of an issue (see Appendix A, *Guided Comprehension: A Teaching Model for Grades 3–8*).

Assessment Options

I observed students and used their multiple applications of Contrast Charts to assess during this lesson.

Guided Comprehension Strategy: Evaluating
Teaching Idea: Thinking Hats

STAGE ONE: Teacher-Directed Whole-Group Instruction

Text: *Bull Run* (Fleischman, 1995)

Explain: I reviewed our goal of evaluating text and explained how Thinking Hats (adapted from DeBono, 1985; see Appendix, page 160) helps us to evaluate by examining narrative or expository text from a number of different perspectives. I explained that we could use this technique with narrative text by examining the story from the perspectives of different characters (for example, *Cinderella* from the perspectives of Cinderella, the stepmother, a stepsister, the fairy godmother, the prince, or a guest at the ball). With expository text, we can explore topics through the eyes of a variety of people involved in the situation (for example, Christopher Columbus's explorations from the perspectives of Columbus, Queen Isabella, King Ferdinand, the leader of the Tainos, Columbus's cabin boy, a crew member from the Santa Maria).

Demonstrate: I demonstrated by using the Cinderella example to assure that students understood how to use Thinking Hats with narrative text. I used an overhead projector and transparencies I had prepared ahead of time to share the story from the perspectives of one of the stepsisters and the fairy godmother. Next, I discussed the application with students and asked what ideas they had to add to these perspectives. They made connections between this technique and others such as Contrast Charts and Mind Portraits, and they readily offered ideas. One student suggested that I include the stepsister's ideas about why and how Cinderella got to go to the ball. Another student suggested that I tell how exhausting it was to be a fairy godmother, traveling from place to place to make people's dreams come true. Then I demonstrated a Thinking Hats discussion in which I played all the parts. I facilitated this by using a graphic organizer that represented the characters involved and who said what about a variety of topics.

My second demonstration focused on expository text. I read aloud a section of *Bull Run*, which describes that famous battle from sixteen different perspectives. I chose the chapter in which James Dacy describes his observation of the battle from a nearby vantage point. Dacy's job was recording war events by sketching them. As I read, I thought aloud about the perspective Dacy offered of the conflict. I recorded his name and perspective on a Thinking Hats planning form for the Battle of Bull Run, which I had placed on the overhead. I continued this process until I had read four different perspectives. This took only a short amount of time because each perspective is only one or two pages long. When the web was complete, I asked three students to join me. I had invited these students to participate the day before and had shared the text with them at that time. Then we conducted a Thinking Hats discussion, followed by the students' analyses of what they saw and heard as well as what they would have added to the discussion.

Guide: I guided the students by having them work in small groups to complete a Thinking Hats Map as I read another variety of selections from *Bull Run*. I was careful to include one of the students who had assisted me with the demonstration in each of the groups. After I finished reading, I guided students in the cooperative learning activity Jigsaw II. I asked each student to choose the role he or she wanted to portray. Then we reorganized the groups by role. For example, one member of each home group selected the perspective of Toby Boyce, an 11-year-old fife player, and they all temporarily moved into the same group to become experts on this character's view of the battle. We did the same for all four perspectives. I guided students' discussion for a short time.

GUIDED COMPREHENSION: PERSPECTIVES
EVALUATING: THINKING HATS

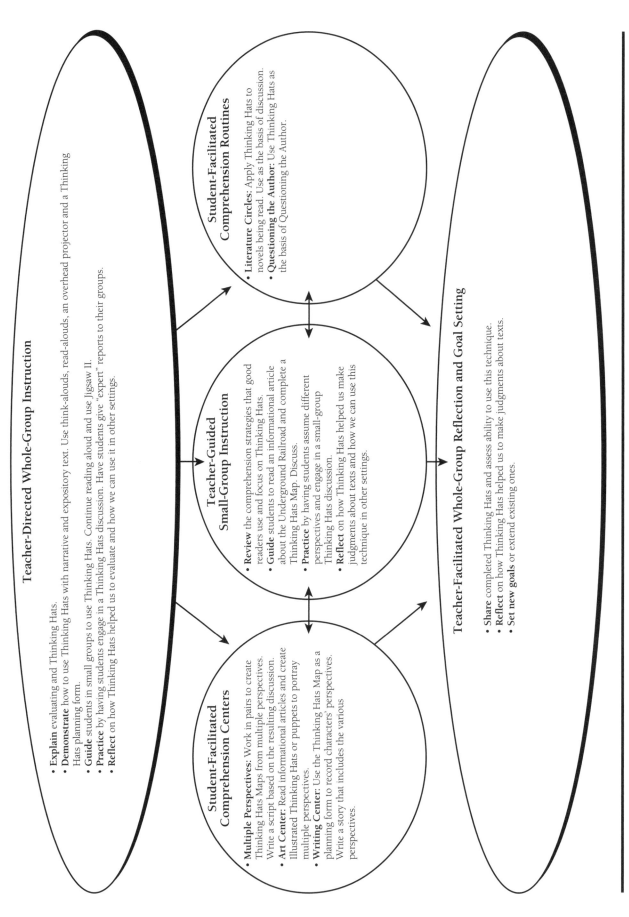

Teacher-Directed Whole-Group Instruction

- **Explain** evaluating and Thinking Hats.
- **Demonstrate** how to use Thinking Hats with narrative and expository text. Use think-alouds, read-alouds, an overhead projector and a Thinking Hats planning form.
- **Guide** students in small groups to use Thinking Hats. Continue reading aloud and use Jigsaw II.
- **Practice** by having students engage in a Thinking Hats discussion. Have students give "expert" reports to their groups.
- **Reflect** on how Thinking Hats helped us to evaluate and how we can use it in other settings.

Student-Facilitated Comprehension Centers

- **Multiple Perspectives:** Work in pairs to create Thinking Hats Maps from multiple perspectives. Write a script based on the resulting discussion.
- **Art Center:** Read informational articles and create Illustrated Thinking Hats or puppets to portray multiple perspectives.
- **Writing Center:** Use the Thinking Hats Map as a planning form to record characters' perspectives. Write a story that includes the various perspectives.

Teacher-Guided Small-Group Instruction

- **Review** the comprehension strategies that good readers use and focus on Thinking Hats.
- **Guide** students to read an informational article about the Underground Railroad and complete a Thinking Hats Map. Discuss.
- **Practice** by having students assume different perspectives and engage in a small-group Thinking Hats discussion.
- **Reflect** on how Thinking Hats helped us make judgments about texts and how we can use this technique in other settings.

Student-Facilitated Comprehension Routines

- **Literature Circles:** Apply Thinking Hats to novels being read. Use as the basis of discussion.
- **Questioning the Author:** Use Thinking Hats as the basis of Questioning the Author.

Teacher-Facilitated Whole-Group Reflection and Goal Setting

- **Share** completed Thinking Hats and assess ability to use this technique.
- **Reflect** on how Thinking Hats helped us to make judgments about texts.
- **Set new goals** or extend existing ones.

Guided Comprehension in Action: Lessons for Grades 3–8 by Maureen McLaughlin and Mary Beth Allen ©2002. Newark, DE: International Reading Association. May be copied for classroom use.

Practice: Students practiced by returning to their home groups, where each "expert" contributed to the discussion from his or her chosen perspective.

Reflect: We reflected on how using ideas like Thinking Hats helped us to evaluate text. One student observed that the reader really needs to know the information to speak from that perspective. Then we discussed how we could use Thinking Hats in other settings.

STAGE TWO: Teacher-Guided Small-Group Instruction

Text: Informational articles (Texts varied according to students' abilities.)

Review: First I reviewed the comprehension strategies that good readers use, and then I focused on evaluating using Thinking Hats. I reminded students that we could use this technique with both narrative and expository text and that today we would be reading expository text. I also noted that although the original technique focused on six perspectives, it also worked with three, four, or five perspectives (see Appendix, page 167).

Guide: I guided students as they read an informational article about the Underground Railroad. During reading they jotted some notes on their organizers, and when they finished reading I guided their completion of the Thinking Hats Web (I used five perspectives this time because there were five students in the group). Students were quite proficient in determining perspectives from which this topic could be viewed. They also quickly realized that only two perspectives were addressed in the article. To determine the remaining perspectives, they brainstormed what other voices might need to be heard. The article addressed adult slaves and the slave owners. The students added slave children, members of the Underground Railroad, and law officers.

Practice: The group practiced by choosing perspectives, taking a few minutes to prepare, and then discussing the Underground Railroad from five different perspectives. It was interesting to observe the dynamics of the discussion. When the law officer said he thought that slaves should be free, another group member noted that he could not say that because the laws supported the slave owners. The law officer replied that although his job required him to defend the laws, on a personal level he was against slavery. This led to an enlightening discussion about what people are expected to believe and what they really believe.

Reflect: We reflected on how Thinking Hats helped us to think about situations in different ways and to make judgments about texts. One student also observed that the activity was a great "mind expander."

Student-Facilitated Comprehension Centers

Multiple Perspectives Center: Many of the students wanted to read more from *Bull Run* and other texts that offered different perspectives on situations, so I placed a number of books and articles at the multiple perspectives center. Students worked in pairs to complete Thinking Hats Maps from multiple perspectives. Then they used them to conduct discussions.

Art Center: At this center, students read informational articles and used what they learned to create Illustrated Thinking Hats (see Appendix, page 168). They used the form provided to draw the various perspectives and shared them with a peer. An example of Jorge's work is featured in Figure 12. Other students worked in pairs to read an article and create puppets to dramatize a discussion from various perspectives.

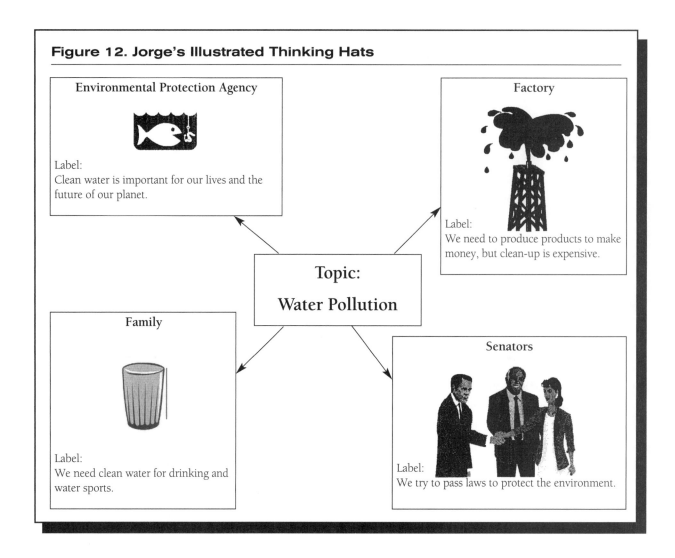

Figure 12. Jorge's Illustrated Thinking Hats

Environmental Protection Agency

Label:
Clean water is important for our lives and the future of our planet.

Factory

Label:
We need to produce products to make money, but clean-up is expensive.

Topic:
Water Pollution

Family

Label:
We need clean water for drinking and water sports.

Senators

Label:
We try to pass laws to protect the environment.

Writing Center: Instead of completing the Thinking Hats Map after reading, students used it as a planner to describe the perspectives of at least four different characters they would include in stories they wrote. Cristin's planner is shown in Figure 13.

Student-Facilitated Comprehension Routines

Literature Circles: Students adapted Thinking Hats to the number of group members and used the technique with the book they were reading.

Questioning the Author: Students adapted Thinking Hats to question the author. They based each perspective on a different character's thinking and used the completed Questioning Hats to query the author about why she had included such perspectives in the story.

STAGE THREE: Teacher-Facilitated Whole-Group Reflection and Goal Setting

Share: It was a festival of sharing because everything presented had multiple perspectives. In small groups, students shared a variety of Thinking Hats experiences including maps they had

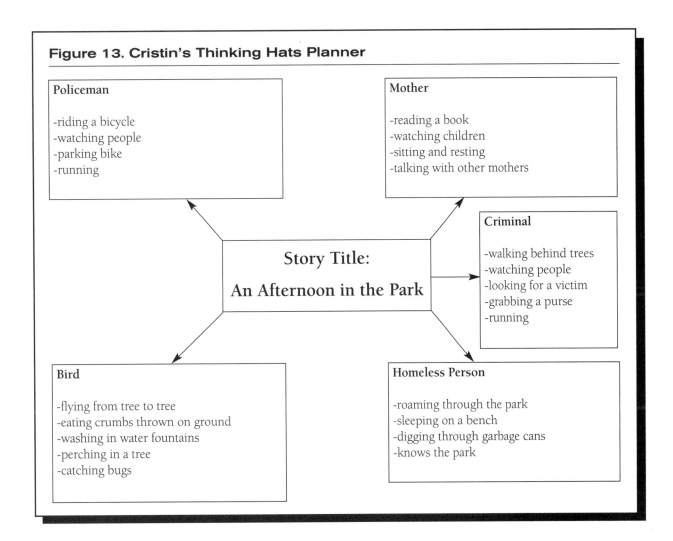

Figure 13. Cristin's Thinking Hats Planner

Policeman

-riding a bicycle
-watching people
-parking bike
-running

Mother

-reading a book
-watching children
-sitting and resting
-talking with other mothers

Story Title:

An Afternoon in the Park

Criminal

-walking behind trees
-watching people
-looking for a victim
-grabbing a purse
-running

Bird

-flying from tree to tree
-eating crumbs thrown on ground
-washing in water fountains
-perching in a tree
-catching bugs

Homeless Person

-roaming through the park
-sleeping on a bench
-digging through garbage cans
-knows the park

drawn, maps used as planners, stories and scripts they had written, and applications from the comprehension routines. In whole group, someone from each small group offered highlights of their sharing experiences and the students talked about how Thinking Hats fostered in-depth thinking and discussion. We all took active roles, and it was a great sharing experience. Everyone felt positive about his or her ability to use this technique.

Reflect: We reflected on the many ways in which Thinking Hats helped us to expand our perspectives and evaluate texts. Students also noted that they thought this technique helped them to monitor their comprehension because it "made us think all the time."

Set New Goals: We decided that after learning several techniques for evaluating texts that we had achieved our goal. So we focused on more fully integrating our knowledge of evaluating with other comprehension strategies while reading narrative and expository text.

Assessment Options

I used a lot of observation during the different stages of Guided Comprehension and students' applications of Thinking Hats for assessment purposes.

THEME RESOURCES

Texts

Anderson, L.H. (1999). *Speak*. New York: Farrar, Straus & Giroux.

Ashby, R., & Ohrn, D.G. (Eds.). (1995). *Herstory: Women who changed the world*. New York: Viking.

Bennett, C., & Gottesfeld, J. (2001). *Anne Frank and me*. New York: G.P. Putnam's Sons.

Bray, R.L. (1995). *Martin Luther King*. New York: Greenwillow.

Bray, R.L. (1995). *Martin Luther King*. New York: Greenwillow Books.

Brokaw, T. (1998). *The greatest generation*. New York: Random House.

Brokaw, T. (1999). *The greatest generation speaks: Letters and reflections*. New York: Random House.

Bunting, E. (2001). *Riding the tiger*. New York: Houghton Mifflin.

Carroll, A. (Ed.). (2001). *War letters: Extraordinary correspondence from American Wars*. New York: Scribner.

DiSpezio, M. (1999). *Optical illusions magic*. New York, Sterling.

Fleischman, P. (1995). *Bull Run*. New York: HarperCollins.

Frank, A. (1993). *Anne Frank: The diary of a young girl*. New York: Prentice Hall.

Garland, S. (1994). *I never knew your name*. New York: Ticknor and Fields.

Gates, H.L., & West, C. (2000). *The African-American century: How Black Americans helped shape our country*. New York: Simon & Schuster.

Gold, A.L. (1997). *Memories of Anne Frank: Reflections of a childhood friend*. New York: Scholastic.

Harness, C. (2001). *Remember the ladies: 100 great American women*. New York: HarperCollins.

Hesse, K. (1992). *Letters from Rifka*. New York: Trumpet Book Club.

Hesse, K. (2001). *Witness*. New York: Scholastic.

Hoose, P. (2001). *We were there, too! Young people in American history*. New York: Farrar, Straus & Giroux.

Jacobs, F. (1992). *The Tainos: The people who welcomed Columbus*. New York: G.P. Putnam.

James, S. (1991). *Dear Mr. Blueberry*. New York: Margaret K. McElderry.

Jennings, P., & Brewster, T. (2000). *The century for young people*. New York: Random House.

Krull, K. (2000). *Lives of extraordinary women*. New York: Harcourt.

McDonough, Y.Z. (1997). *Anne Frank*. New York: Henry Holt.

Parks, R. (with Reed, J.D.). (1996). *Dear Mrs. Parks: A dialogue with today's youth*. New York: Lee & Low.

Rappaport, D. (2001). *Martin's big words: The life of Dr. Martin Luther King, Jr.* New York: Hyperion.

Ringgold, F. (1999). *If a bus could talk: The true story of Rosa Parks*. New York: Simon & Schuster.

Roop, P., & Roop, C. (Eds.). (1990). *Columbus: My journal 1492–1493*. New York: Avon.

Scieszka, J. (1989). *The true story of the 3 little pigs!* New York: Viking Penguin.

Van der Rol, R., & Verhoeven, R. (1993). *Anne Frank: Beyond the diary*. New York: Viking.

Yolen, J. (1992). *Encounter*. New York: Harcourt Brace Jovanovich.

Websites

Media Literacy Clearinghouse
www.med.sc.edu/medialit

Military Women Veterans
userpages.aug.com/captbarb

The New York Times Learning Network

   www.nytimes.com/learning

USA Today

   www.usatoday.com

Performance Extensions Across the Curriculum

Social Studies

- Explore alternative views of historical events (Columbus's discovery of America, the perception of Native Americans, the Vietnam War) or current events.

- Explore alternative views of issues in society (the destruction of the rain forest, overpopulation, salary caps in professional sports, nuclear power).

Science

- Research current scientific developments (cloning, using animal organs for human transplants, germ warfare) and examine each topic from a variety of perspectives. Consider issues such as who or what initiated these developments, who is most likely to benefit from them, and who controls them.

- Research environmental science and explore topics such as global warming and pollution from multiple perspectives. Consider viewpoints such as those of large corporations, individual people, animals, and plant life. Consider issues such as who has the power to affect the environment and who is powerless to effect change. Develop a community plan to help the environment.

Art

- Use the Internet to take virtual tours of great museums such as the Van Gogh Museum in Amsterdam, the Musee d'Orsay and Louvre in Paris, and the Metropolitan Museum of Art in New York City. Review paintings and sculptures from a variety of perspectives and express personal responses by creating original works of art.

- Explore works of art that have emerged during historically significant periods. For example, review the artwork of the children who were in concentration camps during the Holocaust. Contemplate what the artists were hoping to communicate through their work. Consider their work from the perspectives of their families, U.S. citizens during World War II, soldiers, descendants of Holocaust victims, museum visitors, and others. Consider issues such as who had power during the Holocaust and whose voices were perceived to be discounted.

- Compare and contrast artists from different time periods or who use different mediums; examine the works of M.C. Escher that deal with perspectives (Day and Night, Ascending and Descending, Concave and Convex) and describe both perspectives.

Culminating Activity

A Celebration of Multiple Perspectives: Invite parents and community members to a celebration of learning across the curriculum. Display multiple perspectives performances and have students serve as guides and discussants. Live performances can include dramatizations of historical or scientific events as seen from multiple perspectives. Be sure to have the students issue personal invitations to their parents.

CHAPTER 3

Whodunit? The Nature of Mysteries

As readers, we are readily engaged by mysteries. We want to know "whodunit," but we also take pleasure in the process of decoding the clues to assure that every piece of the puzzle fits. Our students are equally fascinated by this genre. Perhaps it is the problem-solving nature of mysteries or that these stories challenge us to think through complex possibilities; whatever the reason, mysteries are motivational.

Although the nature of mysteries remains constant, the text levels and the settings in which the mysteries occur vary. For example, young readers can enjoy this genre by reading the mysterious cases of Cam Jansen and Encyclopedia Brown. Other mystery series like Nancy Drew and the Hardy Boys have become classics for intermediate readers. The Sherlock Holmes series and the writings of Edgar Allan Poe provide more experienced readers with mysteries to solve. The mystery genre also extends to the content areas. For example, readers are invited to contemplate the mysteries of Stonehenge, the pyramids, Shakespeare, Mozart, and the Titanic in books such as *Unsolved Mysteries of History*. Content-area mystery series include History Detectives (*Ancient Egypt*, *Ancient Greece*, *The Aztecs*, *The Romans*).

The Sample Theme-Based Plan for Guided Comprehension: Mysteries (see Figure 14) presents a sampling of goals, state standards, assessments, texts, technology resources, comprehension strategies, teaching ideas, comprehension centers, and comprehension routines. The plan begins by delineating examples of student goals and related state standards. The student goals for this theme include the following:

- using appropriate comprehension strategies
- describing and discussing the characteristics of this genre
- writing mysteries
- communicating effectively

These goals support the following state standards:

- learning to read independently
- reading, analyzing, and interpreting literature

Figure 14. Sample Theme-Based Plan for Guided Comprehension: Mysteries

Goals and Connections to State Standards

Students will

- use appropriate comprehension strategies. Standard: learning to read independently
- describe and discuss characteristics of mysteries. Standard: reading, analyzing, and interpreting literature
- write and dramatize mysteries that incorporate characteristics of the genre. Standards: types and quality of writing
- communicate effectively. Standards: types and quality of writing; speaking and listening

Comprehension Strategies

1. Previewing
2. Monitoring
3. Summarizing
4. Summarizing

Teaching Ideas

Probable Passages
Say Something
Lyric Summaries
Mystery Cubes

Comprehension Centers

Students will apply the comprehension strategies and related teaching ideas in the following comprehension centers:

Art Center
Drama Center
Mystery Center

Research and Technology Center
Writing Center

Comprehension Routines

Students will apply the comprehension strategies and related teaching ideas in the following comprehension routines:

Literature Circles
Questioning the Author
Reciprocal Teaching

Assessment

The following measures can be used for a variety of purposes, including diagnostic, formative, and summative assessment:

Lyric Summaries
Mystery Cubes
Observation
Probable Passages
Say Something
Student Self-Assessments

Text	Theme	Level
1. *From the Mixed-Up Files of Mrs. Basil E. Frankweiler*	M	5
2. *Cam Jansen and the Scary Snake Mystery*	M	3
3. "The Tell-Tale Heart"	M	7
4. *Encyclopedia Brown Takes the Cake*	M	4

Technology Resources

MysteryNet's Kids Mysteries
  kids.mysterynet.com
The Dakota Meadows Eighth-Grade Mysteries
  www.isd77.k12.mn.us/schools/dakota/mystery/
  contents.html
The Moonlit Road
  www.themoonlitroad.com

- types and quality of writing
- speaking and listening

Examples of assessments used in the theme-based Guided Comprehension lessons include observation, strategy applications, and student self-assessments. Comprehension strategies and related teaching ideas that are featured in the lessons include the following:

- Previewing: Probable Passages
- Monitoring: Say Something
- Summarizing: Lyric Summaries
- Summarizing: Mystery Cubes

The texts used in teacher-directed whole-group instruction include *From the Mixed-Up Files of Mrs. Basil E. Frankweiler*, *Cam Jansen and the Scary Snake Mystery*, "The Tell-Tale Heart," and *Encyclopedia Brown Takes the Cake*. References for additional texts at a variety of levels, including those employed in teacher-guided small-group instruction and the student-facilitated comprehension centers and routines are included in the Theme Resources at the end of the chapter.

In this theme, students' independent strategy applications occur at the art, drama, mystery, research and technology, and writing comprehension centers. Comprehension routines, another setting in which students apply the strategies, include Literature Circles, Questioning the Author, and Reciprocal Teaching.

GUIDED COMPREHENSION LESSONS

Guided Comprehension Strategy: Previewing
Teaching Idea: Probable Passages

STAGE ONE: Teacher-Directed Whole-Group Instruction

Text: *From the Mixed-Up Files of Mrs. Basil E. Frankweiler* (Konigsburg, 1967)

Explain: I explained to students the importance of previewing before reading by activating background knowledge, predicting, and setting purposes for reading. I then explained predicting in greater detail by telling students that the author provides clues to use for prediction and today we will have words to help us make predictions before reading and during reading. I showed them the Probable Passages form (adapted from Wood, 1984; see Appendix A, *Guided Comprehension: A Teaching Model for Grades K–8*) and told them that we would use selected words from the story to make predictions about each part of the story.

Demonstrate: I placed the following words on the overhead: *Claudia, Jamie, Metropolitan Museum of Art, statue, Mrs. Basil E. Frankweiler, Michelangelo, clues, files, proof, run away, secret*. I read aloud all the words and explained the meaning of each one by making connections or giving synonyms. I then started thinking aloud about the story. I predicted that the main characters in the story were Claudia and Jamie, and I wrote, "The main characters in this story are Claudia and Jamie." Next I thought aloud about the setting and wrote, "The setting is the Metropolitan Museum of Art in New York City." Then I explained to the students that we would use the other words to make predictions about the rest of the story.

Guide: I engaged the students in a discussion about what the problem (mystery) might be, based on the clue words. We then agreed that the problem was probably a Michelangelo statue was missing from the museum, so I wrote in the next section, "The mystery in this story is someone stole a famous Michelangelo statue from the museum and Claudia and Jamie need to find out who did it." Next, we looked at the words to predict some possible events in the story. Together, we came up with, "Mrs. Basil E. Frankweiler knew a secret about who stole the statue." I encouraged the students to work in pairs to predict two more things that might have happened, based on the clue words. Each pair shared one idea with the class, and I recorded them on the chart. The following are samples of the students' predictions:

Setting:	The setting is the Metropolitan Museum of Art in New York City.

Characters:	The main characters in this story are Claudia and Jamie.

Problem:	The mystery in this story is someone stole a famous Michelangelo statue from the museum and Claudia and Jamie need to find out who did it.

Events:	1. Mrs. Basil E. Frankweiler knows a secret about who stole the statue.
	2. The thief left some clues in the museum that helped Claudia and Jamie figure out who did it.
	3. Claudia and Jamie found the mixed up files in Mrs. Basil E. Frankweiler's office and were able to solve the mystery.

Solution:	The thief was someone who worked in the museum and when he tried to run away, Claudia and Jamie were able to catch him and take back the statue.

GUIDED COMPREHENSION: MYSTERIES
PREVIEWING: PROBABLE PASSAGES

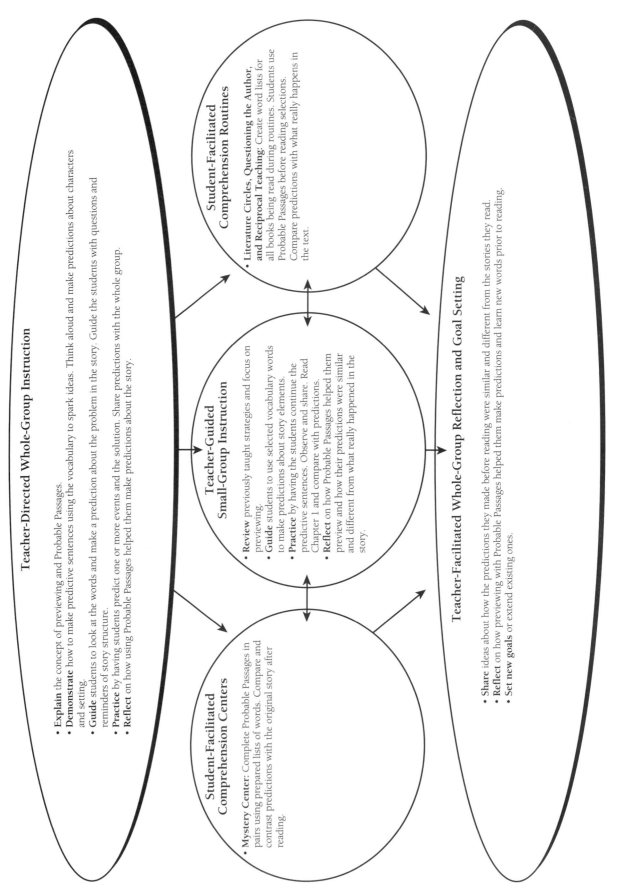

Teacher-Directed Whole-Group Instruction

- **Explain** the concept of previewing and Probable Passages.
- **Demonstrate** how to make predictive sentences using the vocabulary to spark ideas. Think aloud and make predictions about characters and setting.
- **Guide** students to look at the words and make a prediction about the problem in the story. Guide the students with questions and reminders of story structure.
- **Practice** by having students predict one or more events and the solution. Share predictions with the whole group.
- **Reflect** on how using Probable Passages helped them make predictions about the story.

Student-Facilitated Comprehension Routines

- **Literature Circles, Questioning the Author, and Reciprocal Teaching:** Create word lists for all books being read during routines. Students use Probable Passages before reading selections. Compare predictions with what really happens in the text.

Teacher-Guided Small-Group Instruction

- **Review** previously taught strategies and focus on previewing.
- **Guide** students to use selected vocabulary words to make predictions about story elements.
- **Practice** by having the students continue the predictive sentences. Observe and share. Read Chapter 1 and compare with predictions.
- **Reflect** on how Probable Passages helped them preview and how their predictions were similar and different from what really happened in the story.

Student-Facilitated Comprehension Centers

- **Mystery Center:** Complete Probable Passages in pairs using prepared lists of words. Compare and contrast predictions with the original story after reading.

Teacher-Facilitated Whole-Group Reflection and Goal Setting

- **Share** ideas about how the predictions they made before reading were similar and different from the stories they read.
- **Reflect** on how previewing with Probable Passages helped them make predictions and learn new words prior to reading.
- **Set new goals** or extend existing ones.

Practice: I had the students complete the Probable Passages form by using the words to predict a solution to the story. We discussed their ideas, and then I started to read the story aloud to the students. I encouraged them to refer to their Probable Passage form to refine or modify their predictions as we continued with the story. When I finished reading, we discussed how our predictions were confirmed or disconfirmed.

Reflect: Finally, we reflected on how predicting helped us understand the text and focus our reading, and how we could use it in other settings. The students were very surprised that their predictions were so different than what actually happened, but they reflected that it motivated them to keep reading because they wanted to find out what did happen.

STAGE TWO: Teacher-Guided Small-Group Instruction

Text: *The Dollhouse Murders* (Wright, 1983) (Texts varied according to students' abilities.)

Review: I reviewed the comprehension strategies good readers use and visited the process of previewing using Probable Passages. I put selected words from the story on a chart and introduced them to the students. I told them we were going to use these words to make predictions about our new story.

Guide: I guided the students to use the words to make predictions. We did the setting and characters together. Then in pairs, they completed the rest of the Probable Passages. I guided with prompts and reminders. The students shared their predictions, and then they were ready to start reading. I asked the students to read the first chapter. I listened to each student in the group whisper-read to make sure that the text was appropriate. After they finished reading the chapter, we revisited the Probable Passages to determine if our original predictions were on target and how we could modify or refine them. We discussed the clues we had so far from the text and the original words.

Practice: After we refined and revised predictions, I had the students finish the story on their own. I met with the group periodically to revisit predictions and discuss clues from the story.

Reflect: We reflected on the importance of predicting before and during the reading of stories and how authors provide us clues to help us refine or revise our predictions.

Student-Facilitated Comprehension Centers

Mystery Center: I created lists of words for several mystery stories and left them at this center. Students used them to complete Probable Passages as prereading activities for the mysteries of their choice. I asked the students to keep track of revised or modified predictions in their Guided Comprehension Journals. We shared these in Stage Three.

Student-Facilitated Comprehension Routines

Literature Circles: Students completed Probable Passage forms for the book *The Westing Game*, which they were reading for their Literature Circle. They shared their predictions before setting goals for reading. Although students used the circle roles for discussion, I asked them to also share revised predictions as they met to discuss the book. Students kept track of predictions using a Double-Entry Journal in their Guided Comprehension Journals.

Questioning the Author and Reciprocal Teaching: Students used word lists I had supplied to create Probable Passages for the books they were beginning to read. In Questioning the Author, students used this to preview the text before creating queries. In Reciprocal Teaching, students used it during the predicting phase.

STAGE THREE: Teacher-Facilitated Whole-Group Reflection and Goal Setting

Share: Students shared completed examples of the projects and readings from Stage Two.

Reflect: Then we reflected on how predicting motivated us to read the stories and how being aware of an author's clues helped us make better predictions. We also discussed how predicting helped us understand the story and gave us a reason to keep reading.

Set New Goals: Finally, students set goals for using a variety of previewing techniques to help them better understand text.

Assessment Options

I used observation, the completed Probable Passages, and responses recorded in Guided Comprehension Journals as assessments.

Guided Comprehension Strategy: Monitoring
Teaching Idea: Say Something

STAGE ONE: *Teacher-Directed Whole-Group Instruction*

Text: *Cam Jansen and the Scary Snake Mystery* (Adler, 1997)

Explain: First I explained to students the importance of monitoring their understanding while they are reading a text. Then I explained that, in a mystery, the reader needs to keep track of many clues to try to figure out who did the crime and why. I told the students that using Say Something (adapted from Short, Harste, & Burke, 1996; see Appendix A, *Guided Comprehension: A Teaching Model for Grades 3–8*) during reading was a way to think about what they were reading and share their ideas with someone else. This way we can keep track of what we are thinking about while we are reading.

Demonstrate: Next, I read the first chapter of *Cam Jansen* aloud and used a Say Something about what had happened so far. I made sure to focus on the clues the author had provided and said, "It is interesting that Cam can take pictures with her mind. I'll bet that helps her remember exact clues when she is trying to solve a mystery." I told the students that I was going to read additional chapters, and I would stop at various places and ask them to say something about the clues and the story.

Guide: I read Chapter 2 of the story, stopping at three points to guide students to Say Something about the text. I realized that I needed to prompt them with some general concepts that they might say something about. I suggested focusing on an interesting clue, a prediction, a question they had, a connection, or a feeling. Once I gave them some suggestions, they were able to share some interesting ideas. I encouraged students to share in small groups, and then some students shared with the class. We talked about what a meaningful contribution would be and set that as the goal for practice.

Practice: I read aloud Chapter 3, stopping twice for pairs of students to Say Something. I encouraged students to share their ideas with the whole class. I circulated around the room to monitor the conversations and offer support as necessary. We continued this process throughout the reading of the book. Most of the students' comments focused on predictions and connections, such as "I think Cam's photographic memory will help her find out who took the camera" and "This reminds me of a time when someone stole my brand new watch, and I looked around for clues but never found out who did it."

Reflect: I guided the students to reflect on the importance of thinking about what they were reading and use the new information to help them understand. We talked about how using Say Something really helped us engage with the book and how sharing our ideas gave us some other perspectives on thinking.

STAGE TWO: *Teacher-Guided Small-Group Instruction*

Text: *Bunnicula: A Rabbit-Tale of Mystery* (Howe & Howe, 1979) (Texts varied according to students' abilities.)

Review: First I reviewed with the students the strategies good readers use to make sense of text and then I focused them on monitoring by using Say Something.

Guide: I guided the students to make predictions about the book, based on the cover and back-cover summary. I then had them start to read the first chapter. I listened to each student whisper-read a small portion of text to check for fluency. After students had read the first three pages of

GUIDED COMPREHENSION: MYSTERIES
MONITORING: SAY SOMETHING

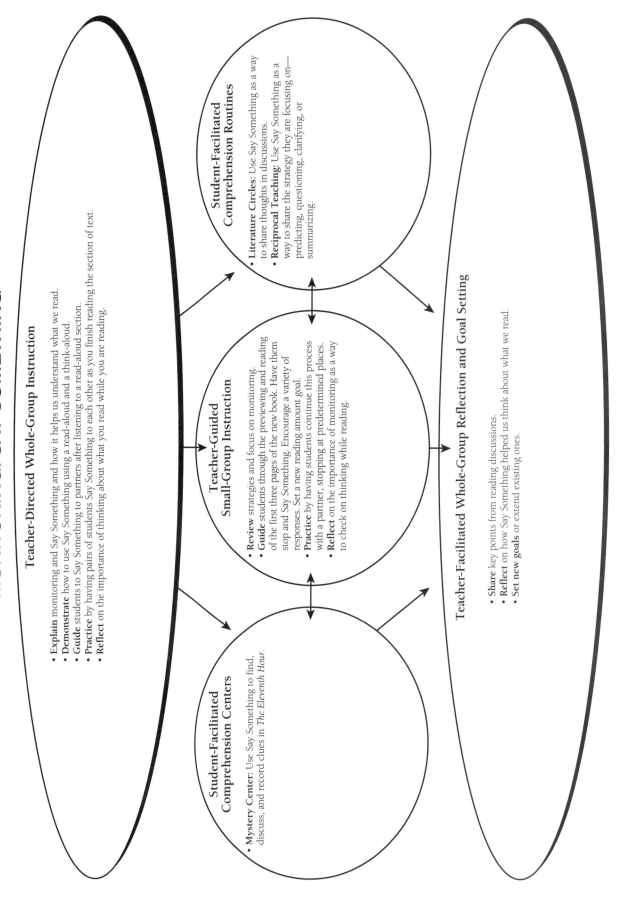

Teacher-Directed Whole-Group Instruction

- **Explain** monitoring and Say Something and how it helps us understand what we read.
- **Demonstrate** how to use Say Something using a read-aloud and a think-aloud.
- **Guide** students to Say Something to partners after listening to a read-aloud section.
- **Practice** by having pairs of students Say Something to each other as you finish reading the section of text.
- **Reflect** on the importance of thinking about what you read while you are reading.

Student-Facilitated Comprehension Centers

- **Mystery Center:** Use Say Something to find, discuss, and record clues in *The Eleventh Hour.*

Teacher-Guided Small-Group Instruction

- **Review** strategies and focus on monitoring.
- **Guide** students through the previewing and reading of the first three pages of the new book. Have them stop and Say Something. Encourage a variety of responses. Set a new reading amount goal.
- **Practice** by having students continue this process with a partner, stopping at predetermined places.
- **Reflect** on the importance of monitoring as a way to check on thinking while reading.

Student-Facilitated Comprehension Routines

- **Literature Circles:** Use Say Something as a way to share thoughts in discussions.
- **Reciprocal Teaching:** Use Say Something as a way to share the strategy they are focusing on—predicting, questioning, clarifying, or summarizing.

Teacher-Facilitated Whole-Group Reflection and Goal Setting

- **Share** key points from reading discussions.
- **Reflect** on how Say Something helped us think about what we read.
- **Set new goals** or extend existing ones.

text, I had them stop and Say Something to the group. I encouraged a variety of responses, such as predictions, connections, clue identifications, character development, and questions. Students read the next three pages of text, and at the end of the designated section, they stopped and said something related to the story.

Practice: Students finished reading the first chapter and used Say Something with a partner. Students stopped at least two more times in the chapter to say something. They recorded these responses in their Guided Comprehension Journals. We used these to spark discussion during the next small-group time. We continued this process throughout the reading of *Bunnicula*.

Reflect: After the first chapter, I encouraged the students to think about how using Say Something helped them make sense of the text. They responded that it really made them think about what they were reading, and they also commented that they learned new ideas when they heard their partners' comments. I asked them to continue to use this process as they read the book on their own. I met with students regularly to discuss the story, share ideas, and reflect on the process.

Student-Facilitated Comprehension Centers

Text: *The Eleventh Hour: A Curious Mystery* (Base, 1989) (Texts varied according to students' abilities.)

Mystery Center: I provided multiple copies of *The Eleventh Hour* and a clue organizer (see Appendix, page 169). Students read it in small groups and used Say Something after every two pages to discuss and highlight clues. I provided a clue sheet as a guide for them to keep track of the clues they were gathering and the suspect they had in mind at each point of the story.

Student-Facilitated Comprehension Routines

Literature Circles: Students used Say Something to promote discussion about the mysteries they were reading (Cam Jansen, Nancy Drew, *The Westing Game*). They read together, determined where they would stop reading, and then used Say Something, first in pairs, and then in the whole group.

Reciprocal Teaching: Students focused their Say Something responses on one of the strategies—predicting, clarifying, questioning, or summarizing. They kept notes of their ideas in their Guided Comprehension Journals to facilitate discussion and sharing both here and in Stage Three.

STAGE THREE: Teacher-Facilitated Whole-Group Reflection and Goal Setting

Share: Students shared and discussed their applications of Say Something from Stage Two in small groups. Then each group reported to the whole class.

Reflect: We reflected on how Say Something helped us monitor as we read. The students noted that they enjoyed this technique because it helped them focus their thinking while reading. Then we discussed how their comments became deeper and more meaningful as they practiced this technique. Everyone felt good about their ability to use this technique.

Set New Goals: We decided to extend our use of Say Something to expository text.

Assessment Options

I used observation during guided small groups and made notes about students' contributions. I also reviewed students' notes in their Guided Comprehension Journals and noted their contributions to whole-group discussions. The clue organizer from the mystery center provided information about the students' abilities to use the clues to solve the mystery.

Guided Comprehension Strategy: Summarizing
Teaching Idea: Lyric Summaries

STAGE ONE: Teacher-Directed Whole-Group Instruction

Text: "The Tell-Tale Heart" (Poe, 1981)

Explain: I explained summarizing and focused on using Lyric Summaries (see Appendix A, *Guided Comprehension: A Teaching Model for Grades 3–8*) with narrative text. I engaged in direct explanation of the elements that needed to be included in a meaningful story summary. Then I described how Lyric Summaries differed from other summaries that we had written. I explained that we would be selecting a familiar tune—such as the theme song from a television show—to use as the music for our Lyric Summaries and that we would format our writing as actual song lyrics.

Demonstrate: To demonstrate, I used "The Tell-Tale Heart." It had served as the introductory selection of our mystery unit, and I had just finished reading it aloud the day before.

Noting that we had different musical tastes, I pointed out that all of us had exposure to television show themes. I offered two suggestions and invited students to add their ideas. We examined our list, considered the tone of the story, and decided on *The Addams Family* theme. Several students noted *The Brady Bunch* and *I Love Lucy* were just too cheerful for Poe. We ran through several renditions of the theme, analyzing the rhythm pattern. The students also felt rhyme was important.

Our next step was to choose the essential story information. I used a think-aloud to begin the summary. "How did the story begin? The two men were neighbors. Did they get along? Yes, at least in the beginning they were fine. I think this is a good place to start." I wrote the information on an overhead transparency.

Guide: Students then volunteered information, which I recorded on a chart, of the narrative elements on the transparency. When we thought we had everything we needed, we reviewed the entire list. The class evaluated each item ("Is it necessary? If you left it out, would the story be the same?") and checked for sequence. Then we began writing the lyrics. I picked the first two ideas from our list (the old man and the mad man, neighbors) and explained that these would have to be expressed in the identified rhythm. Continuing my think-aloud, I composed the first line, demonstrating how to change word choices to make them fit. I initially used *neighbor* as an end word, then remarked that it might be difficult to find a rhyming word. At this point, some of the students jumped in with suggestions of their own. For example, *mad man* became *young man* because they thought it sounded too much like the character was angry.

Practice: Students took over the lyric-writing responsibilities with my continued guidance. They proposed numerous lines plus changes in ideas, word order, and word choices throughout the process. They voted on any significant changes.

Reflect: When we completed our whole-group Lyric Summary, we reflected on what information needed to be included in a good summary, and how writing Lyric Summaries helped us comprehend. Then we discussed how we would use them with other types of texts in other settings. Our whole-group Lyric Summary for "The Tell-Tale Heart" by Edgar Allan Poe, set to the theme from *The Addams Family*, follows on page 46:

GUIDED COMPREHENSION: MYSTERIES
SUMMARIZING: LYRIC SUMMARIES

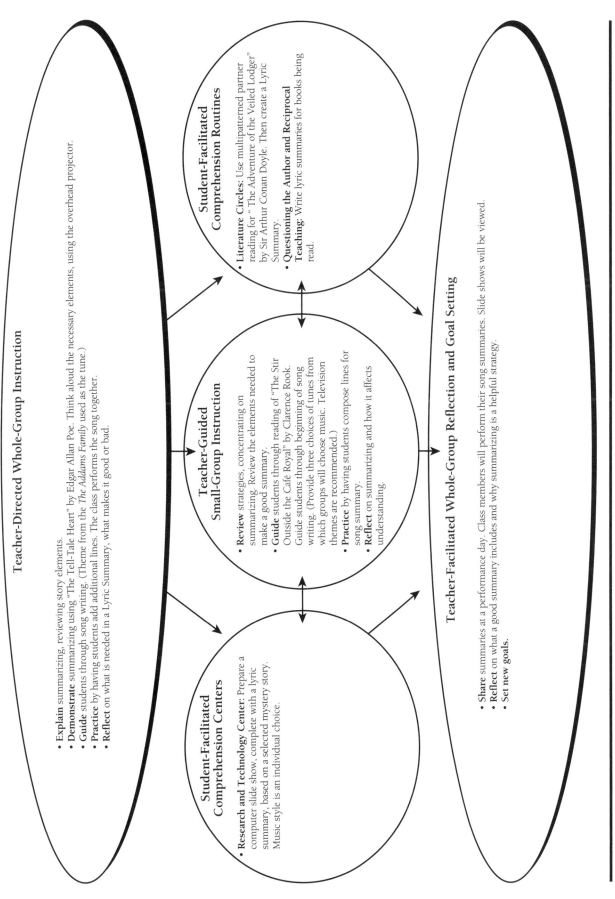

Teacher-Directed Whole-Group Instruction

- **Explain** summarizing, reviewing story elements.
- **Demonstrate** summarizing using "The Tell-Tale Heart" by Edgar Allan Poe. Think aloud the necessary elements, using the overhead projector.
- **Guide** students through song writing. (Theme from the *The Addams Family* used as the tune.)
- **Practice** by having students add additional lines. The class performs the song together.
- **Reflect** on what is needed in a Lyric Summary, what makes it good or bad.

Student-Facilitated Comprehension Routines

- **Literature Circles:** Use multipatterned partner reading for " The Adventure of the Veiled Lodger" by Sir Arthur Conan Doyle. Then create a Lyric Summary.
- **Questioning the Author and Reciprocal Teaching:** Write lyric summaries for books being read.

Teacher-Guided Small-Group Instruction

- **Review** strategies, concentrating on summarizing. Review the elements needed to make a good summary.
- **Guide** students through reading of "The Stir Outside the Café Royal" by Clarence Rook. Guide students through beginning of song writing. (Provide three choices of tunes from which groups will choose music. Television themes are recommended.)
- **Practice** by having students compose lines for song summary.
- **Reflect** on summarizing and how it affects understanding.

Student-Facilitated Comprehension Centers

- **Research and Technology Center:** Prepare a computer slide show, complete with a lyric summary, based on a selected mystery story. Music style is an individual choice.

Teacher-Facilitated Whole-Group Reflection and Goal Setting

- **Share** summaries at a performance day. Class members will perform their song summaries. Slide shows will be viewed.
- **Reflect** on what a good summary includes and why summarizing is a helpful strategy.
- **Set new goals.**

The young man and the old man
As neighbors living they can,
They didn't have a problem,
Until he saw his eye.

The eye was weird and creepy,
It made him feel so freaky,
He had to kill the old man,
He was so very scared.

Thumpety-thump- click, click,
Thumpety-thump- click, click,
Thumpety-thump, thumpety-thump,
Thumpety-thump- click, click.

He feared the blue evil eye,
That looked to him like the sky,
The old man just had to die,
He practiced every night.

Watched the old man every night,
Snuck in and opened the light,
Tried not to give him a fright.
And then the night arrived.

Thumpety-thump- click, click,
Thumpety-thump- click, click,
Thumpety-thump, thumpety-thump,
Thumpety-thump- click, click.

He woke him with a noise,
Who's there? The old man's voice,
After an hour passed,
He killed the blind old man.

Someone had heard a yell,
The cops rang at the bell,
He thought they heard the thumping,
Thump of the old man's heart.

Thumpety-thump- click, click,
Thumpety-thump- click, click,
Thumpety-thump, thumpety-thump,
Thumpety-thump- click, click.

Our man was very nervous,
He huffed and puffed and cursed,
And finally he declared,
Himself the murderer bold!

Thumpety-thump- click, click,
Thumpety-thump- click, click,
Thumpety-thump, thumpety-thump,
Thumpety-thump- click, click.

STAGE TWO: Teacher-Guided Small-Group Instruction

Text: *More Five-Minute Mysteries* (Weber, 1991) (Texts varied according to students' abilities.)

Review: I reviewed the comprehension strategies that good readers use and concentrated on summarizing. I reminded students that we summarize different types of text in different ways and that we would be focusing on narrative summaries.

Guide: I guided students to read the short story "Chasing the Bank Robbers" by offering prompts about previewing and the essential elements of mysteries. After they finished reading, I guided them in creating a Lyric Summary. We brainstormed the essential information from the story. Then we reviewed the list of music selections from Stage One and decided to use the theme song from *Gilligan's Island*. We used the information students had provided and supported the students as we wrote the first two lines.

Practice: The students completed the summary, and I offered my assistance when it was requested. Then we all sang the Lyric Summary, and one student observed, "Summarizing this way was a lot of fun." We all agreed.

Reflect: We reflected on how Lyric Summaries helped us understand what we had read. Students noted that extracting the information necessary for writing the lyrics was very helpful. They also said using music was a great idea and that the Lyric Summaries helped them to understand and remember what they had read.

Student-Facilitated Comprehension Centers

Research and Technology Center: Students worked in trios to prepare a PowerPoint slide show. The shows included a Lyric Summary based on a mystery they had recently read and music they had downloaded from one of several sources provided from the Internet.

Student-Facilitated Comprehension Routines

Literature Circles: Pairs of students used a partner reading pattern to read a Sherlock Holmes mystery such as "The Adventure of the Veiled Lodger." While reading they recorded notes in their Guided Comprehension Journals. Then each pair discussed its mystery with the group. Finally, group members wrote a Lyric Summary, with each verse of the song focusing on a different Sherlock Holmes mystery.

Reciprocal Teaching: Students wrote Lyric Summaries based on the books they had most recently read.

Questioning the Author: Students created Lyric Summaries based on their author queries and responses for the book they had just finished reading.

STAGE THREE: Teacher-Facilitated Whole-Group Reflection and Goal Setting

Share: Students sang the Lyric Summaries they had created during Stage Two and shared their PowerPoint slide shows.

Reflect: We reflected on what good narrative summaries need to include and how summarizing helped us understand what we had read. We also discussed Lyric Summaries. Students' comments ranged from "It was fun!" to "It was challenging." One student remarked that you really had to know the story well to extract the information that was essential to the summary. Another noted that he had never done anything like this and he never liked summarizing before, but he liked it now. All the students were pleased with their efforts. Most important, all said they understood summarizing better.

Set New Goals: We decided to extend our goal by using Lyric Summaries with expository text.

Assessment Options

I observed students throughout the Guided Comprehension process and used completed Lyric Summaries to assess students' understanding and application of summarizing using this technique. I also used students' self-assessment during Stage Three as an information source.

Guided Comprehension Strategy: Summarizing
Teaching Idea: Mystery Cubes

STAGE ONE: *Teacher-Directed Whole-Group Instruction*

Text: *Encyclopedia Brown Takes the Cake: The Case of the Missing Garlic Bread* (Sobol, 1997)

Explain: I started by explaining the concept of summarizing and what needs to be included when summarizing a mystery. I showed the students a completed Mystery Cube that included the title, the characters (usually detective, criminal, victim), the setting, the problem (the mystery), the key events (clues to help solve the mystery), and the solution (see Appendix, pages 160 and 170).

Demonstrate: Next, I gave pairs of students copies of the text and I read aloud a short mystery from *Encyclopedia Brown Takes the Cake: The Case of the Missing Garlic Bread*. After reading, I thought aloud as I completed the first two sides of the Mystery Cube (title and characters). I demonstrated how to revisit the text to help with remembering the information and with spelling.

Guide: Then I used guiding questions (Where did this story take place? What was the case about?) to help the students complete the next two sides of the cube—setting and problem. After that, I guided the students to begin the next side of the cube—the key events. I helped them summarize the events into three or four main clues that Encyclopedia Brown found.

Practice: After I observed the students meeting success finding specific information, I allowed them to complete the cubes in pairs. Each pair used the text to finish the clues and write the solution. Then we shared several summaries based on the information on the cubes and discussed them as a class.

Reflect: Finally, I helped the students to review the key points of a mystery and reflect on how summarizing helped us to identify the most important ideas. We also discussed how we could use summarizing in other settings.

STAGE TWO: *Teacher-Guided Small-Group Instruction*

Text: *Encyclopedia Brown Takes the Cake: The Case of the Missing Watchgoose* (Sobol, 1997). (Texts varied according to students' abilities.)

Review: I reviewed the key points of summarizing a mystery and reminded the students of the other strategies good readers use. Then I focused on using Mystery Cubes to summarize.

Guide: Next I guided the students to make predictions about the mystery based on the title and their previous experience with reading mysteries. Then I had the students read the first two pages of the mystery and asked them to be able to tell the detective and the crime when they were finished reading. I listened to individuals whisper-read as a way to check for fluency. This helped me verify that the book was the appropriate level for each student. When all students finished, I had them record the detective and the crime on their Mystery Cube. I then had students predict what happened to the watchgoose, and cite clues from the story to support their predictions. Next I guided the students to read the next page of the story and offer additional clues about the missing watchgoose. When they finished, I asked the students to share and then record their ideas on their cubes.

Practice: The students finished reading the mystery, and we shared additional clues and made predictions about the solution. Then we checked in the back of the book to see if our predictions

GUIDED COMPREHENSION: MYSTERIES
SUMMARIZING: MYSTERY CUBES

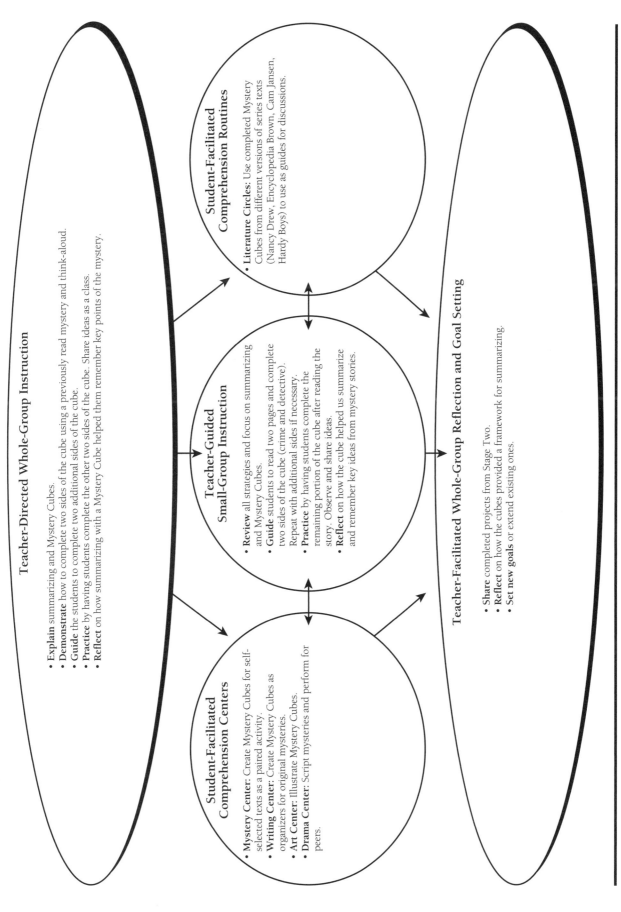

Teacher-Directed Whole-Group Instruction

- **Explain** summarizing and Mystery Cubes.
- **Demonstrate** how to complete two sides of the cube using a previously read mystery and think-aloud.
- **Guide** the students to complete two additional sides of the cube.
- **Practice** by having students complete the other two sides of the cube. Share ideas as a class.
- **Reflect** on how summarizing with a Mystery Cube helped them remember key points of the mystery.

Student-Facilitated Comprehension Routines

- **Literature Circles:** Use completed Mystery Cubes from different versions of series texts (Nancy Drew, Encyclopedia Brown, Cam Jansen, Hardy Boys) to use as guides for discussions.

Teacher-Guided Small-Group Instruction

- **Review** all strategies and focus on summarizing and Mystery Cubes.
- **Guide** students to read two pages and complete two sides of the cube (crime and detective). Repeat with additional sides if necessary.
- **Practice** by having students complete the remaining portion of the cube after reading the story. Observe and share ideas.
- **Reflect** on how the cube helped us summarize and remember key ideas from mystery stories.

Student-Facilitated Comprehension Centers

- **Mystery Center:** Create Mystery Cubes for self-selected texts as a paired activity.
- **Writing Center:** Create Mystery Cubes as organizers for original mysteries.
- **Art Center:** Illustrate Mystery Cubes.
- **Drama Center:** Script mysteries and perform for peers.

Teacher-Facilitated Whole-Group Reflection and Goal Setting

- **Share** completed projects from Stage Two.
- **Reflect** on how the cubes provided a framework for summarizing.
- **Set new goals** or extend existing ones.

were correct. Finally, the students summarized the story by completing the rest of the Mystery Cube. This is the information that Angela and David included on their Mystery Cube:

Setting: This morning at a plant nursery
Detective: Encyclopedia Brown
Mystery: Christopher Columbus Day is missing.
Victim: A watchgoose
3 Clues: Lady with a knapsack, three feathers, two men
Solution: The two men stole and ate the goose

Reflect: We reflected by sharing summaries and revealing the points in the story when we figured out the solution. Others shared how they were tricked into thinking the culprit was someone else. Then we discussed how the Mystery Cubes helped us summarize the story and talked about using them with other mystery books.

Student-Facilitated Comprehension Centers

Mystery Center: Students completed Mystery Cubes based on stories they had previously read. They used the completed cubes as the bases of book talks during Stage Three.

Writing Center: Some students completed Mystery Cubes and then used them as planning organizers for writing new mysteries. I placed some bags with ideas for each part of the mystery (characters, setting, mystery, clues, and solution) to provide assistance for students who needed additional support.

Art Center: Students visited this center to illustrate their original mysteries and produce their completed books.

Drama Center: Students scripted and practiced performing Readers Theatre versions of the mysteries they read.

Student-Facilitated Comprehension Routines

Literature Circles: Students created Mystery Cubes for mysteries that they had already read. For example, one group had read different versions of Cam Jansen stories, so they completed Mystery Cubes based on these stories and used them to share story summaries.

STAGE THREE: Teacher-Facilitated Whole-Group Reflection and Goal Setting

Share: In small groups, students shared the Mystery Cubes and stories they had created in Stage Two and discussed how well they were able to use them.

Reflect: As a whole group, we reflected on the importance of including key ideas in summaries and how summarizing helped us understand what we had read.

Set New Goals: We decided to extend our goal to learning other ways to create summaries.

Assessment Options

I observed students during all stages of Guided Comprehension. I made note of those students who were contributing and those who needed additional support. I also viewed their completed cubes to determine their success in effectively summarizing mysteries. I also noted the reflections we made and the goal we set in Stage Three.

THEME RESOURCES

Texts

Adler, D. (1997). *Cam Jansen and the scary snake mystery*. New York: Scholastic.

Adler, J. Cam Jansen Mystery Series. New York: Scholastic.

Alexander, W. (1990). *The clue kids: The case of the funny money man*. Mahwah, NJ: Troll.

Ardagh, P. (1999). *History detectives: Ancient Egypt*. New York: Peter Bedrick Books.

Aron, P. (2000). *Unsolved mysteries of history: An eye-opening investigation into the most baffling events of all time*. New York: John Wiley & Sons.

Avi. (1989). *The man who was Poe*. New York: Avon.

Base, G. (1989). *The eleventh hour: A curious mystery*. New York: Harry N. Abrams.

Bunting, E. (1989). *The ghost children*. New York: Clarion.

Coleman, M. Internet Detectives Series. New York: Bantam Skylark.

Conford, E. (1988). *A case for Jenny Archer*. Boston: Little, Brown.

Dixon, R.W. The Hardy Boys Series. New York: Grosset & Dunlap.

Frost, E. (1979). *Mystery of the runaway sled*. Mahwah, NJ: Troll.

Giff, P.R. (1987). *The powder puff puzzle*. New York: Dell.

Hahn, M.D. (1990). *The dead man in Indian Creek*. New York: Avon.

Haven, K. (1994). *Marvels of science: 50 fascinating 5-minute reads*. Englewood, CO: Libraries Unlimited.

Hildrick, E.W. (1982). *The case of the felon's fiddle*. Macmillan.

Hinter, P.C. Clue Jr. Series. New York: Scholastic.

Howe, D., & Howe, J. (1979). *Bunnicula: A rabbit-tale of mystery*. New York: Avon.

Howe, J. (1982). *Howliday Inn*. New York: Atheneum.

Howe, J. (1983). *The celery stalks at midnight*. New York: Avon.

Howe, J. (1992). *Return to Howliday Inn*. New York: Atheneum

Keene, C. (1977). *The clue in the old album*. New York: Grosset & Dunlap.

Keene, C. The Nancy Drew Mystery Series. New York: Grosset & Dunlap.

Keene, C. The Nancy Drew Notebooks Series. New York: Pocket Books.

Keller, H. (1998). *Angela's top secret computer club*. New York: Greenwillow.

Konigsburg, E.L. (1986). *From the mixed-up files of Mrs. Basil E. Frankweiler*. New York: Aladdin.

Mckean, T. (1987). *The search for Sara Sanderson*. New York: Avon.

Nixon, J.L. (2000). *Nobody's there*. New York: Delacorte.

Poe, E.A. (1981). *The tell-tale heart and other writings by Edgar Allan Poe*. New York: Bantam Doubleday Dell.

Raskin, E. (1997). *The westing game*. New York: Scott Foresman.

Sharmat, M. (1992). *Nate the great and the stolen base*. New York: Putnam.

Snyder, Z.K. (1986). *The Egypt game*. New York: Yearling.

Sobol, D.J. (1967). *Two-minute mysteries*. New York: Scholastic.

Sobol, D.J. (1982). *Encyclopedia Brown takes the cake: The case of the missing garlic bread and the case of the missing watchgoose*. New York: Scholastic.

Sobol, D.J. (1985). *Encyclopedia Brown: Boy detective*. Bantam Skylark.

Stein, R.L. The R.L. Stein Mystery Series. New York: Scholastic.

Warner, G.C. The Boxcar Children Series. New York: Scholastic.

Weber, K. (1991). *More five minute mysteries*. Philadelphia: Running Press.

Wright, B.R. (1983). *The dollhouse murders*. New York: Scholastic.

Websites

Candlelight Stories: Kids' Mystery Contest
   www.candlelightstories.com/D001/Mystery.asp

Mysteries.com
   www.mysteries.com

The Mystery Reader
   www.themysteryreader.com

MysteryNet's Kids Mysteries
   kids.mysterynet.com

MysteryNet's Kids Mysteries: The Case of the Ruined Roses (Solve-it 28)
   kids.mysterynet.com/solveit

Performance Extensions Across the Curriculum

Social Studies

• Use *Unsolved Mysteries of History* to explore historical mysteries, such as the following:
   Who really invented printing?
   Who built Stonehenge?
   Did Mary, Queen of Scots, kill her husband?
   Who wrote Shakespeare's plays?
   Why were the Pyramids built?
   Did the Trojan War really happen?
   How did the Seven Wonders of the World become the Seven Wonders?

• Journey back in time and use the History Detective Series to solve mysteries of different cultures.

Science

• Research the mysteries of science using *Marvels of Science: 50 Fascinating 5-Minute Reads* by Kendal Haven.

• Visit the website http://www.smm.org/catal to investigate the mysteries uncovered at the archeological site of Catalhöyük in central Turkey.

• Explore other archeological sites and share mysteries that have been uncovered.

Math

• Explore the mysteries of number games and try to solve how the patterns work.

• Solve or design and solve number patterns or mystery word problems.

• Visit Math Maven's Mysteries at http://teacher.scholastic.com/maven to work on the math mystery word problems. Write original math mystery problems and have peers try to solve and explain.

Art

• Explore the surreal paintings of Magritte, Dali, or Miro. Try to figure out the mystery of the message communicated in the art and explore the connections among ideas represented in the paintings.

Music

- Develop theme music for a Readers Theatre production of scenes from your favorite mystery.
- Create background music for a mystery you have written.
- Create a PowerPoint slide presentation for a mystery you have read or written. Download music to enhance the story.

Culminating Activity

Whodunit? A Celebration of Mysteries: Use students' performances from the mystery theme to create a mysterious atmosphere. Have students dramatize a series of minimysteries. Invite parents and community members to participate in an action mystery. Create a variety of stations where students can explain the mystery performances from across the curriculum to the visitors. Have students hold an autographing session for copies of *Whodunit*, a class book of mysteries across the curriculum.

CHAPTER 4

Favorite Authors: Eve Bunting, Jon Scieszka, Gary Soto, and Gary Paulsen

Authors are writers who share unique perspectives on a variety of topics. Their books may be humorous, sad, or thought provoking. They may write to entertain, to persuade, or to inform. They may share life experiences, offer insights into social or historical issues, or serve as tour guides on imaginative journeys. Authors have engaging styles that motivate us to read, and consequently, we have favorite authors. Eve Bunting, Jon Scieszka, Gary Soto, and Gary Paulsen are a few of ours. (Resources for planning themes about other favorite authors—Judy Blume, Beverly Cleary, Patricia Polacco, and Jerry Spinelli—can be found in Chapter 8.)

We chose Eve Bunting because she has written on such a wide variety of topics with such expertise. Whether telling the emotional story of an adult's first reading experiences in *The Wednesday Surprise*, recounting the Los Angeles riots in *Smoky Nights*, relating a story of homeless life in *Fly Away Home*, or acknowledging Vietnam veterans in *The Wall*, Bunting writes from a perspective of knowledge and candor.

Jon Scieszka is one of our favorite authors because his writing is so entertaining. He has said that he writes to make kids laugh; we think he knows that applies to kids of all ages. From *The True Story of the 3 Little Pigs!* to *The Stinky Cheese Man and Other Fairly Stupid Tales*, *Math Curse*, and *Baloney (Henry P.)*, Scieszka and illustrator Lane Smith seem to have a secret knowledge of exactly what makes us laugh. They have also provided us with a permanent ticket to time travel in the Time Warp Trio series which includes such titles as *Your Mother Was a Neanderthal*, *Knights of the Kitchen Table*, *It's All Greek to Me*, and *The Good, the Bad, and the Goofy*.

Another favorite author, Gary Soto, writes short stories, books, poetry, and plays. He also recently ventured into the biography genre by authoring *Jessie De La Cruz: A Profile of a United Farm Worker*. Although the themes of his works are universal, Soto draws heavily on his Mexican-American heritage in his writing. In addition to being an author, he is a professor of creative writing at the University of California, Riverside. Among our favorite Soto titles are *Baseball in April and Other Stories*, *The Skirt*, *Novio Boy*, *Taking Sides*, *Canto Familiar*, and *Neighborhood Odes*.

Gary Paulsen, our final favorite author, has written picture books, young adult novels, adult novels, and two autobiographical volumes: *Eastern Sun, Winter Moon* and *Guts*. Whenever Paulsen shares his literacy history, he is quick to note that his life changed one cold night when he went into a library to get warm. The librarian offered him a library card and that's what sparked his interest in reading. Paulsen frequently writes about his life experiences. For example, in *Winterdance* he chronicles his participation in the Iditarod, a grueling 1,180-mile dogsled race across Alaska.

The Sample Theme-Based Plan for Guided Comprehension: Favorite Authors (see Figure 15) presents a sampling of goals, state standards, assessments, texts, technology resources, comprehension strategies, teaching ideas, comprehension centers, and comprehension routines. The plan begins by delineating examples of student goals and related state standards. The student goals for this theme include the following:

- using appropriate comprehension strategies
- interpreting literature, including describing and discussing characteristics of writers' styles
- writing retellings and reviews
- communicating effectively

These goals support the following state standards:

- learning to read independently
- reading, analyzing, and interpreting literature
- types and quality of writing
- speaking and listening

Samples assessments include observation, strategy applications, and student self-assessments. The Guided Comprehension lessons are based on the following strategies and corresponding teaching ideas:

- Making Connections: Save the Last Word for Me
- Knowing How Words Work: Context Clues
- Summarizing: Comic Strip Summaries
- Evaluating: Evaluative Questioning

Terrible Things: An Allegory of the Holocaust, Baloney (Henry P.), Taking Sides, and *Winterdance: The Fine Madness of Running the Iditarod* are the texts used in Stage One for teacher-directed whole-group instruction. Numerous additional theme-related texts, including those used in teacher-guided small-group instruction and the student-facilitated comprehension centers and routines are presented in the Theme Resources at the end of the chapter.

Examples of Comprehension Centers students use during Stage Two of Guided Comprehension include art, favorite author, research and technology, and writing. Students also engage in strategy application in comprehension routines such as Literature Circles, Questioning the Author, and Reciprocal Teaching. Sample website resources—including sites for favorite authors Eve Bunting, Jon Scieszka, Gary Soto, and Gary Paulsen—complete the overview.

Figure 15. Sample Theme-Based Plan for Guided Comprehension: Favorite Authors

Goals and Connections to State Standards | Students will

- use appropriate comprehension strategies. Standard: learning to read independently
- interpret literature. Standard: reading, analyzing, and interpreting literature
- write retellings and reviews. Standard: types and quality of writing
- communicate effectively. Standards: types and quality of writing; speaking and listening

Comprehension Strategies

1. Making Connections
2. Knowing How Words Work
3. Summarizing
4. Evaluating

Teaching Ideas

Save the Last Word for Me
Context Clues
Comic Strip Summaries
Evaluative Questioning

Comprehension Centers

Students will apply the comprehension strategies and related teaching ideas in the following comprehension centers:

Art Center
Favorite Author Center
Research and Technology Center
Writing Center

Comprehension Routines

Students will apply the comprehension strategies and related teaching ideas in the following comprehension routines:

Literature Circles
Questioning the Author
Reciprocal Teaching

Assessment

The following measures can be used for a variety of purposes, including diagnostic, formative, and summative assessment:

Book Reviews
Chapter Word Maps
Comic Strip Summaries
Context Clue Organizers

Observation
Retellings
Save the Last Word Cards
Students' Self-Assessments

Text	Title	Theme	Level
1.	*Terrible Things: An Allegory of the Holocaust*	FA	4
2.	*Baloney (Henry P.)*	FA	3
3.	*Taking Sides*	FA	5
4.	*Winterdance: The Fine Madness of Running the Iditarod*	FA	7

Technology Resources

Book Page Children's Interview: Eve Bunting
www.bookpage.com/9705bp/childrens/
evebunting.html

The New York Public Library: Chat With Jon Scieszka
www.nypl.org/branch/kids/authorchat.html

The Official Gary Soto Website
www.garysoto.com

Books@Random: Gary Paulsen
www.randomhouse.com/features/garypaulsen/
about.html

GUIDED COMPREHENSION LESSONS

Favorite Author Eve Bunting
Guided Comprehension Strategy: Making Connections
Teaching Idea: Save the Last Word for Me

STAGE ONE: Teacher-Directed Whole-Group Instruction

Text: *Terrible Things: An Allegory of the Holocaust* (1996)

Explain: I explained to the students that good readers make connections to texts before reading, during reading, and after reading. I reminded them that we make text-self, text-text, and text-world connections. I told them that we were going to focus on making connections to Eve Bunting books during and after reading. I explained to them that during reading we would make connections verbally and after reading we would engage in an activity titled Save the Last Word for Me (Short, Harste, & Burke, 1996; see Appendix A, *Guided Comprehension: A Teaching Model for Grades 3–8*).

Demonstrate: I introduced the book by having students think about and then "quickwrite" about terrible things. When sharing my quickwrite, I noted that I thought war, murder, and mean people were terrible things. Then students shared their views from their quickwrites, and I started reading the book aloud. I made sure my voice was very loud whenever the terrible things were around, and I made my voice soft and sweet when the little rabbit was speaking. I stopped at three places in the story to have the students make connections. I modeled at the first stopping point after the birds were taken away. I said, "This reminds me of when someone is being made fun of and nobody speaks up." The students made connections at the other two stopping points. After I finished reading the text, I showed the students how to engage in Save the Last Word for Me (see Appendix, page 171). I told them that we would each find something within the text that really affected us or that we thought was really important. We would write that on side one of an index card, and then we would explain why we chose it on the other side. I demonstrated this process on an overhead transparency. Here is what I wrote:

Side One	Side Two
"The Terrible Things don't need a reason. Just be glad it wasn't us they wanted." Big Rabbit	I thought this was very selfish. If the animals had helped each other, they may have been able to be saved.

I covered side two and showed the students what I wrote on side one. Then I explained that when the students were finished writing their cards, they would share side one with others in their group. Once they read side one aloud, the others in the group would react to or comment on what was shared. After everyone in the group had responded, the person who shared side one would read side two of his or her card. I read my side one to the students and asked for some responses. Then I shared what I had written on side two of my card.

Guide: I guided the students to think about a part of the book that they thought was interesting or worth discussing. I told them to write it on one side of an index card. I reread parts of the story to help refresh their minds. I guided them to write why they chose that part on side two of their

GUIDED COMPREHENSION: FAVORITE AUTHORS
MAKING CONNECTIONS: SAVE THE LAST WORD FOR ME

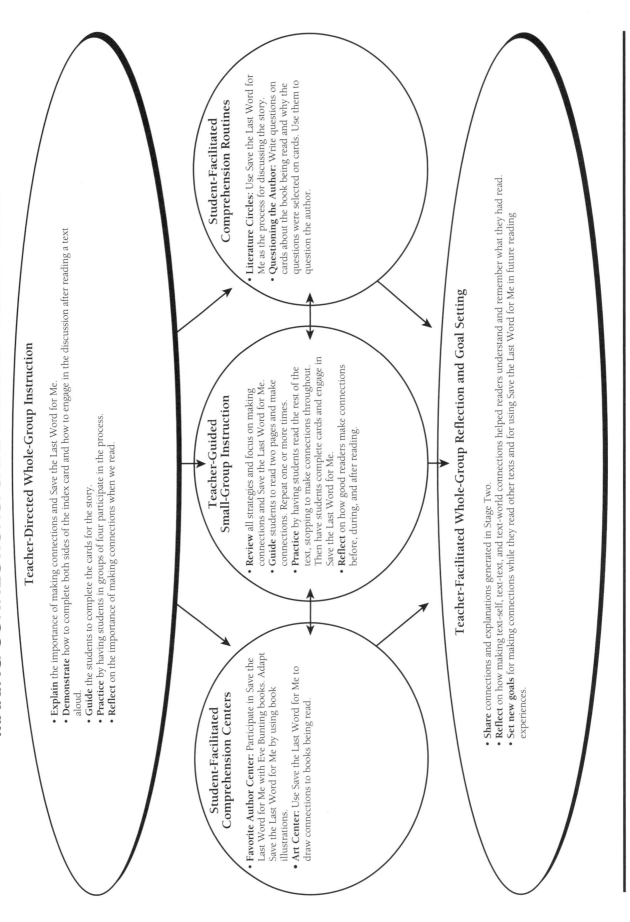

Teacher-Directed Whole-Group Instruction

- **Explain** the importance of making connections and Save the Last Word for Me.
- **Demonstrate** how to complete both sides of the index card and how to engage in the discussion after reading a text aloud.
- **Guide** the students to complete the cards for the story.
- **Practice** by having students in groups of four participate in the process.
- **Reflect** on the importance of making connections when we read.

Student-Facilitated Comprehension Routines

- **Literature Circles:** Use Save the Last Word for Me as the process for discussing the story.
- **Questioning the Author:** Write questions on cards about the book being read and why the questions were selected on cards. Use them to question the author.

Teacher-Guided Small-Group Instruction

- **Review** all strategies and focus on making connections and Save the Last Word for Me.
- **Guide** students to read two pages and make connections. Repeat one or more times.
- **Practice** by having students read the rest of the text, stopping to make connections throughout. Then have students complete cards and engage in Save the Last Word for Me.
- **Reflect** on how good readers make connections before, during, and after reading.

Student-Facilitated Comprehension Centers

- **Favorite Author Center:** Participate in Save the Last Word for Me with Eve Bunting books. Adapt Save the Last Word for Me by using book illustrations.
- **Art Center:** Use Save the Last Word for Me to draw connections to books being read.

Teacher-Facilitated Whole-Group Reflection and Goal Setting

- **Share** connections and explanations generated in Stage Two.
- **Reflect** on how making text-self, text-text, and text-world connections helped readers understand and remember what they had read.
- **Set new goals** for making connections while they read other texts and for using Save the Last Word for Me in future reading experiences.

Guided Comprehension in Action: Lessons for Grades 3–8 by Maureen McLaughlin and Mary Beth Allen ©2002. Newark, DE: International Reading Association. May be copied for classroom use.

cards. I circulated and engaged some students in conversation about their choices. This helped them focus on what to write on side two.

Practice: Once all students completed their cards, I put them in groups of four to engage in Save the Last Word for Me. I used an overhead projector to remind them of the process for sharing:

- Decide who will share first.
- First person reads side one of the index card.
- All other members take turns responding to what the first person shared.
- After everyone has had a chance to share, first person reads side two of the index card and has the last word.
- Repeat the process with another student.

The following are some samples of what the students wrote:

Nicholas

Side One

Little Rabbit survived the Terrible Things and said he would go warn the other animals.

Side Two

I wish he had thought to do this before the Terrible Things wiped out all the animals in his part of the woods. If the animals had worked together, they might have been able to fight back against the Terrible Things.

Hannah

Side One

Little Rabbit was left all by himself.

Side Two

This made me feel sad because all his friends were taken away and he was all alone. This also made me feel scared because now he would have to try to protect himself from the Terrible Things and he is so small and they are so huge and mean.

Reflect: We reflected on the importance of making connections while reading and how this helped us comprehend better. The students said that it was really fun to use Save the Last Word for Me because it was interesting to hear what others wrote on side one and what everyone thought about those ideas. They also liked the structure of the activity and said it kept everyone on task. Finally, we talked about how and when we could use this idea in other settings.

STAGE TWO: Teacher-Guided Small-Group Instruction

Text: *So Far From the Sea* (1998) (Texts varied according to students' abilities.)

Review: I reviewed the comprehension strategies good readers use and then focused on making connections using Save the Last Word for Me.

Guide: I introduced the new book we were going to read, *So Far From the Sea*. I had students make predictions by finishing this sentence: "This reminds me of...." The students read the first two pages and shared what connection they were making. Then they read the next two pages and shared connections. One student made the connection to World War II and then to *Terrible Things*. This sparked a long discussion on how horribly many people were treated during that time. Students continued to read silently and share connections after every two pages.

Practice: After the students finished reading the text, I asked them to write a connection that was important to them on an index card. Next, I asked them to explain why they chose that idea. The students then discussed their cards using the Save the Last Word for Me format.

Reflect: We reflected on how making connections helped us think about the text in a personal way, and students reported that sharing helped them make bigger and broader connections.

Student-Facilitated Comprehension Centers

Favorite Author Center: I placed several Eve Bunting books at the center and the students noted their connections and explanations on index cards. They used Save the Last Word for Me to share these in small groups and during Stage Three. Other students adapted Save the Last Word for Me by using sticky notes to mark an illustration that they found especially interesting or meaningful. Then they used that illustration in place of the usual information on side one. Other students in the group commented on the illustration, and the person who selected the illustration had the last word.

Art Center: Students used Save the Last Word for Me to draw connections they were making during the reading of Eve Bunting books including *The Wednesday Surprise*, *The Wall*, and *Fly Away Home*. They shared these with peers in this stage and later during Stage Three.

Student-Facilitated Comprehension Routines

Literature Circles: Students read *The Hideout* by Eve Bunting. They used Save the Last Word for Me as the process for discussing each chapter.

Questioning the Author: Students used an adaptation of Save the Last Word for Me as a process for QtA. They read agreed upon sections of *The Ghost Children* and recorded their queries on index cards, instead of the usual side one information. When they shared with the group, the other members predicted the author's responses, and the person who wrote the query had the last word.

STAGE THREE: Teacher-Facilitated Whole-Group Reflection and Goal Setting

Share: Students in small groups shared insights they gained from their applications of Save the Last Word for Me in Stage Two. Then one student from each group reported to the whole class.

Reflect: We reflected on how Save the Last Word for Me helped us to make connections with text. Then students engaged in self-assessment. Everyone felt competent in using this technique and their applications supported their thinking. Students also noted that they enjoyed the structure of using the index cards to write what they were going to share. They said it helped them remember points for discussion and connections that they had made while reading. Many students said they liked that this activity assured that everyone had a turn to share what he or she thought was important.

Set New Goals: We decided to stay with our current goal and made plans to make connections and use Save the Last Word for Me in other settings.

Assessment Options

I observed students in all stages of Guided Comprehension, and this helped me determine their ability to make connections. I also collected students' completed index cards and assessed the depth of their connections and their explanations. Some students were very deep thinkers; others were more superficial thinkers. I will use this process again with other texts to help all students make more thoughtful connections.

Favorite Author Jon Scieszka
Guided Comprehension Strategy:
Knowing How Words Work
Teaching Idea: Context Clues

STAGE ONE: Teacher-Directed Whole-Group Instruction

Text: *Baloney (Henry P.)* (2001)

Explain: I explained knowing how words work and focused on Context Clues (see Appendix A, *Guided Comprehension: A Teaching Model for Grades 3–8*). I explained that there were several different kinds of Context Clues, and we often use more than one type to determine a word's meaning. I told the students that we would be learning about the following types of Context Clues (Vacca & Vacca, 2002):

- Example-Illustration—provides an example or illustration to describe the word
- Logic—provides a connection (such as a simile) to the word
- Root Words and Affixes—provides meaningful roots and affixes that the reader uses to determine meaning
- Grammar—provides syntactical cues that allow for reader interpretation

I noted that Context Clues can be used when reading all kinds of text, and that we would study them in the context of our theme, Favorite Author Jon Scieszka. I learned through discussion that many of the students were familiar with Context Clues, but they lacked knowledge of the different types.

Demonstrate: I demonstrated by using a think-aloud, read-aloud, and overhead projector. I thought aloud about what I did when I came to a word I did not know while reading. I illustrated by using a sentence containing a nonsense word and demonstrating how the other words in the sentence helped me determine its possible meaning or synonym. Next, I introduced *Baloney (Henry P.)*, noting that it contained many situations in which we could use Context Clues to determine the meaning of words. I used the Context Clue Organizer (see Appendix, page 172) on the overhead to record our three-step process: locate, define, verify. I noted that the organizer had three columns: one for the words I don't understand, one for the words' possible meanings, and one to place a check mark to indicate that I had verified the meaning in the sentence.

Then I began reading aloud, stopping periodically to think aloud when I encountered a word I did not know. The first word I did not know was *zimulis*. The context was the sentence *I misplaced my trusty zimulis* in a story about an alien student trying to explain his tardiness to his teacher. I wrote *zimulis* in the left column of the organizer. I thought about what the context told me about this word. The text told me what topic it was related to (logic) and what part of speech it was (grammar). Knowing just that much would have allowed me to try several school-related nouns, but the text also provided an illustration (example—illustration) of a pencil. I thought aloud that "pencil" worked well with the other clues. A pencil is school-related, and it is a noun. I recorded *pencil* in the second column of the organizer. I substituted *pencil* for *zimulis* in the sentence and verified that it worked. Then I recorded a checkmark in the third column. This was followed by a brief discussion. One of the students noted that using Context Clues was like math: We could use the clues to make a guess and then try it out to see if it worked.

GUIDED COMPREHENSION: FAVORITE AUTHORS
KNOWING HOW WORDS WORK: CONTEXT CLUES

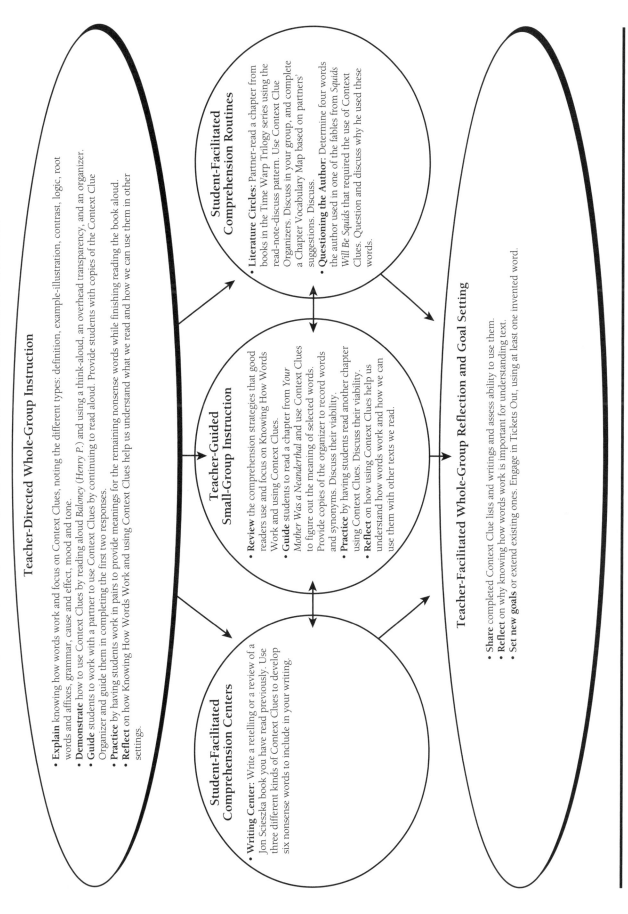

Teacher-Directed Whole-Group Instruction

- **Explain** knowing how words work and focus on Context Clues, noting the different types: definition, example-illustration, contrast, logic, root words and affixes, grammar, cause and effect, mood and tone.
- **Demonstrate** how to use Context Clues by reading aloud *Baloney (Henry P.)* and using a think-aloud, an overhead transparency, and an organizer.
- **Guide** students to work with a partner to use Context Clues by continuing to read aloud. Provide students with copies of the Context Clue Organizer and guide them in completing the first two responses.
- **Practice** by having students work in pairs to provide meanings for the remaining nonsense words while finishing reading the book aloud.
- **Reflect** on how Knowing How Words Work and using Context Clues help us understand what we read and how we can use them in other settings.

Student-Facilitated Comprehension Routines

- **Literature Circles:** Partner-read a chapter from books in the Time Warp Trilogy series using the read-note-discuss pattern. Use Context Clue Organizers. Discuss in your group, and complete a Chapter Vocabulary Map based on partners' suggestions. Discuss.
- **Questioning the Author:** Determine four words the author used in one of the fables from *Squids Will Be Squids* that required the use of Context Clues. Question and discuss why he used these words.

Teacher-Guided Small-Group Instruction

- **Review** the comprehension strategies that good readers use and focus on Knowing How Words Work and using Context Clues.
- **Guide** students to read a chapter from *Your Mother Was a Neanderthal* and use Context Clues to figure out the meaning of selected words. Provide copies of the organizer to record words and synonyms. Discuss their viability.
- **Practice** by having students read another chapter using Context Clues. Discuss their viability.
- **Reflect** on how using Context Clues help us understand how words work and how we can use them with other texts we read.

Student-Facilitated Comprehension Centers

- **Writing Center:** Write a retelling or a review of a Jon Scieszka book you have read previously. Use three different kinds of Context Clues to develop six nonsense words to include in your writing.

Teacher-Facilitated Whole-Group Reflection and Goal Setting

- **Share** completed Context Clue lists and writings and assess ability to use them.
- **Reflect** on why knowing how words work is important for understanding text.
- **Set new goals** or extend existing ones. Engage in Tickets Out, using at least one invented word.

Guided Comprehension in Action: Lessons for Grades 3–8 by Maureen McLaughlin and Mary Beth Allen ©2002. Newark, DE: International Reading Association. May be copied for classroom use.

I continued reading and used Context Clues to determine the meaning of *deski*. I recorded *deski* in the first column of the organizer and thought aloud about what clues the context offered. I again used logic and grammar clues to determine that *deski* was a school-related noun. This time I also used the root word *desk* as a clue (root words and affixes). Then I noticed that there was also an illustration (example—illustration). I thought that *deski* meant desk, so I recorded *desk* in the second column of the organizer. Then I substituted *desk* for *deski* in the sentence to verify its meaning. It worked, so I put a check mark in the third column of the organizer.

Guide: I continued to read aloud, inviting pairs of students to determine the possible meanings of the next two words we did not know. I recorded *torakku* on the organizer on the overhead, and students recorded it on the copies of the Context Clue Organizer that I had provided. Next, I asked the students to think about the clues offered by the context to determine the meaning of this word. They used logic to determine it was some kind of large container because the desk was placed inside it. They used grammar to determine it was a noun because *in* is a preposition and *torakku* was the object of the preposition. Finally, they used the illustration to determine that it was a type of truck or similar outer-space vehicle that was large enough to transport the desk. We recorded *truck* on the organizers and then substituted it for *torakku* in the sentence. It worked and we placed check marks in the third column of our organizers.

Practice: I read aloud to the end of the book and had students work in pairs to determine the meaning of the nonsense words we encountered. Each time, we recorded the word and its possible meanings on the organizers. Then we verified our words in the context of the sentences to see if they made sense and marked the outcome in the third column of the organizer. A section of our completed organizer is featured in Figure 16.

Reflect: We reflected on how using Context Clues helps us understand the meanings of words, and students expressed interest in learning about the other types of clues. One student described Context Clues as "just like using clues to solve a mystery." We also talked about how we could use Context Clues with other texts in other settings.

Figure 16. Context Clue Organizer

Unknown Word	Possible Meaning	Verification
zimulis	pencil	✓
deski	desk	✓
torakku	truck	✓

STAGE TWO: Teacher-Guided Small-Group Instruction

Text: *Your Mother Was a Neanderthal* (1993) (Texts varied according to students' abilities.)

Review: I began by reminding students about the comprehension strategies active readers use and focused on knowing how words work using Context Clues.

Guide: I introduced the text, *Your Mother Was a Neanderthal*, and guided students' reading and use of Context Clues while reading Chapter 1. I provided Context Clue Organizers (see Appendix, page 172) for each student and reminded students about our locate-define-verify system. I monitored as they used the three-step process and recorded the unknown words, their possible meanings, and verifications on the organizers. Then we discussed students' responses.

Practice: Students practiced by reading Chapter 2 and identifying, defining, and verifying words' meanings using Context Clues. They used their Context Clue Organizers to record their responses. Then we discussed their choices.

Reflect: We reflected on how Context Clues help us understand how words work and how we can use them to determine word meanings when reading other kinds of texts in other settings.

Student-Facilitated Comprehension Centers

Writing Center: Students chose to write either a retelling or a review of a Jon Scieszka book they had read previously. They used a Context Clue Organizer to develop nonsense words to include in their writing. Then they switched writings with another student and used Context Clues and a blank copy of the Context Clue Organizer to determine the meaning of the nonsense words. Finally, the students shared their retellings or reviews. Figure 17 shows Makiko's retelling of *The Frog Prince Continued* and the Context Clue Organizer she used when planning.

Figure 17. Makiko's Retelling of *The Frog Prince Continued*

The story begins by telling the ending of the original fairytale. It says that the pruha and the frog prince lived happily ever after, but then the story moves on to what really happened. They really weren't happy. The pruha didn't like that the prince hung around the house so much or that he hopped on the furniture. The prince didn't feel like going out, but one day they had a big fight and the pruha said he should go back to being a frog. The prince went back to the forest to find a drusee who could turn him back into a frog. He met some ruses from other fairytales, but none of them could help him until he met Cinderella's Fairy Godmother and she accidentally turned him into a whizco like the one Cinderella went to the ball in. By then it was dark and the frog prince was lost and the forest was scary. Then all he wanted was to be himself again and go homeas to see the pruha. He was sad and scared, but when the clock struck midnight he wasn't a whizco anymore. He ran homeas and kissed the pruha and they both turned into frogs and hopped away.

Context Clue Organizer

Real Word	Nonsense Word	Verification
princess	pruha	✓
witch	drusee	✓
carriage	whizco	✓
home	homeas	✓

Student-Facilitated Comprehension Routines

Literature Circles: Students partner-read chapters of their current books (*Your Mother Was a Neanderthal*, *Knights of the Kitchen Table*, or *The Good, the Bad, and the Goofy*) using the read-note-discuss pattern. When they noted a word meaning they determined by using Context Clues, they discussed it and recorded the necessary information on the Context Clue Organizer. In their group meeting, they used their completed organizers to discuss vocabulary and develop a Chapter Word Map (see Figure 18 and Appendix, page 173).

Questioning the Author: Students worked in groups to question the author about four of his vocabulary choices that required the use of Context Clues in selected fables from *Squids Will Be Squids: Fresh Morals for Beastly Fables*. They questioned and discussed why the author made the choices he did. Then they suggested synonyms the author could have used and verified them by placing them in the context of the story.

STAGE THREE: Teacher-Facilitated Whole-Group Reflection and Goal Setting

Share: Students shared their applications of Context Clues from Stage Two in small groups and assessed their ability to use them. One member of each group then reported to the whole group. Students enjoyed sharing their organizers, retellings, reviews, chapter maps, and queries.

Reflect: When we reflected on using these Context Clues, students commented that they felt capable using them. Their applications from Stage Two supported their thinking.

Set New Goals: We decided to stay with our current goal and learn about other types of Context Clues.

Assessment Options

I observed students in all stages of Guided Comprehension. I also reviewed their completed Context Clue Organizers, retellings, reviews, and Chapter Word Maps.

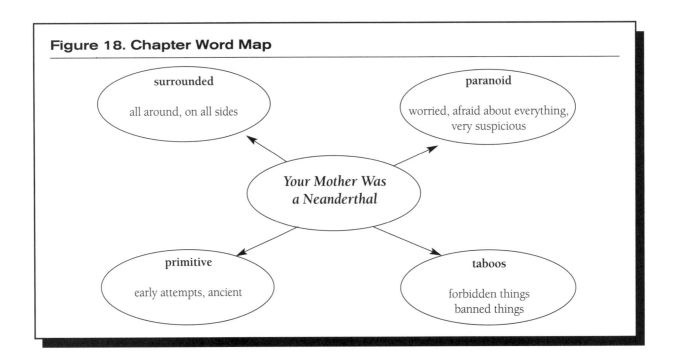

Figure 18. Chapter Word Map

Favorite Author Gary Soto
Guided Comprehension Strategy: Summarizing
Teaching Idea: Comic Strip Summaries

STAGE ONE: Teacher-Directed Whole-Group Instruction

Text: *Taking Sides* (1991)

Explain: In this lesson, I integrated visualizing and summarizing to teach my students how to create Comic Strip Summaries (see Appendix, page 161). I combined the two strategies to make use of students' fondness for drawing and to reteach a simple summary. I explained visualization, asking them to close their eyes and to try and "see" in their minds what I described, which was from the novel we were about to read. Many of them had not focused on visualizing before, so it was a bit difficult at first. Then I moved on to something with which almost every student was familiar—the comic strip. Displaying several pages of Sunday comics, I pointed out and thought aloud about the separate cells, the simple story line, the way in which the characters were introduced, and how the story ended in only a few cells. We then reviewed summarizing orally, using a story I had finished reading aloud the week before.

Demonstrate: To begin the demonstration, I used a 10-cell template of a comic strip, which I pinned to the bulletin board. This would be the drawing board for our comic strip summary. Then I recalled the important information about the beginning of the story Gary Soto tells in *Taking Sides* and wrote it on the chalkboard. (I had recently shared this book through read-aloud as part of our study of Gary Soto's writing.) When I finished, I did a think-aloud of the important information from that part of the story as I quickly sketched in the first two cells and added a descriptive statement for each.

Guide: I continued to summarize sections of the book and guide students in small groups to use the information to develop summary statements. Then students sketched the additional cells. We continued to work through the novel using this process.

Practice: Students practiced by using the remaining chapters to visualize and draw. The students then discussed their thoughts and visualizations.

Reflect: When finished, we discussed what effect the periodic summarizing and drawing had on our understanding and enjoyment of the book. One particular student was elated that he was able to use drawing—what he felt was his true talent—instead of completing worksheets, as he often did in other classes.

STAGE TWO: Teacher-Guided Small-Group Instruction

Text: *Boys at Work* (1996) (Texts varied according to students' abilities.)

Review: I reviewed the strategies good readers use and focused our lesson on summarizing using Comic Strip Summaries.

Guide: I guided my students through their reading of the conclusion of *Taking Sides*, a book we had been reading during our study of Gary Soto's works. Then I encouraged them to discuss the story with a partner and offer ideas that would be important to include in a summary. I recorded their suggestions about characters and setting and guided students to use those ideas to begin creating a group Comic Strip Summary.

Practice: Students practiced by continuing to discuss, summarize, and draw the important events in the story using a comic strip template. I monitored the students' progress throughout this activity.

GUIDED COMPREHENSION: FAVORITE AUTHORS
SUMMARIZING: COMIC STRIP SUMMARIES

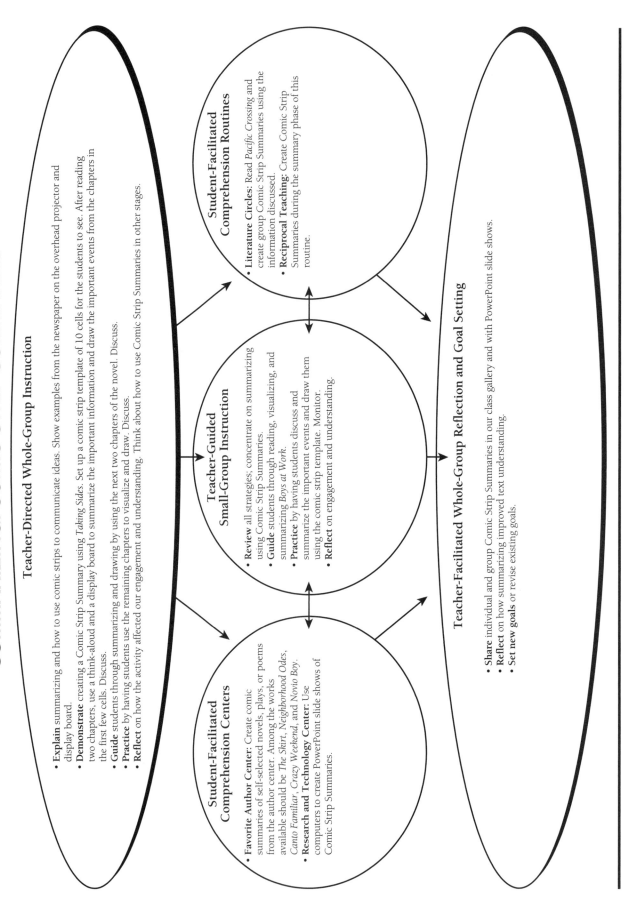

Teacher-Directed Whole-Group Instruction

- **Explain** summarizing and how to use comic strips to communicate ideas. Show examples from the newspaper on the overhead projector and display board.
- **Demonstrate** creating a Comic Strip Summary using *Taking Sides*. Set up a comic strip template of 10 cells for the students to see. After reading two chapters, use a think-aloud and a display board to summarize the important information and draw the important events from the chapters in the first few cells. Discuss.
- **Guide** students through summarizing and drawing by using the next two chapters of the novel. Discuss.
- **Practice** by having students use the remaining chapters to visualize and draw. Discuss.
- **Reflect** on how the activity affected our engagement and understanding. Think about how to use Comic Strip Summaries in other stages.

Student-Facilitated Comprehension Centers

- **Favorite Author Center:** Create comic summaries of self-selected novels, plays, or poems from the author center. Among the works available should be *The Skirt, Neighborhood Odes, Canto Familiar, Crazy Weekend,* and *Novio Boy.*
- **Research and Technology Center:** Use computers to create PowerPoint slide shows of Comic Strip Summaries.

Teacher-Guided Small-Group Instruction

- **Review** all strategies; concentrate on summarizing using Comic Strip Summaries.
- **Guide** students through reading, visualizing, and summarizing *Boys at Work.*
- **Practice** by having students discuss and summarize the important events and draw them using the comic strip template. Monitor.
- **Reflect** on engagement and understanding.

Student-Facilitated Comprehension Routines

- **Literature Circles:** Read *Pacific Crossing* and create group Comic Strip Summaries using the information discussed.
- **Reciprocal Teaching:** Create Comic Strip Summaries during the summary phase of this routine.

Teacher-Facilitated Whole-Group Reflection and Goal Setting

- **Share** individual and group Comic Strip Summaries in our class gallery and with PowerPoint slide shows.
- **Reflect** on how summarizing improved text understanding.
- **Set new goals** or revise existing goals.

Guided Comprehension in Action: Lessons for Grades 3–8 by Maureen McLaughlin and Mary Beth Allen ©2002. Newark, DE: International Reading Association. May be copied for classroom use.

Reflect: We reflected on engagement and understanding of Comic Strip Summaries. Then we talked about how we could use them in other settings.

Student-Facilitated Comprehension Centers

Favorite Author Center: Students visited this center and created Comic Strip Summaries of self-selected Gary Soto novels or poems they had read previously (see Figure 19). Among the works

Figure 19. Comic Strip Summaries

available were *The Skirt* (novel), *Neighborhood Odes* (poetry collection), *Canto Familiar* (poetry collection), *Crazy Weekend* (novel), and *Novio Boy* (play).

Research and Technology Center: Students visited this center and used computers to create PowerPoint slide shows of Comic Strip Summaries based on Gary Soto's work.

Student-Facilitated Comprehension Routines

Literature Circles: Students read *Pacific Crossing* and used it as the basis of their discussions. Then they created group Comic Strip Summaries based on the book.

Reciprocal Teaching: Students created Comic Strip Summaries during the summary phase.

STAGE THREE: Teacher-Facilitated Whole-Group Reflection and Goal Setting

Share: At the conclusion of the unit, room dividers were brought in, and all the comic strips were exhibited on them. This proved to be highly successful. We even invited other classes to view our work.

Reflect: We reflected on the engagement and enjoyment Comic Strip Summaries provided for all students, including those who struggled with traditional writing assignments. We also reflected on how summarizing improved understanding by providing an opportunity to synthesize the important information about the story.

Set New Goals: Feeling confident with our ability to use Comic Strip Summaries, we decided to extend our goal about summarizing to using Lyric Summaries.

Assessment Options

I used observation and students' completed Comic Strip Summaries as assessments.

Favorite Author Gary Paulsen
Guided Comprehension Strategy: Evaluating
Teaching Idea: Evaluative Questioning

STAGE ONE: Teacher-Directed Whole-Group Instruction

Text: *Winterdance: The Fine Madness of Running the Iditarod* (1994)

Explain: I began by explaining how using Evaluative Questioning (see Appendix A, *Guided Comprehension: A Teaching Model for Grades 3–8*) helps us to make judgments about the text. I reminded students that when we evaluate, we make judgments and we need to support our thinking with sound reasoning. Then I explained how to structure Evaluative Questions using signal words such as *defend*, *judge*, and *justify* (what do you think).

Demonstrate: I demonstrated how to create and use Evaluative Questioning by reading aloud the first chapter of *Winterdance*. Before reading I shared the title with the students and they immediately made connections to what we had already learned about Gary Paulsen's life, especially his participation in the Iditarod. As I read, I stopped periodically to think aloud about Evaluative Questions that I had and wrote them on an overhead transparency. For example, I paused after reading "I grabbed, snatched with my hand as the wind hit, but it was too sudden, too wild, and I was torn from the sled, taken by the wind, tumbling end over end down the mountain" on page six. I thought aloud about an Evaluative Question I had: "How could Gary Paulsen justify risking his life and the dogs' lives for this grueling Iditarod training?" I wrote the question on an overhead transparency and underlined the signal word *justify*. Next, I demonstrated that responding to Evaluative Questions involved what I had already read in this book, what I already knew about Gary Paulsen and his life experiences, and any prior knowledge I had about such circumstances. We discussed possible responses and I continued to read. I stopped again on page 14 after reading about the author's use of math: "If you broke trail with snowshoes at half a mile an hour and it was eighty miles to camp—where there was food for the dogs—it would take 160 hours." My Evaluative Question this time was, "What do I think Gary's chances of surviving would be if he chose to break trail?" We discussed possible responses and decided that based on weather, lack of food, time, and distance, his chances were nonexistent.

Guide: I continued to read aloud and guided students to work in pairs to use the signal words to structure Evaluative Questions. I asked them to structure one question based on the next section I read. Many of their questions focused on the last paragraph in Chapter 1:

> and I thought that any sane man who was in his forties and had a good career going would quit now, would leave the dogs, end it now and go back to the world and sanity and I knew what scared me wasn't the canyon and wasn't the hook hanging by one prong but the knowledge, the absolute fundamental knowledge that I could not stop, would not stop, would never be able to stop running dogs of my own free will. (p. 18)

Students structured questions requiring the author and them to defend why he should quit or why he should continue. We shared and discussed all their questions and possible answers, which resulted in quite a lively debate.

Practice: I read the beginning sections of Chapter 2 aloud and the students continued to work in pairs to create additional Evaluative Questions and to formulate possible responses. The students

GUIDED COMPREHENSION: FAVORITE AUTHORS
EVALUATING: EVALUATIVE QUESTIONS

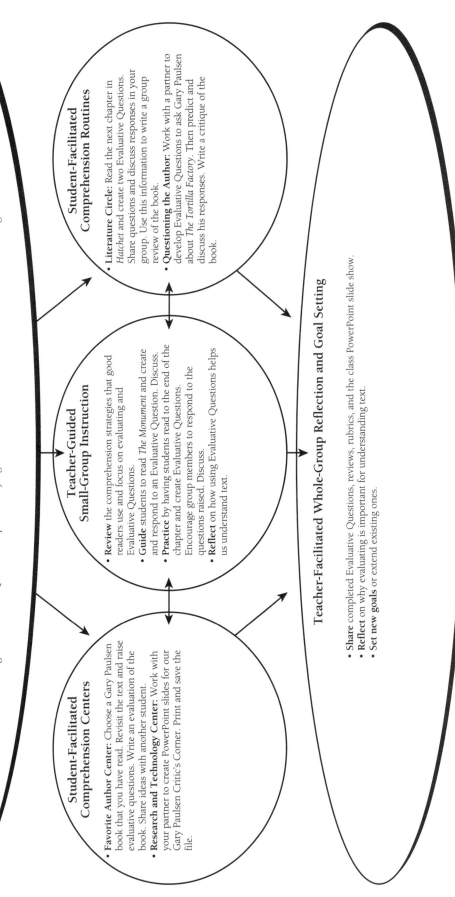

Teacher-Directed Whole-Group Instruction

- **Explain** evaluating and how to use Evaluative Questions to make judgments about text.
- **Demonstrate** how to create and use Evaluative Questions. Use *Winterdance*, a read-aloud, a think-aloud, and an overhead projector or chalkboard. Remind students of the signal words for Evaluative Questions and how they can be used to structure questions. Read the first chapter aloud and then create Evaluative Questions and respond to them. Discuss.
- **Guide** students in pairs to use Evaluative Questions. Read aloud another section of Chapter 1 and have each pair of students develop an Evaluative Question and respond to it. Share and discuss.
- **Practice** by finishing reading the chapter aloud and having students work in pairs to create additional Evaluative Questions. Share and respond to the questions.
- **Reflect** on how evaluating and Evaluative Questions help us make judgments about text and how we can use them in other settings.

Student-Facilitated Comprehension Routines

- **Literature Circle:** Read the next chapter in *Hatchet* and create two Evaluative Questions. Share questions and discuss responses in your group. Use this information to write a group review of the book.
- **Questioning the Author:** Work with a partner to develop Evaluative Questions to ask Gary Paulsen about *The Tortilla Factory*. Then predict and discuss his responses. Write a critique of the book.

Teacher-Guided Small-Group Instruction

- **Review** the comprehension strategies that good readers use and focus on evaluating and Evaluative Questions.
- **Guide** students to read *The Monument* and create and respond to an Evaluative Question. Discuss.
- **Practice** by having students read to the end of the chapter and create Evaluative Questions. Encourage group members to respond to the questions raised. Discuss.
- **Reflect** on how using Evaluative Questions helps us understand text.

Student-Facilitated Comprehension Centers

- **Favorite Author Center:** Choose a Gary Paulsen book that you have read. Revisit the text and raise evaluative questions. Write an evaluation of the book. Share ideas with another student.
- **Research and Technology Center:** Work with your partner to create PowerPoint slides for our Gary Paulsen Critic's Corner. Print and save the file.

Teacher-Facilitated Whole-Group Reflection and Goal Setting

- **Share** completed Evaluative Questions, reviews, rubrics, and the class PowerPoint slide show.
- **Reflect** on why evaluating is important for understanding text.
- **Set new goals** or extend existing ones.

Guided Comprehension in Action: Lessons for Grades 3–8 by Maureen McLaughlin and Mary Beth Allen ©2002. Newark, DE: International Reading Association. May be copied for classroom use.

liked creating their own questions, and I found that even struggling readers were able to create and respond to Evaluative Questions.

Reflect: I asked the students to reflect on how using Evaluative Questioning helped them to make judgments about text. Shelby responded with "I like these questions because what I think matters and I have a lot of sources I can use to think of a response. It's not like when the answer is right there in the book."

STAGE TWO: Teacher-Guided Small-Group Instruction

Text: *The Monument* (1991) (Texts varied according to students' abilities.)

Review: I reviewed the comprehension strategies that all good readers use such as previewing and visualizing. Then I focused on evaluating and Evaluative Questioning.

Guide: I previewed *The Monument* and guided students' reading of the opening chapter. I asked them to create one evaluative question and think about possible responses. Several of the students focused on this passage from page 4 when Rocky (Rachel Ellen Turner) says, "I mean I want to know every little thing that's going to happen and not have any surprises. But I can't and that sometimes makes me mad." Students' questions focused on justifying Rocky's perspective. Other students questioned the author's use of the name Rocky for the girl in the story and asked that he and they defend his choice. They also made personal connections to his thinking.

Practice: The students continued to read Chapters 2 and 3 of *The Monument*, creating two Evaluative Questions as they read. We discussed their Evaluative Questions and possible answers. Questions included, "What do you think it was like for Rocky to be an abandoned orphan?" "How would you defend Rocky's feelings of rejection when she was not selected for adoption?" "How would you justify Rocky's feelings when she learned that her adoptive parents were alcoholics?" "How would Gary Paulsen (or you) justify his use of his life circumstance (alcoholic parents) in this book?" The students' queries resulted in a lively discussion.

Reflect: I asked the students how creating and responding to Evaluative Questions helped them to understand text. Deron said that creating Evaluative Questions reminded him of predicting because he wanted to read ahead to see if his ideas and the author's were similar.

Student-Facilitated Comprehension Centers

Favorite Author Center: The students chose a book that they had already read by Gary Paulsen. They revisited the text to develop four Evaluative Questions. Then they used their knowledge of the book, the responses to the Evaluative Questions, and a Book Review Planner (see Appendix, page 174) to write a critique. They posted the completed reviews in our Critics' Corner.

Research and Technology Center: Pairs of students selected a related topic, such as Gary Paulsen's life or the Iditarod, and researched it using a variety of sources. Then they used the information to create a PowerPoint slide presentation using clip art, sound, and animation. They saved their presentation and shared them in Stage Three.

Student-Facilitated Comprehension Routines

Literature Circles: The students finished reading the last two chapters of *Hatchet* individually. Then they wrote and responded to two Evaluative Questions. When all the group members had completed these tasks, they met and used their Evaluative Questions as the basis of discussion. Finally, they used what they learned to write a group book review.

Questioning the Author: The students worked with a partner to develop Evaluative Questions to ask Gary Paulsen about *The Tortilla Factory*. Then they predicted his responses. After discussing these issues, the group members used the Book Review Planner and wrote a composite review of *The Tortilla Factory*, which they posted in our Critics' Corner.

STAGE THREE: Teacher-Facilitated Whole-Group Reflection and Goal Setting

Share: Students shared their applications of Evaluative Questions from Stage Two with the class.

Reflect: We reflected on what we had learned and how Evaluative Questioning helped us to evaluate text.

Set New Goals: Students assessed their abilities to use Evaluative Questioning and we decided to stay with this goal and learn how to use Discussion Webs (Alvermann, 1991), another technique for evaluating.

Assessment Options

I observed students in all stages of the process, focusing on their ability to create and respond to Evaluative Questions. I also reviewed students' applications during Stage Two, including their contributions to the PowerPoint presentation.

THEME RESOURCES

Texts

Bunting, E. (1989). *The ghost children*. Boston: Houghton Mifflin.

Bunting, E. (1989). *The Wednesday surprise*. New York: Clarion Books.

Bunting, E. (1990). *The wall*. New York: Clarion Books.

Bunting, E. (1991). *Fly away home*. New York: Clarion Books.

Bunting, E. (1991). *The hideout*. Orlando, FL: Harcourt Brace Jovanovich.

Bunting, E. (1994). *Smoky nights*. Orlando, FL: Harcourt Brace Jovanovich.

Bunting, E. (1994). *Terrible things: An allegory of the Holocaust*. New York: Harper and Row.

Bunting, E. (1998). *So far from the sea*. New York: Clarion Books.

Paulsen, G. (1987). *Hatchet*. New York: Bradbury Press.

Paulsen, G. (1990). *Woodsong*. New York: Bradbury Press.

Paulsen, G. (1991). *The monument*. New York: Dell.

Paulsen, G. (1993). *Eastern sun, winter moon: An autobiographical odyssey*. New York: Harcourt Brace Jovanovich.

Paulsen, G. (1994). *Winterdance: The fine madness of the Iditarod*. Toronto: Harcourt Brace Jovanovich.

Paulsen, G. (1995). *The tortilla factory*. New York: Harcourt Brace.

Paulsen, G. (1995). *Dogsong*. New York: Aladdin Paperbacks.

Paulsen, G. (1996). *Brian's winter*. New York: Delacorte.

Paulsen, G. (2001). *Guts: The true stories behind Hatchet and the Brian books*. New York: Delacorte.

Scieszka, J. (1989). *The true story of the 3 little pigs!* New York: Viking Penguin.

Scieszka, J. (1991). *The frog prince continued*. New York: Viking Penguin.

Scieszka, J. (1992). *The stinky cheese man and other fairly stupid tales*. New York: Penguin Books.

Scieszka, J. The Time Warp Trio series. New York: Viking.

Scieszka, J. (1995). *Math curse*. New York: Viking.

Scieszka, J. (1998). *Squids will be squids: Fresh morals for beastly fables*. New York: Viking Penguin.

Scieszka, J. (2002). *Hey kid, want to buy a bridge?* New York: Viking.

Scieszka, J., & Smith, L. (2001). *Baloney* (Henry P.). New York: Viking.

Soto, G. (1990). *Baseball in April and other stories*. San Diego: Harcourt Brace Jovanovich.

Soto, G. (1991). *Taking sides*. San Diego: Harcourt Brace Jovanovich.

Soto, G. (1992). *Neighborhood odes*. New York: Scholastic.

Soto, G. (1992). *The skirt*. New York: Delacorte.

Soto, G. (1993). *Too many tamales*. New York: G.P. Putnam's Sons.

Soto, G. (1994). *Crazy weekend*. New York: Scholastic.

Soto, G. (1995). *Canto familiar*. San Diego: Harcourt Brace.

Soto, G. (1995). *Chato's kitchen*. New York: Putnam's.

Soto, G. (1996). *Boys at work*. New York: Yearling.

Soto, G. (1997). *Buried onions*. San Diego: Harcourt Brace.

Soto, G. (1997). *Novio boy*. San Diego: Harcourt Brace.

Soto, G. (2000). *Chato and the party animals*. New York: Putnam.

Websites

Eve Bunting

Book Page Children's Interview: Eve Bunting
    www.bookpage.com/9705bp/childrens/evebunting.html

Educational Paperback Association: Eve Bunting
    www.edupaperback.org/authorbios/Bunting_Eve.html

Eve Bunting: Teacher Resource File
    falcon.jmu.edu/~ramseyil/bunting.htm

Jon Scieszka

Educational Paperback Association: Scieszka, Jon
    www.edupaperback.org/authorbios/Scieszka_Jon.html

Internet School Library Media Center: Jon Scieszka
    falcon.jmu.edu/~ramseyil/scieszka.htm

Kidsreads.com: Jon Scieszka
    www.kidsreads.com/authors/au-scieszka-jon.asp

The New York Public Library: Chat With Jon Scieszka
    www.nypl.org/branch/kids/authorchat.html

Utah Education Network: Jon Scieszka
    www.uen.org/utahlink/activities/view_activity.cgi?activity_id=6145

Gary Soto

Gary Soto: A Teacher Resource File
    falcon.jmu.edu/~ramseyil/soto.htm

The Official Gary Soto Website
    www.garysoto.com

Poets in Person: Gary Soto Home Page
    www.wilmington.org/poets/soto.html

Gary Paulsen

Books@Random: Gary Paulsen
    www.randomhouse.com/features/garypaulsen/about.html

Gary Paulsen: Teacher Resource File
    falcon.jmu.edu/~ramseyil/paulsen.htm

The Internet Public Library: Gary Paulsen
    www.ipl.org/youth/AskAuthor/paulsen.html

Learning About Gary Paulsen
    www.scils.rutgers.edu/~kvander/paulsen.html

Performance Extensions Across the Curriculum

Social Studies

• Use Eve Bunting books to explore social issues (*Fly Away Home*—homelessness, *The Wednesday Surprise*—illiteracy). Gather additional information and develop an action plan to help a community organization that supports the issue.

- Use the book *Dandelions* to introduce the settling of the plains. Investigate the hardships the settlers faced, the motives that drew them to the plains, and how people, such as Native Americans, affected and were affected by the settlers.
- Use Jon Scieszka's Time Warp Trio series to make connections to various aspects of social studies (*Knights of the Kitchen Table*, *Tut Tut*, *2095*).
- Use Gary Soto's books to explore cultures, traditions, and lifestyles of Mexican Americans. Celebrate a World Cultures Day with food, art, music, and traditions from multiple countries, including Mexico.
- Use Gary Paulsen's experiences and novels to make connections to and research Alaska, including the Iditarod.

Science

- Use Gary Paulsen's *Hatchet* and *Brian's Winter* to explore factors needed for survival in various environments and climates. Choose additional climates and environments and record information needed to live there. Use this information as the basis of a *Survivor* episode.

Art

- Investigate various art techniques used in picture books—painting, sketching, paper cutting, collage, etc. Explore how to use a technique employed by your favorite illustrator and create additional illustrations for the book.

Drama

- Use a First Person Experience (McLaughlin, 2000) to become your favorite author or illustrator and share information about life and works with the class at an Author Celebration Night.

Culminating Activity

Author Celebration Night: Invite parents and community members to join teachers and students in an author celebration. Focusing on the idea that we are all authors, invite parents, community members, teachers, and students to contribute writings to be published in an authors' booklet, which will be distributed at the celebration. Parents and community members can join students in presenting displays and engaging in discussions of favorite authors. A favorite local author may present ideas about writing careers and the publishing process. Engage students and teachers from across the curriculum to present investigations of content area-related literature, informational books authored in content area classes, and other related projects. All participants will sign the I Am a Writer mural in the hallway outside the multipurpose room. Provide student-designed bookmarks to commemorate the celebration.

CHAPTER 5

Poetry: Aesthetic and Efferent Stances

In his opening of *Where the Sidewalk Ends*, Shel Silverstein invites dreamers to come in. In "A Time to Talk" and "Stopping by Woods," Robert Frost assures that poetry can convey life's simple yet essential messages. In her poetry, Judith Viorst offers humorous views of the child in all of us, and in her collected works, Maya Angelou provides insight into the ongoing drama of everyday life. All these examples support Rosenblatt's (1980) view that "a poem is an event in which the listener or reader draws on images and feelings and ideas stirred up by the words of the text; out of these is shaped the lived-through experience" (p. 386). It is the transactional nature of such experiences that makes poetry such a viable theme for situating Guided Comprehension.

We can use poetry "to motivate student learning, activate prior knowledge, encourage in-depth processing of concepts, construct personal interpretations, offer a different perspective, encourage students to take an aesthetic stance, extend students' thinking and assess student learning" (Paugh, McLaughlin, Call, & Vandever-Horvath, 2000, p. 137). These possibilities afford us numerous opportunities to make personal connections, explore personal interpretations, and apply comprehension strategies.

The Sample Theme-Based Plan for Guided Comprehension: Poetry (see Figure 20) presents a sampling of goals, state standards, assessments, texts, technology resources, comprehension strategies, teaching ideas, comprehension centers, and comprehension routines. The plan begins by delineating examples of student goals and related state standards. The student goals for this theme include the following:

- using appropriate comprehension strategies
- interpreting poetry
- writing poetry
- communicating effectively

These goals support the following state standards:

- learning to read independently
- reading, analyzing, and interpreting literature
- types and quality of writing
- speaking and listening

Figure 20. Sample Theme-Based Plan for Guided Comprehension: Poetry

Goals and Connections to State Standards

Students will

- use appropriate comprehension strategies. Standard: learning to read independently
- interpret poetry. Standard: reading, analyzing, and interpreting literature
- write poetry. Standards: types and quality of writing
- communicate effectively. Standards: types and quality of writing; speaking and listening

Assessment

The following measures can be used for a variety of purposes, including diagnostic, formative, and summative assessment:

Diamantes   Student Self-Assessments
Observation   Text Transformations
Photographs of the Mind   That Was Then...This Is Now
                      The Rest of the Story

Text	Title	Theme	Level
1.	*LIVES: Poems About Famous Americans*	P	5
2.	*Where the Sidewalk Ends*	P	3
3.	*Voices: Poetry and Art From Around the World*	P	8
4.	*Walking the Bridge of Your Nose*	P	3

Technology Resources

Poetry4Kids
    www.poetry4kids.com
KidzPage
    www.veeceet.com
Yahooligans! Directory: Poetry
    www.yahooligans.com/school_bell/language_arts/
    poetry

Comprehension Strategies

1. Previewing
2. Visualizing
3. Knowing How Words Work
4. Knowing How Words Work

Teaching Ideas

That Was Then...This Is Now
Photographs of the Mind
Diamantes
Text Transformations

Comprehension Centers

Students will apply the comprehension strategies and related teaching ideas in the following comprehension centers:

Art Center   Research and Technology Center
Poetry Center   Writing Center

Comprehension Routines

Students will apply the comprehension strategies and related teaching ideas in the following comprehension routines:

Literature Circles
Questioning the Author
Reciprocal Teaching

Examples of the dynamic assessments used during Guided Comprehension include observation, strategy applications, and student self-assessments. The following comprehension strategies and related teaching ideas are featured in the theme-based lessons:

- Previewing: That Was Then...This Is Now
- Visualizing: Photographs of the Mind
- Knowing How Words Work: Diamantes
- Knowing How Words Work: Text Transformations

LIVES: Poems About Famous Americans, *Where the Sidewalk Ends*, *Voices: Poetry and Art From Around the World*, and *Walking the Bridge of Your Nose* are the texts that are used in teacher-directed whole-group instruction. Additional texts at a variety of levels, including those used in teacher-guided small-group instruction and the student-facilitated comprehension centers and routines, are included in the Theme Resources at the end of the chapter.

In the Guided Comprehension lessons, students apply strategies at a variety of centers, including art, poetry, research and technology, and writing. Literature Circles, Questioning the Author, and Reciprocal Teaching are the comprehension routines in which students engage.

GUIDED COMPREHENSION LESSONS

Guided Comprehension Strategy: Previewing
Teaching Idea: That Was Then...This Is Now

STAGE ONE: Teacher-Directed Whole-Group Instruction

Text: *LIVES: Poems About Famous Americans* (Hopkins, 1999)

Explain: I began by explaining previewing and how That Was Then...This Is Now (see Appendix, page 161) helps us preview what we read. I noted that previewing encompasses activating background knowledge, predicting, and setting a purpose for reading. I introduced the technique by noting that we would each sketch and label what we knew about the topic before reading and record them on the That Was Then side of the organizer. Next, we would share our ideas and discuss the reasoning for our choices in small groups. After reading, we would revisit our sketches and labels, note changes based on what we had read, and record them on the This Is Now side.

Demonstrate: I demonstrated how to use That Was Then...This Is Now by using a poem from *LIVES: Poems About Famous Americans*, a think-aloud, and an overhead projector. I placed an organizer I had previously prepared on the overhead (see Appendix, page 175). Then I noted that the topic I would be reading about was Sacagawea, a Native American woman who helped Lewis and Clark explore. I thought aloud about what I already knew about her and began sketching. I reminded the students that although we are not all great artists, we can all sketch our ideas, and I demonstrated some simple lines and shapes. Then I recorded my summary statement on the That Was Then side of the organizer and explained my reasoning. My summary statement was *Sacagawea was a Native American woman who was a hero because she helped Lewis and Clark explore.*

Next, I read aloud "A Song for Sacagawea" by Jane Yolen. After reading, I thought aloud about what I had learned and drew a new sketch and wrote a new summary statement. This time my summary statement said, *Sacagawea helped Lewis and Clark explore, but she was viewed as a slave won in a bet, not a member of the exploration team.* I recorded this sketch and summary statement on the This Is Now side of the organizer. We discussed how the two sketches and statements differed.

Guide: I guided students to complete That Was Then...This Is Now by sharing the subject of another poem, Harriet Tubman. Students worked in pairs to complete the left side of the organizer and we discussed their sketches, summary statements, and reasoning. Then I read aloud the poem "The Whippoorwill Calls" by Beverly McLoughland, which I had placed on an overhead transparency.

Practice: When I finished reading, students practiced by chatting enthusiastically about what they had learned and how they would change their sketch and statement for the This Is Now side of the organizer. The most dramatic changes focused on including dark backgrounds to accommodate the idea of the Underground Railroad operating at night and drawing Harriet Tubman in camouflage to blend in with the scene. One pair of students changed their representation of Harriet Tubman from a woman to a bird, the metaphor used in the poem. Their work is featured in Figure 21. We shared and discussed the students' work in small groups.

Reflect: We reflected on how That Was Then...This Is Now helps us preview, visualize, and summarize our reading. Students remarked that they especially liked being able to sketch their thinking

GUIDED COMPREHENSION: POETRY
PREVIEWING: THAT WAS THEN...THIS IS NOW

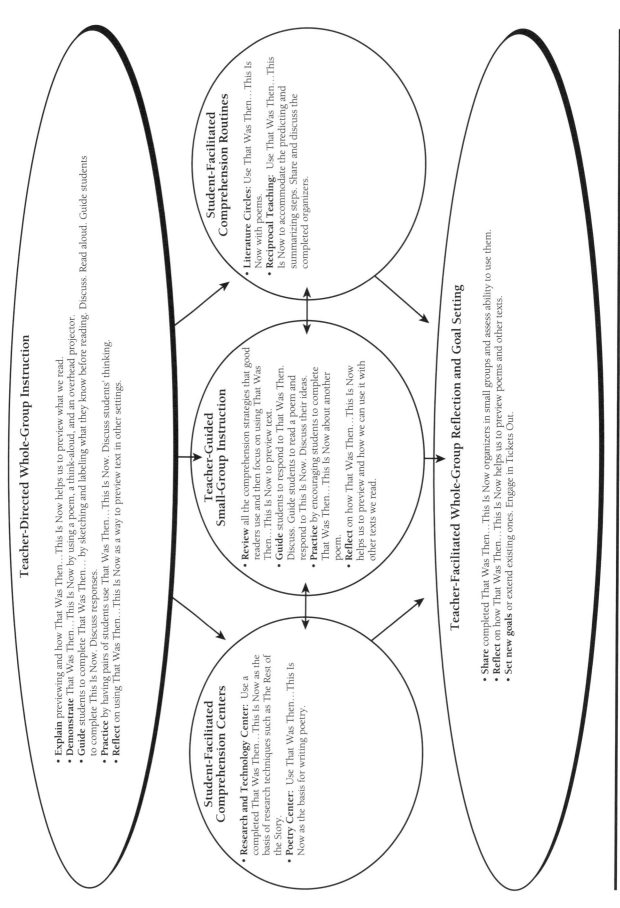

Teacher-Directed Whole-Group Instruction

- **Explain** previewing and how That Was Then...This Is Now helps us to preview what we read.
- **Demonstrate** That Was Then...This Is Now by using a poem, a think-aloud, and an overhead projector.
- **Guide** students to complete That Was Then... by sketching and labeling what they know before reading. Discuss. Read aloud. Guide students to complete This Is Now. Discuss responses.
- **Practice** by having pairs of students use That Was Then...This Is Now. Discuss students' thinking.
- **Reflect** on using That Was Then...This Is Now as a way to preview text in other settings.

Student-Facilitated Comprehension Routines

- **Literature Circles:** Use That Was Then...This Is Now with poems.
- **Reciprocal Teaching:** Use That Was Then...This Is Now to accommodate the predicting and summarizing steps. Share and discuss the completed organizers.

Teacher-Guided Small-Group Instruction

- **Review** all the comprehension strategies that good readers use and then focus on using That Was Then...This Is Now to preview text.
- **Guide** students to respond to That Was Then. Discuss. Guide students to read a poem and respond to This Is Now. Discuss their ideas.
- **Practice** by encouraging students to complete That Was Then...This Is Now about another poem.
- **Reflect** on how That Was Then...This Is Now helps us to preview and how we can use it with other texts we read.

Student-Facilitated Comprehension Centers

- **Research and Technology Center:** Use a completed That Was Then...This Is Now as the basis of research techniques such as The Rest of the Story.
- **Poetry Center:** Use That Was Then...This Is Now as the basis for writing poetry.

Teacher-Facilitated Whole-Group Reflection and Goal Setting

- **Share** completed That Was Then...This Is Now organizers in small groups and assess ability to use them.
- **Reflect** on how That Was Then...This Is Now helps us to preview poems and other texts.
- **Set new goals** or extend existing ones. Engage in Tickets Out.

Figure 21. That Was Then...This Is Now

That Was Then...

This Is Now

Come with me... you will be safe

Harriet Tubman helped a lot of people escape slavery.

Harriet had to act like a bird so she would not get caught.

and that they were surprised in the differences before and after hearing the poems. They also were surprised that poems could be used to share information about the achievements of these people.

STAGE TWO: Teacher-Guided Small-Group Instruction

Text: *LIVES: Poems About Famous Americans* (1999) (Texts varied according to students' abilities.)

Review: I reminded students about the strategies that good readers use and focused on previewing, visualizing, and summarizing in the technique, That Was Then...This Is Now. This was a perfect time to remind students about how comprehension strategies work in concert.

Guide: We focused on Rosa Parks, the subject of the poem we were going to read. ("When Babe Ruth Hit His Last Home Run" and "First Men on the Moon" were among the poems various small groups read.) We discussed what we already knew about Rosa Parks, and I guided students to complete their sketches and summary statements for the That Was Then section of the organizer. Then I guided their reading by suggesting that they think about the This Is Now section of the organizer and what information might be new to them as they were reading.

Practice: Students practiced this technique by completing the organizer after reading. Then we shared That Was Then...This Is Now and explained our reasoning.

Reflect: We reflected on how That Was Then...This Is Now helped us preview, visualize, and summarize and talked about how to use it with other kinds of text in other settings.

Student-Facilitated Comprehension Centers

Research and Technology Center: Students used That Was Then...This Is Now organizers as the basis of researching the life of a famous person or a famous occurrence. They made selections from a list I provided. They recorded what they knew before researching by writing a summary statement and drawing a sketch in the That Was Then section. After researching, they recorded what they knew in the This Is Now section. Some also chose to extend this technique by engaging in The Rest of the Story (McLaughlin, 2000), an inquiry-based investigation that encourages the researcher to go beyond the basic facts generally known about a person, discovery, invention, or event.

Poetry Center: Students used volumes of poetry I provided to complete That Was Then...This Is Now about content area-related poems. Some also completed That Was Then...This Is Now organizers as a springboard for more in-depth research. They reported what they had learned in a variety of ways, including writing poetry.

Student-Facilitated Comprehension Routines

Literature Circles: Students used That Was Then...This Is Now with poems from a variety of sources, including *Voices* and *Words With Wings*. Then they shared the completed organizers and used them as the basis of discussion.

Reciprocal Teaching: Students used That Was Then...This Is Now to accommodate the predicting and summarizing steps. Then they shared and discussed the completed organizers.

STAGE THREE: Teacher-Facilitated Whole-Group Reflection and Goal Setting

Share: Students shared their applications of That Was Then...This Is Now from Stage Two in small groups. Then several students shared in whole group.

Reflect: We reflected on previewing, visualizing, and summarizing and how well we could use That Was Then...This Is Now. Students really enjoyed this technique and talked about how they could use it when reading on their own.

Set New Goals: We decided that we were very successful in applying this technique and that we should extend our goal by learning how to use Anticipation Guides (Readence, Bean, & Baldwin, 2000). At the end of the lesson, students engaged in Tickets Out (see Appendix E, *Guided Comprehension: A Teaching Model for Grades 3–8*).

Assessment Options

I used observation and students' applications of That Was Then...This Is Now as assessments during this lesson.

Guided Comprehension Strategy: Visualizing
Teaching Idea: Photographs of the Mind

STAGE ONE: Teacher-Directed Whole-Group Instruction

Text: *Where the Sidewalk Ends* (Silverstein, 1974)

Explain: I began by explaining visualization and the concept of sketching to aid in expressing the mental images we create while reading. Then I described Photographs of the Mind (Keene & Zimmerman, 1997; see Appendix, page 162) and told the class we would be using the poem "Sarah Cynthia Sylvia Stout Would Not Take the Garbage Out" by Shel Silverstein for demonstration. I asked what they thought the poem was about. Then we discussed responsibilities we have at home and concluded that most of us need reminding to complete such tasks.

Demonstrate: I read "Sarah Cynthia Sylvia Stout" aloud the first time so the students could enjoy the message of the poem. Then I read it again. In the second reading, I stopped one third of the way through and thought aloud about what I was visualizing at that point. I continued to share my thoughts as I sketched the photograph in my mind: Sarah and her assorted types of garbage.

Guide: Then I read aloud the second part of the poem and asked students to share the images that came into their heads. Next, they worked in pairs, sketching their images separately and sharing with their partner.

Practice: After I read the final section of the poem, students practiced by sketching their visualizations of text. I asked students to share their work with the class.

Reflect: We reflected on how visualizing and sketching helped us express and share the mental images we create while reading. Then we talked about how we could use Photographs of the Mind with other kinds of texts in other settings. Students indicated that they enjoyed this technique because it gave them a fun way to record and share their thinking. Alicia's completed Photographs of the Mind for "Sarah Cynthia Sylvia Stout" is featured in Figure 22.

STAGE TWO: Teacher-Guided Small-Group Instruction

Text: *A Swinger of Birches: Poems of Robert Frost for Young People* (Frost, 1982) (Texts varied according to students' abilities.)

Review: I reviewed the comprehension strategies good readers use and then focused on using Photographs of the Mind as a visualization technique.

Guide: I read aloud the poem "A Time to Talk" by Robert Frost for students' enjoyment. Then I distributed copies of a Photographs of the Mind organizer (see Appendix, page 176). I guided students to read the first section of the poem and pause to reflect on and sketch their mental images. Students shared their ideas and sketches with the group.

Practice: Students read the remaining sections of the poem and paused twice to think about their mental images and sketch them. Then they shared and discussed with all the group members.

Reflect: We reflected on how using Photographs of the Mind to share our visualizations helped us understand text. Students remarked that it gave us a way to show what is inside our minds. They also noted that it is sometimes difficult to talk about our ideas, and that drawing them before sharing them made this process easier. Of course, they like to draw and that made this technique especially student friendly.

GUIDED COMPREHENSION: POETRY
VISUALIZING: PHOTOGRAPHS OF THE MIND

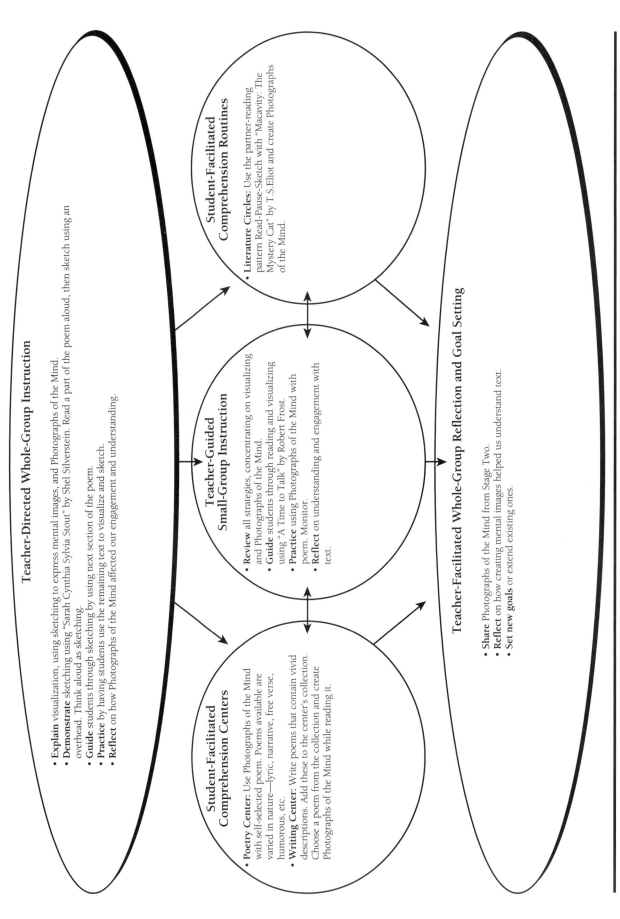

Teacher-Directed Whole-Group Instruction

- **Explain** visualization, using sketching to express mental images, and Photographs of the Mind.
- **Demonstrate** sketching using "Sarah Cynthia Sylvia Stout" by Shel Silverstein. Read a part of the poem aloud, then sketch using an overhead. Think aloud as sketching.
- **Guide** students through sketching by using next section of the poem.
- **Practice** by having students use the remaining text to visualize and sketch.
- **Reflect** on how Photographs of the Mind affected our engagement and understanding.

Student-Facilitated Comprehension Centers

- **Poetry Center:** Use Photographs of the Mind with self-selected poem. Poems available are varied in nature—lyric, narrative, free verse, humorous, etc.
- **Writing Center:** Write poems that contain vivid descriptions. Add these to the center's collection. Choose a poem from the collection and create Photographs of the Mind while reading it.

Teacher-Guided Small-Group Instruction

- **Review** all strategies, concentrating on visualizing and Photographs of the Mind.
- **Guide** students through reading and visualizing using "A Time to Talk" by Robert Frost.
- **Practice** using Photographs of the Mind with poem. Monitor.
- **Reflect** on understanding and engagement with text.

Student-Facilitated Comprehension Routines

- **Literature Circles:** Use the partner-reading pattern Read-Pause-Sketch with "Macavity: The Mystery Cat" by T.S.Eliot and create Photographs of the Mind.

Teacher-Facilitated Whole-Group Reflection and Goal Setting

- **Share** Photographs of the Mind from Stage Two.
- **Reflect** on how creating mental images helped us understand text.
- **Set new goals** or extend existing ones.

Figure 22. Alicia's Photographs of the Mind

Student-Facilitated Comprehension Centers

Poetry Center: I placed an ample supply of poems of varied types (lyric, narrative, free verse, form, humorous, etc.—both published and student authored) at this center. Students self-selected a poem to use for Photographs of the Mind and created their visualizations.

Writing Center: Students wrote poems by creating mental images of their ideas, sketching the images, and using the completed information to write a poem. Students published their poems and added them to the center's supply for other students to use. Then pairs of students read poems from the center's student-authored collection. They completed Photographs of the Mind individually and shared and discussed the results with their partners.

Student-Facilitated Comprehension Routines

Literature Circles: Students worked with a partner to "Read-Pause-Sketch" while reading "Macavity: The Mystery Cat" by T.S. Eliot. I asked students to sketch individual visualizations of the poem, then compare and discuss their drawings with their group. Then students discussed ways to create a composite sketch that would represent the group's visualizations, and then they created it.

STAGE THREE: Teacher-Facilitated Whole-Group Reflection and Goal Setting

Share: Students shared and discussed their Photographs of the Mind applications from Stage Two.

Reflect: We discussed how Photographs of the Mind and other visualization techniques helped us understand what we read. Then they self-assessed their ability to use this and similar techniques.

Set New Goals: We decided to extend our goal of visualizing and learn how to apply Photographs of the Mind to expository texts.

Assessment Options

I observed students in all stages of Guided Comprehension. I also reviewed their applications of Photographs of the Mind in their Guided Comprehension Journals and their composite Photographs of the Mind.

Guided Comprehension Strategy: Knowing How Words Work
Teaching Idea: Diamantes

STAGE ONE: Teacher-Directed Whole-Group Instruction

Text: *Voices: Poetry and Art From Around the World* (Brenner, 2000)

Explain: I explained to my students that we would continue to learn about how words work by focusing on antonyms. I recalled our work on cinquains and explained that today we would be using another form poem, the diamante.

Demonstrate: I demonstrated by selecting a pair of antonyms. I chose *summer* and *winter*. Next, I used an overhead and a think-aloud to think through the form of the diamante (see Appendix, page 177). I noticed that the first and last lines were where the antonyms should be placed. I read the descriptions of the information required for line two: two adjectives describing the subject. I thought aloud about two words to describe summer. I decided on *hot* and *sunny*. Then I moved on to the next line: three participles (*-ing* words) telling about the subject. I thought about summer and decided on *invigorating, energizing*, and *revitalizing*. Then I thought aloud about the next line, which required four nouns: two describing summer and two describing its opposite, winter. I wrote the nouns for summer: *fun* and *freedom*. We talked about my responses for summer, the first half of the diamante, and the need to now address its antonym, winter.

Guide: I guided students to the last line of the diamante, which said *winter*. Then we worked our way toward the middle of the poem. We provided two adjectives to describe winter. Students suggested *demanding* and *cold*.

Practice: Students practiced by working in pairs to suggest lines to complete the diamante. For the three participles, we decided on *restricting, confining*, and *exhausting*. Then we selected *snow* and *sleet* for the two nouns. In our discussion, we noted that we did not mean to sound so negative about winter, but we were focused on offering opposite ideas. Our completed diamante follows.

Summer

Hot, sunny

Invigorating, energizing, revitalizing

Fun freedom snow sleet

restricting, confining, exhausting

demanding, cold

winter

Reflect: We discussed how the diamante format accommodates opposite terms and how we could use the format in other settings. Students noted that they liked the diamantes because they really needed to think to provide the appropriate words. One student said that it reminded him of the cinquain, but it was more involved because it used opposites.

STAGE TWO: Teacher-Guided Small-Group Instruction

Text: *Voices: Poetry and Art From Around the World* (Brenner, 2000) (Texts varied according to students' abilities.)

Review: I reviewed the strategies good readers use and focused on Knowing How Words Work and techniques for using antonyms.

GUIDED COMPREHENSION: POETRY
KNOWING HOW WORDS WORK: DIAMANTES

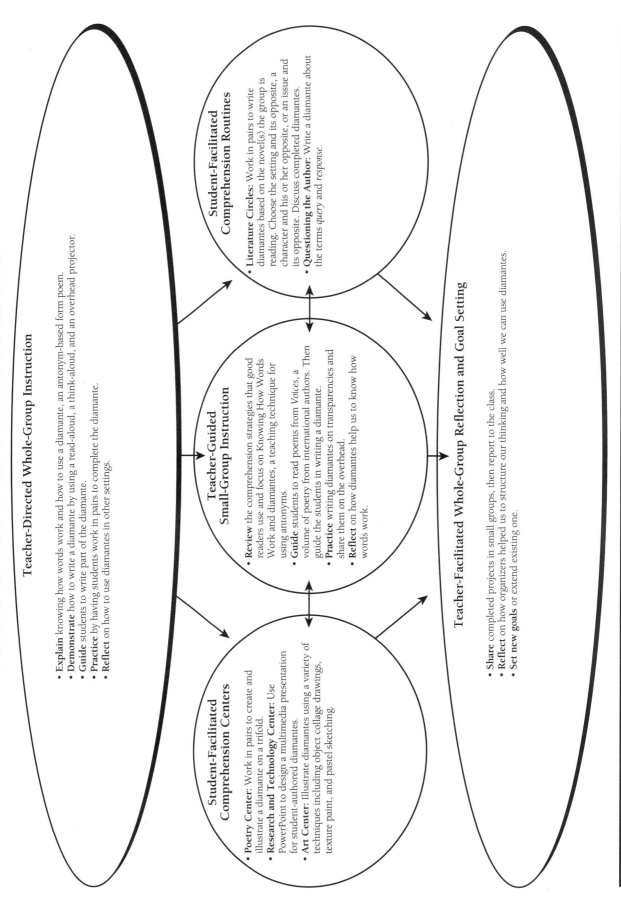

Teacher-Directed Whole-Group Instruction

- **Explain** knowing how words work and how to use a diamante, an antonym-based form poem.
- **Demonstrate** how to write a diamante by using a read-aloud, a think-aloud, and an overhead projector.
- **Guide** students to write part of the diamante.
- **Practice** by having students work in pairs to complete the diamante.
- **Reflect** on how to use diamantes in other settings.

Student-Facilitated Comprehension Routines

- **Literature Circles:** Work in pairs to write diamantes based on the novel(s) the group is reading. Choose the setting and its opposite, a character and his or her opposite, or an issue and its opposite. Discuss completed diamantes.
- **Questioning the Author:** Write a diamante about the terms *query* and *response*.

Teacher-Guided Small-Group Instruction

- **Review** the comprehension strategies that good readers use and focus on Knowing How Words Work and diamantes, a teaching technique for using antonyms.
- **Guide** students to read poems from *Voices*, a volume of poetry from international authors. Then guide the students in writing a diamante.
- **Practice** writing diamantes on transparencies and share them on the overhead.
- **Reflect** on how diamantes help us to know how words work.

Student-Facilitated Comprehension Centers

- **Poetry Center:** Work in pairs to create and illustrate a diamante on a trifold.
- **Research and Technology Center:** Use PowerPoint to design a multimedia presentation for student-authored diamantes.
- **Art Center:** Illustrate diamantes using a variety of techniques including object collage drawings, texture paint, and pastel sketching.

Teacher-Facilitated Whole-Group Reflection and Goal Setting

- **Share** completed projects in small groups, then report to the class.
- **Reflect** on how organizers helped us to structure our thinking and how well we can use diamantes.
- **Set new goals** or extend existing one.

Guided Comprehension in Action: Lessons for Grades 3–8 by Maureen McLaughlin and Mary Beth Allen ©2002. Newark, DE: International Reading Association. May be copied for classroom use.

Guide: I provided diamante forms (see Appendix, page 177) for the students and guided their reading of short poems from *Voices*, a volume of poetry from international authors. We previewed and read "The Sun" and "On the Mountain: Question and Answer." Then students offered suggestions about pairs of opposites based on the poems we read. *Sun* and *moon* was one pair; *mountain* and *valley* was another. We decided on *sun* and *moon*, and I guided the students through the placement of the opposite nouns and the writing of the second and third lines.

Practice: Students practiced in pairs by completing the diamantes on transparencies, sharing them on the overhead, and discussing their choices. This is Stephanie and Fred's completed diamante:

Sun

Yellow, bright

Glistening, radiating, beaming

Heat daylight stars nightlight

Calming, changing, shimmering

White, iridescent

Moon

Reflect: We reflected on writing form poems and students noted that they liked them because, even though they had to use different parts of speech and limited numbers of words, finishing one was "like solving a mystery."

Student-Facilitated Comprehension Centers

Poetry Center: Students worked in pairs to write and illustrate a diamante on a trifold (see Figure 23). The poem was written in the center, an illustration of the first term on the left, and an illustration of the second term on the right. When completed, the poems were shared with another pair of students and then displayed in our Poetry Gallery.

Research and Technology Center: Students used computers to design a multimedia presentation of their diamantes.

Art Center: Students illustrated their diamantes in a variety of ways including object collage drawings, texture paint, and pastel sketching.

Student-Facilitated Comprehension Routines

Literature Circles: Students worked in pairs to write diamantes about the setting of the book and its opposite, a character from the book and his or her opposite, or an issue and its opposite. Then they shared and discussed their completed diamante with their group.

Questioning the Author: Rather than engage in the usual routine, students wrote the following diamante about the terms *query* and *response*:

Query

Collaborative inquisitive

Probing, engaging, conveying

Idea inquiry answer belief

Predicting, determining, clarifying

Shared, reasoned

Response

Figure 23. Diamante/Clip Art Trifold

Subject	Diamante	Opposite
	Ocean	
	Wet salty	
	Rolling, rising, falling	
	Water sea sand earth	
	Scorching, roasting, baking	
	Dry sandy	
	Desert	

STAGE THREE: Teacher-Facilitated Whole-Group Reflection and Goal Setting

Share: Students shared their diamantes in small groups, and then one student from each group reported to the class. There was quite a variety of diamantes and students felt skilled in their ability to use this form.

Reflect: We reflected on how organizers helped us to structure our thinking. Students felt positive about their diamante experiences.

Set New Goals: We decided to extend our goal and learn another technique that would help us learn more about how words work.

Assessment Options

I observed students as much as possible during their writing. I also reviewed and commented on the completed diamantes, illustrations, and technology presentations.

Guided Comprehension Strategy:
Knowing How Words Work
Teaching Idea: Text Transformations

STAGE ONE: Teacher-Directed Whole-Group Instruction

Text: *Walking the Bridge of Your Nose* (Rosen, 1999)

Explain: I explained to the students that we were going to learn more about how words work by engaging in Text Transformations (see Appendix, page 162), a fun writing activity in which we would take existing poems and use them to write new ones. I told them we would be focusing on using interesting words and would use thesauruses to help us. I read two fractured nursery rhymes, "Hickory Dickory Dock" and "Mary Had a Little Lamb," from the book *Walking the Bridge of Your Nose* to show them how we would rewrite existing poems, changing words first and phrases later.

Demonstrate: I had the rhyme "Jack and Jill" written on an overhead transparency (see Appendix, page 178). I read it to the students and told them I was going to use it to write a new rhyme. Then I showed the students the rhyme with some words left out.

> Jack and Jill _____ up the hill
>
> To _____ a pail of water.
>
> Jack fell down and broke his _____
>
> And Jill came _____ after.

I told the students I was going to rewrite this rhyme using synonyms of the words that were left out. I read "Jack and Jill ____" and thought aloud, "Some synonyms for *went* are *traveled, climbed, scurried, trudged*—I think I'll use *trudged*," and I filled in the blank with the word *trudged*. I repeated the process with the word *fetch*, this time using a thesaurus to help me think of words.

Guide: I asked the students to help me think of synonyms for the next two words: *crown* and *tumbling*. I reminded them to look at the context for the word *crown* and note that it was not a king's hat in this context. I listed the synonyms on the overhead. Together we wrote a fractured nursery rhyme:

> Jack and Jill trudged up the hill
>
> To retrieve a pail of water.
>
> Jack fell down and broke his cranium,
>
> And Jill came somersaulting after.

Practice: I gave each pair of students a printed copy of the same rhyme and asked them to use their thesauruses to create a different version of this rhyme using synonyms. Here are some of the synonym rhymes:

> Jack and Jill sauntered up the hill
>
> To obtain a pail of water.
>
> Jack fell down and broke his skull,
>
> And Jill came rolling after

GUIDED COMPREHENSION: POETRY
KNOWING HOW WORDS WORK: TEXT TRANSFORMATIONS

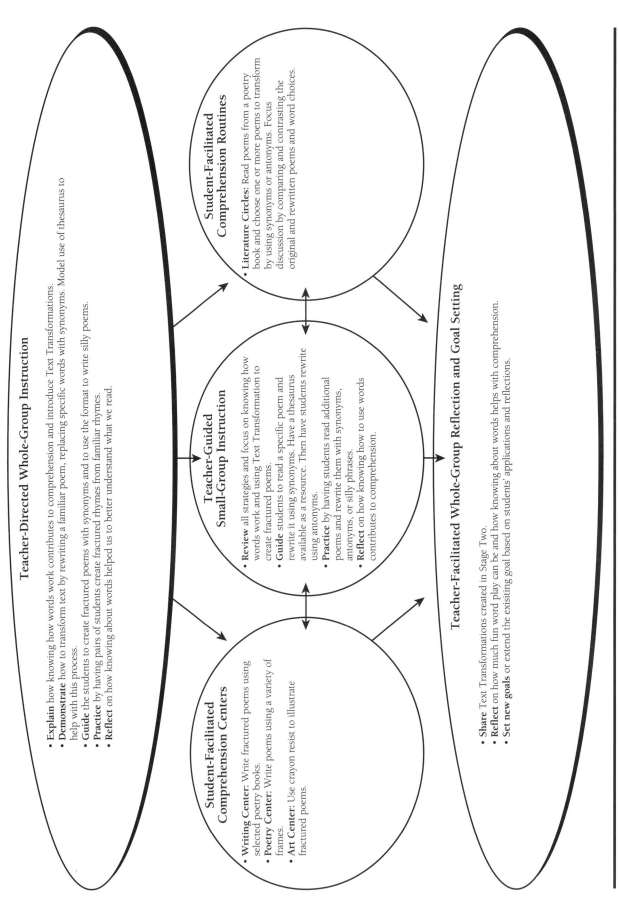

Teacher-Directed Whole-Group Instruction

- **Explain** how knowing how words work contributes to comprehension and introduce Text Transformations.
- **Demonstrate** how to transform text by rewriting a familiar poem, replacing specific words with synonyms. Model use of thesaurus to help with this process.
- **Guide** the students to create fractured poems with synonyms and to use the format to write silly poems.
- **Practice** by having pairs of students create fractured rhymes from familiar rhymes.
- **Reflect** on how knowing about words helped us to better understand what we read.

Student-Facilitated Comprehension Routines

- **Literature Circles:** Read poems from a poetry book and choose one or more poems to transform by using synonyms or antonyms. Focus discussion by comparing and contrasting the original and rewritten poems and word choices.

Teacher-Guided Small-Group Instruction

- **Review** all strategies and focus on knowing how words work and using Text Transformation to create fractured poems.
- **Guide** students to read a specific poem and rewrite it using synonyms. Have a thesaurus available as a resource. Then have students rewrite using antonyms.
- **Practice** by having students read additional poems and rewrite them with synonyms, antonyms, or silly phrases.
- **Reflect** on how knowing how to use words contributes to comprehension.

Student-Facilitated Comprehension Centers

- **Writing Center:** Write fractured poems using selected poetry books.
- **Poetry Center:** Write poems using a variety of frames.
- **Art Center:** Use crayon resist to illustrate fractured poems.

Teacher-Facilitated Whole-Group Reflection and Goal Setting

- **Share** Text Transformations created in Stage Two.
- **Reflect** on how much fun word play can be and how knowing about words helps with comprehension.
- **Set new goals** or extend the exisiting goal based on students' applications and reflections.

Jack and Jill meandered up the hill
To acquire a pail of water.
Jack fell down and broke his noggin,
And Jill came cartwheeling after.

Next, I challenged students to change other words but keep the same form to create a silly rhyme.

Jack and Jill got in a car
To go to see a movie
They went too fast and they ran out of gas
And they didn't think that was very groovy.

Cat and mouse went to a house
To see their friend Pythonous.
He was mad but soon was glad
He had an early dinner.

Reflect: We reflected on how using existing rhymes helps us know more about how words work. Students said they thought it was fun to change the rhymes and that they enjoyed using the thesaurus to help them find lots of synonyms. They also commented on how easy it was to create the silly rhymes once they had worked with the pattern. They said next time they wanted to try creating silly rhymes that kept the rhyming pattern of the original rhyme. I asked them what they could use to help them think of good rhyming words and they suggested the rhyming dictionary that we have in the classroom. I told them I would put that at the writing center so they could use it as a resource in Stage Two.

STAGE TWO: Teacher-Guided Small-Group Instruction

Text: *Something Big Has Been Here* (Prelutsky, 1990) (Texts varied according to students' abilities.)

Review: I reviewed the comprehension strategies readers use and then focused on Knowing How Words Work using synonyms and silly rhymes to learn new words.

Guide: I read the poem "You're Nasty and You're Loud" by Jack Prelutsky and told the students that we're going to rewrite this using synonyms. The original poem goes like this:

You're nasty and you're loud
You're mean enough for two
If I could be a cloud
I'd rain all day on you.

I guided the students to find words that we could replace with synonyms. I had several thesauruses available so we could have a resource to use. We started with *nasty* and brainstormed several words, such as *wicked*, *mean*, and *vicious*. We decided on *vicious*. We then looked at the word *mean* and brainstormed *evil*, *despicable*, and *contemptible*. We decided on *evil*. Finally, we looked at *rain* and replaced it with *drizzle*. Our fractured poem looked like this:

You're vicious and you're loud
You're evil enough for two.
If I could be a cloud
I'd drizzle all day on you.

Next, I guided the students to rewrite the poem and use antonyms. Here are two samples of what they wrote:

> You're lovely and you're quiet
> You're kind enough for two
> If I could be a sun
> I'd shine all day on you.
>
> You're delightful and you're serene
> You're sweet enough for two
> If I could be a rainbow
> I'd sparkle all day on you.

The students used the thesaurus, and when they could not find an exact opposite, I told them to use a word to make as much sense as possible.

Practice: Next, I gave each pair of students a different poem from *Something Big Has Been Here*. I asked them to rewrite the poem using synonyms first, then antonyms, and finally keeping the structure to create a silly poem. They used the thesaurus and rhyming dictionary to help.

Reflect: We reflected on how much fun word play is and how we can use resources to help us know new words. The students said they loved writing fractured poems and were looking forward to doing some others at the writing center.

Student-Facilitated Comprehension Centers

Writing Center: I placed several poetry books, such as *A Light in the Attic*, *Falling Up*, *Something Big Has Been Here*, *A Pizza the Size of the Sun*, and *New Kid on the Block*, at the center. Poems that could be rewritten easily were marked with colored sticky notes. The students chose one or more poems to rewrite with synonyms, antonyms, or silly variations.

Poetry Center: Students used several poetry frames to rewrite the poems inserting their own words. They shared and discussed their poems with at least two other students.

Art Center: Students used crayon resist to illustrate their fractured poems. They shared these in Stage Three and displayed them in our Poetry Gallery.

Student-Facilitated Comprehension Routines

Literature Circles: Students read different poetry books and selected poems to rewrite. They shared the title and author of their poetry books with the group. Then they read the original poems and the transformations they had written. They discussed the words they had replaced and how and why they had chosen them.

STAGE THREE: Teacher-Facilitated Whole-Group Reflection and Goal Setting

Share: Students shared fractured poems they had created in Stage Two. They were excited about these, especially the silly ones.

Reflect: We discussed the importance of learning new words and using them effectively in our reading, speaking, and writing. The students also reflected on how important resources can be, especially when writing.

Set New Goals: Feeling confident in our ability to use Text Transformations, we extended our goal to learn other techniques that would help us understand how words work.

Assessment Options

I used the students' completed rhymes to determine their ability to use different and creative words. I also looked at the reflections they made in their Guided Comprehension Journals. I gathered a lot of information as I watched them work on their rhymes during Stage Two.

THEME RESOURCES

Texts

Adoff, A. (1968). *I am the darker brother: An anthology of modern poems by Negro Americans*. New York: Macmillian.

Adoff, A. (1997). *Love letters*. New York: The Blue Sky Press.

Arnold, A. (1986). *Sport's pages*. New York: Harper & Row.

Brenner, B. (2000). *Voices: Poetry and art from around the world*. Washington, DC: National Geographic Society.

Carle, E. (1989). *Eric Carle's animals animals*. New York: Philomel Books.

de Paola, T. (1988). *Book of poems*. New York: G.P. Putnam's Sons.

Dickenson, E. (1994). *Poetry for young people*. New York: Scholastic.

Eliot, T.S. (1939). *Old possum's book of practical cats*. New York: Harcourt Brace.

Fields, E. (1991). *Shut-Eyetrain and other poems of childhood*. Edgewood Cliffs, NJ: Silver Press.

Fleischman, P. (1988). *Joyful noise: Poems for two voices*. New York: Harper & Row.

Fleischman, P. (2000). *Big talk: Poems for four voices*. Cambridge, MA: Candlewick Press.

Fletcher, R. (1999). *Relatively speaking: Poems about family*. New York: Orchard Books.

Florian, D. (1998). *Insectlopedia*. New York: Scholastic

Florian, D. (1999). *Laugh-eteria*. New York: Scholastic.

Frost, R. (1982). *A swinger of birches: Poems of Robert Frost for young people*. Owings Mills, MD: Stemmer House.

Giovanni, N. (1971). *Spin a soft black song*. New York: The Trumpet Club.

Greenberg, D. (1999). *Whatever happened to Humpty Dumpty and other surprising sequels to Mother Goose poems*. Boston: Little, Brown.

Hill, L. (1990). *Poems & songs of the Civil War*. New York: The Fairfax Press.

Holbrook, S. (1996). *I never said I wasn't difficult*. Honesdale, PA: Boyds Mill Press.

Holbrook, S. (1996). *The dog ate my homework*. Honesdale, PA: Boyds Mill Press.

Holbrook, S. (1998). *Walking on the boundaries of change*. Honesdale, PA: Boyds Mills Press.

Hopkins, L. (1999). *LIVES: Poems about famous Americans*. New York: HarperCollins.

Hudson, W. (1993). *Pass it on: African American poetry for young children*. New York: Scholastic.

Johnson, D. (2000). *Movin' teen poets take voice*. New York: Orchard Books.

Korman, G., & Korman, B. (1992). *The D-poems of Jeremy Bloom: A collection of poems about school, homework, and life (sort of)*. New York: Scholastic.

Lansky, B. (1997). *No more homework! No more tests! Kids favorite funny school poems*. New York: Scholastic.

Loewen, N. (1994). *Voices in poetry by Walt Whitman*. Mankato, MN: Creative Editions.

Numeroff, L. (1999). *Sometimes I wonder if poodles like noodles*. New York: Simon & Schuster.

Paschen, E., & Mosby, R.P. (2001). *Poetry speaks: Hear great poets read their work from Tennyson to Plath*. Naperville, IL: Sourcebooks MediaFusion.

Prelutsky, J. (1983). *The Random House book of poems*. New York: Random House.

Prelutsky, J. (1990). *Something big has been here*. New York: Scholastic.

Prelutsky, J. (1991). *For laughing out loud: Poems to tickle your funny bone*. New York: Alfred A. Knopf.

Prelutsky, J. (1994). *A pizza the size of the sun*. New York: Greenwillow Books.

Prelutsky, J. (1997). *It's raining pigs and noodles*. New York: Scholastic.

Prelusky, J. (1998). *Imagine that: Poems of never was*. New York: Alfred A. Knopf.

Prelutsky, J. (1999). *The 20th century children's poetry treasury*. New York: Random House.

Richelle, B. (2000). *Words with wings: A treasury of African-American poetry and art*. New York: HarperCollins.

Rosen, M. (1999). *Walking the bridge of you nose*. New York: Larousse Kingfisher Chambers.

Silverstein, S. (1974). *Where the sidewalk ends*. New York: Harper & Row.

Silverstein, S. (1981). *A light in the attic*. New York: HarperCollins.

Silverstein, S. (1996). *Falling up*. New York: Harper & Row.

Stevenson, J. (1999). *Candy corn*. New York: Scholastic.

Stevenson, J. (1999). *Popcorn*. New York: Scholastic.

Thomas, J. (1993). *Brown honey in broomwheat tea*. New York: Harper & Row.

Viorst, J. (1981). *If I were in charge of the world and other worries*. New York: Atheneum.

Volakova, H. (1993). *...I never saw another butterfly: Children's drawings and poems from Terezin Concentration Camp*. New York: Schocken Books.

Wise, W. (2000). *Dinosaurs forever*. New York: Dial.

Yolen, J. (1990). *Dinosaur dances*. New York: G.P. Putnam's Sons.

Yolen, J., & Stemple, H. (2001). *Dear mother, dear daughter: Poems for young people*. Honesdale, PA: Wordsong.

Websites

Children's Book Council: Young People's Poetry Week
www.cbcbooks.org/html/poetry_week.html

Favorite Poem Project
www.favoritepoem.org/story/index.html

KidzPage
www.veeceet.com

Poetry Pages for Young Adults
falcon.jmu.edu/~ramseyil/poetry.htm

Poetry4Kids
www.poetry4kids.com

The Site for Young Writers
home.earthlink.net/~ameliaruth/index2.html

Yahooligans! Directory: Poetry
www.yahooligans.com/school_bell/language_arts/poetry

Performance Extensions Across the Curriculum

Social Studies

- Make poetry connections to social studies by exploring issues such as important people in history ("Lincoln" by Carl Sandburg, *I Never Saw Another Butterfly* (children's poetry and illustrations from the Holocaust), or topics in geography (Jack Prelutsky's "New York is in North Carolina").
- Investigate poets who have recited their poems at U.S. presidential inaugurations (Robert Frost for President Kennedy, Maya Angelou for President Clinton) and the poems they shared on those occasions. Use this information to engage in an inquiry-based exploration such as The Rest of the Story or a First Person Experience (McLaughlin, 2000).
- Read or listen to ballads that tell about historic events; create original ballads, songs, or other poems related to areas of study.

Science

- Explore poems that relate to science topics and write poems in response, or research the topics the poems address.
- Create original songs or poems that include researched facts about topics.

- Engage in the ReWrite (Bean, 1997) activity in which students write songs before and after content area study. The ReWrite represents how students' knowledge, perceptions, and feelings have changed after studying the topic.

Math
- Write raps to explain processes for using specific algorithms; write word problems in poetic forms and give to peers to solve.
- Use poetry to engage students in math projects as Colleen and Lynn did when they issued the following invitation to their students:

The Poetry of Algebra
Colleen Connors and Lynn Cunningham, Wallenpaupack High School

Math and English, there is a link
Poetry and Algebra, who would think

Now that we've finished systems of equations
This assignment might try your patience

Our equations contained both x and y
We'll bump up the level, way up high

Creating your own word problem is the task at hand
But we'll spice it up so it won't be so bland

Pick a topic with two unknowns
Like an archeologist finding stones and bones

Write a system that can relate the two
Be sure the solution makes sense to you

When you solve, you can't have half a person
If that's the case, you must change your version

After your system appears to cause no worry
Write some lines that tell your story

Then a poster you will design
I hope this part won't make you whine

The poster should be both colorful and neat
It should be visible from every seat

Your poster should certainly catch one's eye
Anyone looking at it should also know why

On the back your system should appear
The solution process should also be there

The answer should also appear on back
On that side your name shouldn't lack

If you want your work previewed by me
Three days before it's due is when I should see

March 22nd is when the project is due
You may work in groups of no more than two

I hope you enjoy this type of job
It's designed to be fun...not to make you sob

Art
- Explore art techniques used in different poetry books (*Insectlopedia*—water color on brown paper bags), with certain poetry forms (haiku—water color), or by different poets. Have students use these techniques with their original poems or other writings.

Music
- Set poetry to music, turning the poem into song lyrics.
- Interpret a poem through music and dance.

Culminating Activity

Poetry Festival: A Community of Poets: Invite parents and community members to a poetry celebration. Display poetry projects and applications across the curriculum. Feature student poetry performances: readings, artwork, dramatizations, and musical interpretations. Publish and distribute a community poetry book in which student poems appear as well as any contributed by parents, school personnel, and other community members. Create a website and post the booklet there to assure wider access. Limit submissions to one poem per person.

CHAPTER 6

Biography and Autobiography: Knowing Others, Knowing Ourselves

Biographies are stories of people's lives that chronologically recount individual histories. They tell about goals, trials, successes, and failures. We read them to gain insight into the lives of others, which in turn offers us insight into ourselves. Biography is a popular genre that accommodates a wide range of reading tastes. For example, we can gain greater understanding of the intricacies of history by reading biographies of John Adams, Anne Frank, Martin Luther King, and John McCain. We can learn more about inventions and scientific discoveries by investigating the lives of Alexander Graham Bell, the Wright brothers, and James Watson and Francis Crick. We can also gain insights into the arts by reading biographies of musicians, artists, writers, and actors through the ages. Fascination often draws us to this genre, but it is our continuing curiosity that keeps us—and our students—engaged.

The Sample Theme-Based Plan for Guided Comprehension: Biography and Autobiography (see Figure 24) presents a sampling of goals, state standards, assessments, texts, technology resources, comprehension strategies, teaching ideas, comprehension centers, and comprehension routines. The plan begins by delineating examples of student goals and related state standards. The student goals for this theme include the following:

- using appropriate comprehension strategies
- relating essential elements of the biographical format to reading and writing
- writing biographies and autobiographies
- communicating effectively

These goals support the following state standards:

- learning to read independently
- reading, analyzing, and interpreting literature
- types and quality of writing
- speaking and listening

Figure 24. Sample Theme-Based Plan for Guided Comprehension: Biography and Autobiography

Goals and Connections to State Standards | Students will

- use appropriate comprehension strategies. Standard: learning to read independently
- relate essential elements of the biographical format to their reading and writing. Standards: reading, analyzing, and interpreting literature; types of writing
- write biographies and autobiographies. Standard: types and quality of writing
- communicate effectively. Standards: speaking and listening

Assessment

The following measures can be used for a variety of purposes, including diagnostic, formative, and summative assessment:

Autobio- and Bio-Cubes	Student Autobiographies
Bio- and Autobio-Organizers	Student Self-Assessments
Bio-Pyramids	The Rest of the Story
Observation	Thick and Thin Questions

Text	Title	Theme	Level
1.	*Satchel Paige*	B	3
2.	*Bill Peet: An Autobiography*	A	5
3.	Civil War Biographies from http://www.civilwarhome.com	B	4
4.	*Betsy Ross*	B	3

Technology Resources

Arts and Entertainment's Biography
   www.biography.com
Lives: The Biography Resource
   www.amillionlives.com
Biography Maker
   www.bham.wednet.edu/bio/biomak2.htm

Comprehension Strategies

1. Self-Questioning
2. Making Connections/ Summarizing
3. Summarizing
4. Summarizing

Teaching Ideas

Thick and Thin Questions
Biography/ Autobiography Organizer
Bio-Cubes
Bio-Pyramid

Comprehension Centers

Students will apply the comprehension strategies and related teaching ideas in the following comprehension centers:

Art Center   Writing Center
Biography Center
Research and Technology Center

Comprehension Routines

Students will apply the comprehension strategies and related teaching ideas in the following comprehension routines:

Literature Circles
Questioning the Author
Reciprocal Teaching

Assessments used during the Guided Comprehension lessons include observation, a variety of strategy applications, student writing, and student self-assessments. The lessons focus on the following comprehension strategies and related teaching ideas:

- Self-Questioning: Thick and Thin Questions
- Making Connections/Summarizing: Biography/Autobiography Organizer
- Summarizing: Bio-Cubes
- Summarizing: Bio-Pyramids

Biographies or autobiographies of Satchel Paige; Bill Peet; Civil War figures such as Clara Barton, Harriet Tubman, and George Armstrong Custer; and Betsy Ross are the texts used for teacher-directed whole-group instruction. References for other texts at a variety of levels, including those used in teacher-guided small-group instruction and the student-facilitated comprehension centers and routines, are provided in the Theme Resources at the end of the chapter.

Art, biography, research and technology, and writing are among the centers students use during Guided Comprehension. Students also engage in strategy applications in comprehension routines including Literature Circles, Reciprocal Teaching, and Questioning the Author.

GUIDED COMPREHENSION LESSONS

Guided Comprehension Strategy: Self-Questioning
Teaching Idea: Thick and Thin Questions

STAGE ONE: Teacher-Directed Whole-Group Instruction

Text: *Satchel Paige* (Cline-Ransome, 2000)

Explain: I explained self-questioning to students, noting that this strategy, like all the others, required us to think in depth. I explained the concept of Thick and Thin Questions (see Appendix A, *Guided Comprehension: A Teaching Model for Grades 3–8*) using the biography *Satchel Paige*, which I read aloud to the students. I told them that thin questions had small answers that required just a word or phrase. I explained that thick questions had larger answers that required several phrases or sentences and usually needed a combination of information from the text and their own minds. I reminded the students that good readers engage in self-questioning before, during, and after reading and that we would use this process in other texts we read.

Demonstrate: I decided to use large and small sticky notes, as suggested by Harvey and Goudvis (2000). I made a transparency of the Thick and Thin Question form (see Appendix, page 179) so that I could show the students how to record their questions and answers. I showed the students the cover of the book and thought aloud about how important it is to have questions in my mind before I start reading because it helps to focus my reading and gives me purposes for reading. I said, "One question I have as I look at the cover of this book is 'What made Satchel Paige famous?'" I wrote this question in the Thin Question column and told the students that it was a thin question because the answer is probably short and evident in the text. Next, I asked aloud, "What impact did Satchel Paige have on African Americans and baseball?" I recorded this question in the Thick Question column and explained to the students that the answer was probably larger than a word or two. I explained that I knew from prior experience that Satchel Paige pitched a long time ago and that black men were not always welcome in the major leagues then. I also told them that I knew that Satchel was famous so I think that he did influence blacks in baseball. I explained that this is a thick question because it would take information from the text and my mind to answer it.

Guide: Next, I read the first two pages of text to the students. I prompted them to think of a question that had a small answer. They suggested, "Where did Satchel grow up?" and "How did Satchel help his mother?" I recorded these in the Thin Question column. I then guided the students to think of some larger questions that could be answered from the information in the text and from their minds or in other parts of the text. They were having trouble thinking of these because they were so focused on the direct recall questions. I gave them another example: "What evidence is there that Satchel had an 'early gift for throwing?'" and explained that this question had a bigger answer than just one word or phrase. I then read the next two pages and prompted the students with guiding questions such as "What do you know about Satchel?" and "What more do you want to know?" They came up with "Why did Satchel need to earn money?" and "What kind of worker is Satchel? How do you know?" I recorded these in the Thick Question column. I then

GUIDED COMPREHENSION: BIOGRAPHY AND AUTOBIOGRAPHY
SELF-QUESTIONING: THICK AND THIN QUESTIONS

Teacher-Directed Whole-Group Instruction

- **Explain** self-questioning and Thick and Thin Questions.
- **Demonstrate** how to create Thick and Thin Questions using a read-aloud biography.
- **Guide** the students to create Thick and Thin Questions using additional sections of the biography.
- **Practice** by having students create questions in groups of four, using large and small sticky notes. Share questions and answers as a class.
- **Reflect** on how self-questioning helped them understand what they were reading.

Student-Facilitated Comprehension Centers

- **Biography Center:** Create Thick and Thin Questions for self-chosen biographies. Record answers in Guided Comprehension Journals and discuss with a peer.

Teacher-Guided Small-Group Instruction

- **Review** all strategies and focus on self-questioning and Thick and Thin Questions.
- **Guide** students to look at the cover and create Thick and Thin Questions. Then have them read three pages and record questions on sticky notes.
- **Practice** by having students finish the story and record questions at certain points. Use questions as prompts for small-group discussion of text.
- **Reflect** on how Thick and Thin Questions helped us focus on what we were reading.

Student-Facilitated Comprehension Routines

- **Literature Circles:** Use Thick and Thin Questions to prompt discussion of biographies.
- **Questioning the Author:** Create thick questions to query the author.

Teacher-Facilitated Whole-Group Reflection and Goal Setting

- **Share** Thick and Thin Questions and answers generated in Stage Two.
- **Reflect** on how the self-questioning helped them understand what they had read.
- **Set new goals** or extend existing ones.

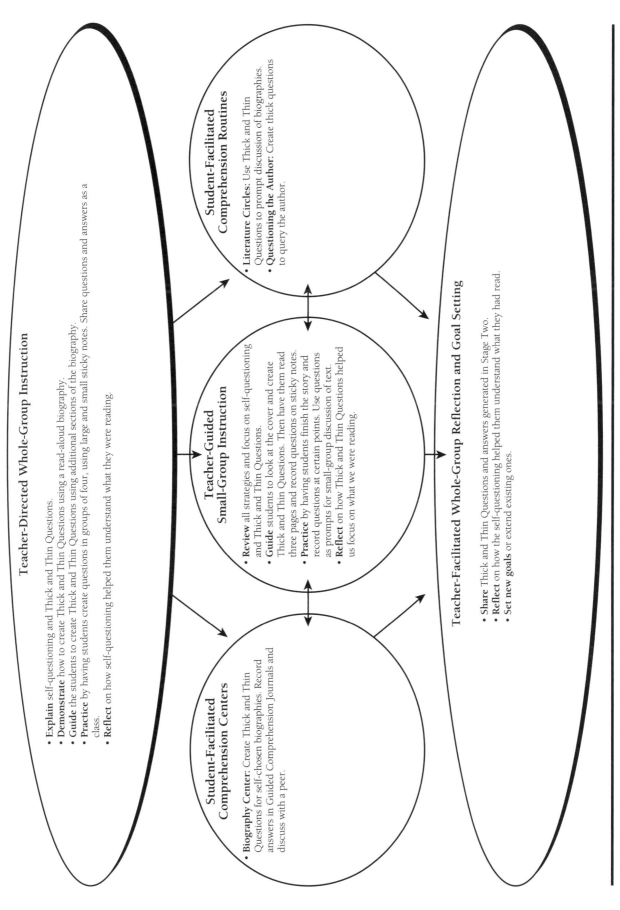

Guided Comprehension in Action: Lessons for Grades 3–8 by Maureen McLaughlin and Mary Beth Allen ©2002. Newark, DE: International Reading Association. May be copied for classroom use.

repeated this process with the next two pages of text. The students were able to create Thick and Thin Questions. I felt they were able to try this on their own so I gave each group of four students a stack of large and small sticky notes. I demonstrated how to record thin questions on the small sticky notes and thick questions on the larger notes.

Practice: I read the next two pages of text aloud and asked each group to create one thin and one thick question. Each group shared questions and possible answers. Other students contributed additional responses to the thick questions. I continued this process throughout the reading of Satchel Paige's biography.

Reflect: The students reflected on how the questions really helped to focus them as they listened to the story. They also shared that the thick questions made them think about larger connections within the text and their own minds. We talked about ways they could use self-questioning when they read, and they set goals for using questioning when they read on their own.

STAGE TWO: Teacher-Guided Small-Group Instruction

Text: *Helen Keller* (Davidson, 1969) (Texts varied according to students' abilities.)

Review: I reviewed the comprehension strategies good readers use and then focused on self-questioning and Thick and Thin Questions.

Guide: I showed the students the cover of the new book they were going to read, *Helen Keller*. I encouraged them to think of a Thin and Thick Question to give them a focus for reading. I started by asking, "What was Helen Keller's disability?" I explained that was a thin question because it had a short answer. Then I asked, "What kinds of hardships did Helen Keller face because of her disability?" I explained why that was a thick question and we used the questions to set purposes for reading. I asked the students to read the first chapter on their own. When they finished, we discussed that the text had provided the answer to the thin question I had raised, but not the thick question. We decided we would keep that question in mind as we continued to read the book. We created new Thick and Thin Questions and students read the next chapter.

Practice: The students created responses to the questions as they read the next two chapters. They also created new Thick and Thin Questions on sticky notes. We used these questions as prompts to discuss the biography the next time we met in small groups. I continued this process as a way to prompt discussion and monitor students' understanding as they completed this biography. These are some of the Thick and Thin Questions students raised:

Thick Questions

- How will Annie get Helen to learn self-control?
- Why was Helen so difficult toward Annie?
- What might Annie try next?

Thin Questions

- What is Annie's job?
- Why was Helen angry with Annie?
- What caused the worst fight Helen and Annie had?

Reflect: I encouraged the students to reflect on the importance of self-questioning when they read and on the difference between questions with small and large answers. We discussed how this helped them think and understand what they were reading. They agreed that it helped to give them a purpose for wanting to read more.

Student-Facilitated Comprehension Centers

Biography Center: I placed large and small sticky notes at the center and had the students record Thick and Thin Questions on them. I asked them to place the sticky notes and appropriate answers in their Guided Comprehension Journals so I could review and comment on them.

Student-Facilitated Comprehension Routines

Literature Circles: Students read the same biography and used Thick and Thin Questions recorded on sticky notes as the prompts for their discussions. Students took turns posing questions to and getting answers from the group before they shared their own answers. They continued this process throughout the reading of the biography. They placed their sticky notes and answers in their Guided Comprehension Journals.

Questioning the Author: Students involved in QtA focused their questions on "thick" answers. They recorded their queries on large sticky notes and used them to engage in this process. They made notes about the answers in their Guided Comprehension Journals.

STAGE THREE: Teacher-Facilitated Whole-Group Reflection and Goal Setting

Share: In small groups, students used their Guided Comprehension Journals to share examples of Thick and Thin Questions they had created in Stage Two.

Reflect: In whole group, I reminded the students about the importance of self-questioning while reading and asked them to think about how it helped them understand the text. They agreed that the questions helped give them a reason to continue reading and in many instances clarified ideas for them as they shared answers. They got into a discussion on the value of thin questions and we came to a consensus that thin questions were valuable, but they should not be the only kind of question we think about. I then had the students think about how they could use this questioning technique in other reading settings.

Set New Goals: We engaged in self-assessment and decided to extend our current goal by learning about Evaluative Questioning.

Assessment Options

I observed students during all stages of Guided Comprehension and made notes about contributions and interactions. I also read their Guided Comprehension Journals to gather evidence about their ability to create Thick and Thin Questions. The students' self-assessments during comprehension centers and routines provided additional information about their understanding.

Guided Comprehension Strategy: Making Connections/ Summarizing
Teaching Idea: Biography/Autobiography Organizer

STAGE ONE: Teacher-Directed Whole-Group Instruction

Text: *Bill Peet: An Autobiography* (Peet, 1989)

Explain: I showed the students several autobiographies and then focused on *Bill Peet: An Autobiography*. I read the first five pages and asked the students to tell me the kind of information we had learned so far about Bill Peet. I recorded their ideas on the Biography/Autobiography Organizer (see Appendix, page 180). Next, I asked the students how Bill Peet's book was different from the biographies we had read. They said that this book was about an author. I prompted them to discover that Peet had written about his own life. Then we revisited the book and looked for evidence to support this. We discovered the pronoun *I* was frequently used by the author. We discussed how we use pronouns like *I*, *we*, and *our* when we write in the first person. I continued to read from Bill Peet's autobiography and recorded information about his life on the organizer. I used this experience with Bill Peet's autobiography to segue into the students writing their autobiographies.

Demonstrate: I made an overhead of the Biography/Autobiography Organizer and explained it to the students. Then, I started to think aloud about some of the facts about me that would go onto the organizer. I proceeded to fill it in by thinking aloud and recording ideas in the organizer. First I wrote my name in the center. Then I thought out loud about the Interests and Hobbies section and wrote, "I like to read, golf, and walk my dog." After I had filled in information in each section, I demonstrated how to start writing my autobiography. I thought aloud about how I wanted it to start and then wrote on the overhead, *I knew very early in my life that I wanted to be a teacher when I grew up*. I continued to draft the text, thinking aloud about the choices I made for words and organization.

Guide: Next, I gave students an organizer and asked them to think about what they remembered about their early life. I guided them to think about important events that happened or key people who influenced them. I had them fill in at least two items for their early life. We repeated this process for the rest of the subtopics: family and friends, accomplishments, interests, and other important facts. This is the information Ryan listed on his organizer:

Early Life:	Became a big brother.
	Had a part in the fourth-grade play.
Important People:	Mom, Dad, Sister
Interests and Hobbies:	Soccer, Basketball, Harry Potter books, Cooking

I encouraged the students to give a brief description for each thing they listed. I then guided them to start their autobiographies. We brainstormed different ways they could start them—with an anecdote, a question, or an interesting fact. I encouraged students to discuss with the people in their groups ways to start their autobiographies.

Practice: I had the students start their autobiographies and told them they could work on them more in Stage Two.

Reflect: I encouraged the students to make connections between their autobiographies and the biographies we had read. I also prompted them to focus on what key information needs to be included in biographies and autobiographies.

GUIDED COMPREHENSION: BIOGRAPHY AND AUTOBIOGRAPHY
MAKING CONNECTIONS: BIOGRAPHY/AUTOBIOGRAPHY ORGANIZER

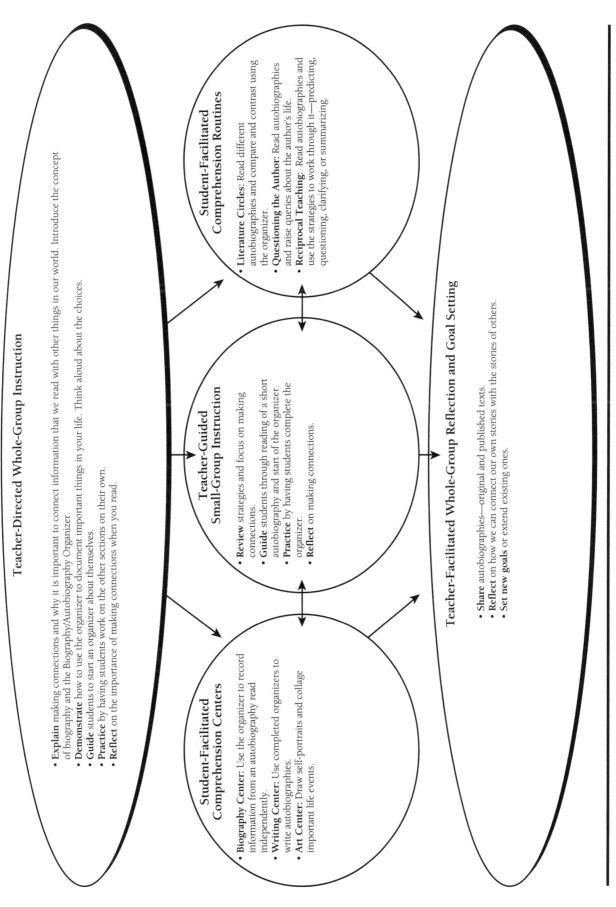

Teacher-Directed Whole-Group Instruction

- **Explain** making connections and why it is important to connect information that we read with other things in our world. Introduce the concept of biography and the Biography/Autobiography Organizer.
- **Demonstrate** how to use the organizer to document important things in your life. Think aloud about the choices.
- **Guide** students to start an organizer about themselves.
- **Practice** by having students work on the other sections on their own.
- **Reflect** on the importance of making connections when you read.

Student-Facilitated Comprehension Routines

- **Literature Circles:** Read different autobiographies and compare and contrast using the organizer.
- **Questioning the Author:** Read autobiographies and raise queries about the author's life.
- **Reciprocal Teaching:** Read autobiographies and use the strategies to work through it—predicting, questioning, clarifying, or summarizing.

Teacher-Guided Small-Group Instruction

- **Review** strategies and focus on making connections.
- **Guide** students through reading of a short autobiography and start of the organizer.
- **Practice** by having students complete the organizer.
- **Reflect** on making connections.

Student-Facilitated Comprehension Centers

- **Biography Center:** Use the organizer to record information from an autobiography read independently.
- **Writing Center:** Use completed organizers to write autobiographies.
- **Art Center:** Draw self-portraits and collage important life events.

Teacher-Facilitated Whole-Group Reflection and Goal Setting

- **Share** autobiographies—original and published texts.
- **Reflect** on how we can connect our own stories with the stories of others.
- **Set new goals** or extend existing ones.

STAGE TWO: Teacher-Guided Small-Group Instruction

Review: I reviewed the comprehension strategies readers use and then focused on using graphic organizers to help make connections and summarize. I also reviewed the kind of information that makes an effective biography or autobiography.

Guide: Each student had a volume of *Something About the Author*, a biographical and autobiographical reference series that I borrowed from our school library. They previewed the life of the author and shared ideas with the group. I had them read the first page of the autobiography silently and then share what information they had learned about the author. I had them think about how this autobiography is like the one they started and asked them to think about other pieces of information they may want to include in their own. We repeated this with the next two pages.

Practice: I had the students begin writing their autobiographies independently and use the ideas from the text to think of other ideas they could add to their autobiography.

Reflect: I encouraged the students to reflect on what is the important information that needs to be included in biographies and autobiographies. I also had them think about how the various authors are similar and different from them.

Student-Facilitated Comprehension Centers

Biography Center: Students read at least one autobiography independently and used the structure of this to help them complete their own. They also charted the information from the text on the graphic organizer.

Writing Center: Students used the organizer to continue drafting autobiographies.

Art Center: Then they went to the Art Center to create self-portraits and collages to represent key points in their lives. The used these with their autobiographies to tell about themselves.

Student-Facilitated Comprehension Routines

Literature Circles: Students each read a different biography, completed the organizer, and used it as a structure for comparing and contrasting each person's life.

Questioning the Author: Students involved in QtA read the same autobiography and created questions they wanted to ask the author.

Reciprocal Teaching: Students read the same biography and used predicting, questioning, clarifying, and summarizing to work through it.

STAGE THREE: Teacher-Facilitated Whole-Group Reflection and Goal Setting

Share: Students shared work they completed in Stage Two. They enjoyed hearing about one another's lives, and they got some new ideas to include in their own stories.

Reflect: Then we reflected on summarizing the information that needs to be included in biographies and autobiographies and what it was like to author the stories of our lives.

Set New Goals: We felt confident that we had become quite good at summarizing a variety of text types as well as our lives, so we decided to set new goals about evaluating.

Assessment Options

I observed students during all stages of Guided Comprehension and made notes about contributions and interactions. The students' organizers and drafts provided excellent information about their ability to note the essential information as well as write effectively. I used their self-evaluations to document contribution in routines.

Guided Comprehension Strategy: Summarizing
Teaching Idea: Bio-Cubes

STAGE ONE: Teacher-Directed Whole-Group Instruction

Text: Civil War Biographies from http://www.civilwarhome.com

Explain: I began by engaging in direct explanation of summarizing, focusing on expository text and the components of a biography. Then I explained that a Bio-Cube (see Appendix, page 163) provides a structure for summarizing a person's life.

Demonstrate: I used a brief Civil War biography (Clara Barton, Harriet Tubman, George Armstrong Custer) to demonstrate summarizing. These biographies are available at http://www.civilwarhome.com. Next, I used a think-aloud and an overhead transparency to strengthen the understanding of my lesson. I then reviewed the information needed to complete the six sides of the Bio-Cube (see Appendix, page 170): (1) the subject's name, birth date, and birthplace; (2) a statement about personal background; (3) something the person struggled with or overcame; (4) why this person should be remembered; (5) an epitaph; and (6) an illustration. Then I read the text, pausing occasionally to think aloud about the Bio-Cube components and to mark necessary information with sticky notes. After reading the text, I demonstrated how I had used the information to complete a Bio-Cube, which I had prepared prior to class. Then I used the Bio-Cube to create an oral summary.

Guide: I read aloud another short biography and began to create a Bio-Cube. I began by noting the information for the first side of the cube. Then I guided pairs of students to provide information for the next two sides. We discussed students' ideas and added the information they suggested to the cube.

Practice: The students practiced summarizing by working in pairs to complete the Bio-Cubes. Then they shared with their partner an oral summary based on the biography. Finally, the students shared and discussed their Bio-Cube and summary with another pair of students.

Reflect: We reflected on how the Bio-Cubes helped us understand what was important about people's lives and how we can use Bio-Cubes in other settings. The students enjoyed creating their Cubes and enjoyed discussing their summaries with other group members. The information from our group Bio-Cube is featured in Figure 25.

STAGE TWO: Teacher-Guided Small-Group Instruction

Text: *Anne Frank* (McDonough, 1997) (Texts varied according to students' abilities.)

Review: I reminded students about the comprehension strategies that good readers use and focused on using summarizing with Bio-Cubes.

Guide: I guided the students in reading *Anne Frank*, the picture book. We began by discussing what we already knew about Anne Frank and then read to learn new or more detailed information. As they read, the students coded the information needed to complete the Bio-Cube. Then I assisted the students in completing the first two sections of the Bio-Cube and provided support as needed.

Practice: The students practiced this activity by completing the Bio-Cube and developing an oral summary. The students then shared and discussed their summaries.

Reflect: We reflected on how summarizing helps us understand what we read and how Bio-Cubes help us summarize people's lives.

GUIDED COMPREHENSION: BIOGRAPHY AND AUTOBIOGRAPHY
SUMMARIZING: BIO-CUBES

Teacher-Directed Whole-Group Instruction

- **Explain** summarizing, focusing on expository text and the components of a biography. Explain that a Bio-Cube provides a structure for summarizing a person's life.
- **Demonstrate** by using a short biography such as *Martin Luther King* or a Civil War biography, a think-aloud, and an overhead transparency of a precut cube form. Use the completed cube to create an oral summary.
- **Guide** students to complete a Bio-Cube based on a brief biography read aloud. Begin by working with the students to complete the first two components.
- **Practice** by having students work in pairs to complete the cubes and share oral summaries based on them. Share and discuss with another pair.
- **Reflect** on how Bio-Cubes helped us understand what was important about people's lives and how we can use Bio-Cubes in other settings.

Student-Facilitated Comprehension Routines

- **Literature Circle:** Use the subject of the biography you just finished reading to create a Bio-Cube.
- **Questioning the Author:** Use selected biographies from *Something About the Author* to query the authors about the influence of their lives on their work. Create Bio-Cubes.

Teacher-Guided Small-Group Instruction

- **Review** the comprehension strategies that good readers use and focus on summarizing using Bio-Cubes.
- **Guide** students to read a brief biography (the picture book *Anne Frank* or *Gandhi* or a biography from *Lives of Extraordinary Women, Lives of the Presidents, Lives of Athletes, Lives of the Artists, Lives of the Writers, Lives of the Musicians*) and code the information needed to complete the Bio-Cube. Guide students to complete the first two sections of the cube. Provide support as needed.
- **Practice** by having students complete the Bio-Cube and develop oral summaries. Discuss.
- **Reflect** on summarizing and Bio-Cubes.

Student-Facilitated Comprehension Centers

- **Research and Technology Center:** Access http://www.amillionlives.com to create a Bio-Cube about a famous person of your choice. Research further to discover The Rest of the Story. Use at least two sources and the form provided.
- **Biography Center:** Read and create mobiles that include information from Bio-Cubes.
- **Writing and Art Centers:** Use the forms provided to complete and illustrate a square for our class autobiographical quilt.

Teacher-Facilitated Whole-Group Reflection and Goal Setting

- **Share** Bio-Cubes, Autobio-Cubes, quilt squares, and summaries created in Stage Two and assess ability to use them.
- **Reflect** on how summarizing helped us when reading and how summaries of different kinds of text require different components.
- **Set new goals** or extend existing ones.

Guided Comprehension in Action: Lessons for Grades 3–8 by Maureen McLaughlin and Mary Beth Allen ©2002. Newark, DE: International Reading Association. May be copied for classroom use.

Figure 25. Group Bio-Cube

Clara Barton
Born December 25, 1821, in Oxford, Massachusetts, USA

Personal Background:
        youngest of five children
        middle-class family
        educated at home
        started teaching school at age 15

Issue She Overcame:
        obtaining medical supplies for wounded soldiers

Why She Should Be Remembered:
        traveled with ambulances to nurse soldiers during Civil War
        founded the American Red Cross
        established free public school in New Jersey

Epitaph:
        devoted life to helping others

Illustration:
        Clara Barton nursing Civil War soldiers

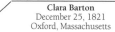

Student-Facilitated Comprehension Centers

Research and Technology Center: Students accessed http://www.amillionlives.com to create a Bio-Cube about a famous person of their choice. Then they conducted further research to discover The Rest of the Story (McLaughlin, 2000), which is information not generally learned about the person's life. The students used at least two research sources.

Biography Center: Students chose to read books such as *Martin Luther King* or *Martin's Big Words* to create illustrated mobiles that contained the same information as the Bio-Cubes. The mobile format provided additional room for the illustrations. Figure 26 shows an example of a mobile in progress.

Writing and Art Centers: Some students completed Auto-Bio Cubes and others used the Autobiography Quilt Square Pattern (see Appendix, page 181) to organize information for their squares in our class autobiography quilt. Then they went to the Art Center to design their quilt square.

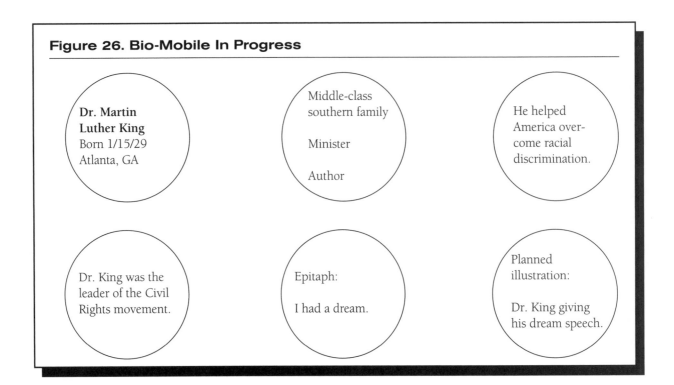

Figure 26. Bio-Mobile In Progress

Dr. Martin Luther King
Born 1/15/29
Atlanta, GA

Middle-class southern family

Minister

Author

He helped America overcome racial discrimination.

Dr. King was the leader of the Civil Rights movement.

Epitaph:

I had a dream.

Planned illustration:

Dr. King giving his dream speech.

Student-Facilitated Comprehension Routines

Literature Circles: The students used the subject of the biography they just finished reading and created a Bio-Cube for that person. Then the group members used their completed cubes to prompt discussion.

Questioning the Author: Students read the biography of the author of their current book and raised queries about connections between the author's life experiences and the book he or she had written. Students had previously obtained copies of the author's biography from *Something About the Author*. Students also made a group Bio-Cube about the author's life and created oral summaries.

STAGE THREE: Teacher-Facilitated Whole-Group Reflection and Goal Setting

Share: We began by sharing the Bio-Cubes, mobiles, Autobio-Cubes, and summaries created in Stage Two. Next, we discussed our abilities to create Bio-Cubes and use them to create oral summaries.

Reflect: We reflected on how summarizing helped us understand our reading and how summarizing different kinds of text required different components.

Set New Goals: Feeling confident with our ability to use summarizing, we set new goals for learning multiple ways to evaluate text.

Assessment Options

I observed students throughout the Guided Comprehension process and used their completed Bio-Cubes, oral summaries, and other applications from Stage Two as assessments.

Guided Comprehension Strategy: Summarizing
Teaching Idea: Bio-Pyramid

STAGE ONE: Teacher-Directed Whole-Group Instruction

Text: *Betsy Ross* (Wallner, 1994)

Explain: I explained to the students that we were going to work on summarizing the key information we read in biographies and we were going to use a format called a Bio-Pyramid (see Appendix A, *Guided Comprehension: A Teaching Model for Grades 3–8*). I helped the students connect this pyramid to the Narrative Pyramid we had completed a few weeks ago. I explained that this looked similar but that we would be recording specific facts we learned after reading a biography. I used the biography *Betsy Ross* that I had read to them the day before. We had recorded essential information from the text on a large chart paper, and we used these notes to complete the Bio-Pyramid.

Demonstrate: I had a copy of the Bio-Pyramid form on an overhead transparency and distributed one for each of the students. I read each of the items we would be recording and focused the students on the number of words for each line. Then I thought aloud, "Well, the first two lines are easy. Line one is the person's name and so I will write *Betsy Ross* on that line. Line two needs two describing words so I will record *talented seamstress.*" I reminded the students that I needed to make sure that the information I put in the pyramid was essential, followed the format, and made sense.

Guide: I then read line three and asked the students to identify some possibilities to describe Betsy's childhood. We revisited our chart of notes and saw that she was the eighth of 17 children. The students wanted to include that, but they were having trouble fitting in brothers and sisters in a three-word phrase. I prompted them to think of another word meaning "brothers and sisters," and they said "siblings." We then generated the phrase *had sixteen siblings* and I recorded it on the overhead and had the students write it on their pyramid. We then worked on line four and five together. After reviewing our notes again, we created the phrases *husband killed by explosion* and *made flag for George Washington*. At that point, I felt the students understood the process and I told them they would finish the pyramid in pairs. I encouraged them to refer to the chart of notes we had to help them make their decisions about what to write.

Practice: The students worked on lines six, seven, and eight in pairs. We shared many possibilities with the class, and I recorded several of them on the overhead. An example of one of the completed pyramids follows:

Betsy Ross

Talented seamstress

Had sixteen siblings

Husband killed by explosion

Made flag for George Washington

Worked as an upholsterer in Philadelphia

Taught her children and grandchildren to sew

She gets credit for sewing first American flag

GUIDED COMPREHENSION: BIOGRAPHY AND AUTOBIOGRAPHY
SUMMARIZING: BIO-PYRAMID

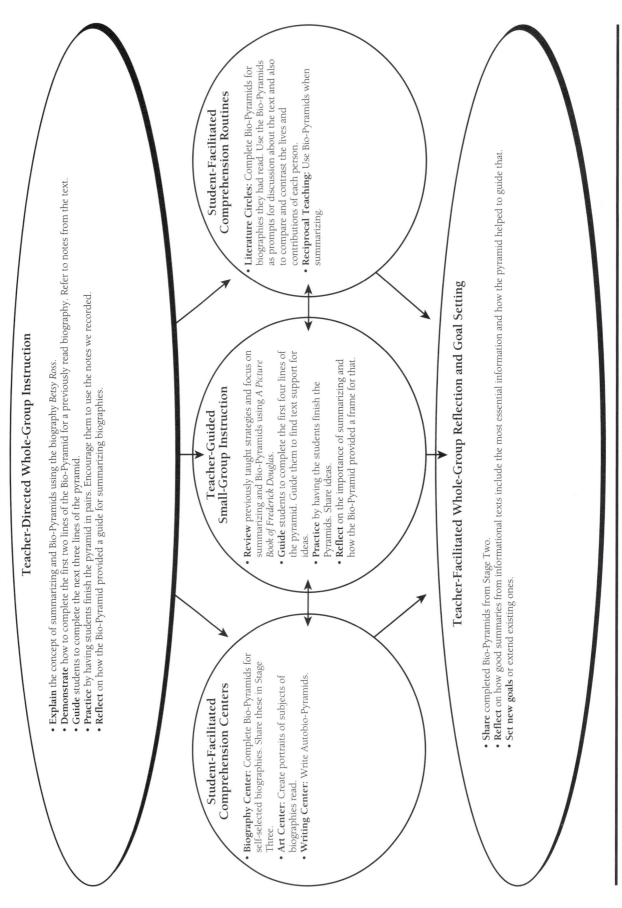

Teacher-Directed Whole-Group Instruction

- **Explain** the concept of summarizing and Bio-Pyramids using the biography *Betsy Ross*.
- **Demonstrate** how to complete the first two lines of the Bio-Pyramid for a previously read biography. Refer to notes from the text.
- **Guide** students to complete the next three lines of the pyramid.
- **Practice** by having students finish the pyramid in pairs. Encourage them to use the notes we recorded.
- **Reflect** on how the Bio-Pyramid provided a guide for summarizing biographies.

Student-Facilitated Comprehension Routines

- **Literature Circles:** Complete Bio-Pyramids for biographies they had read. Use the Bio-Pyramids as prompts for discussion about the text and also to compare and contrast the lives and contributions of each person.
- **Reciprocal Teaching:** Use Bio-Pyramids when summarizing.

Teacher-Guided Small-Group Instruction

- **Review** previously taught strategies and focus on summarizing and Bio-Pyramids using *A Picture Book of Frederick Douglas*.
- **Guide** students to complete the first four lines of the pyramid. Guide them to find text support for ideas.
- **Practice** by having the students finish the Pyramids. Share ideas.
- **Reflect** on the importance of summarizing and how the Bio-Pyramid provided a frame for that.

Student-Facilitated Comprehension Centers

- **Biography Center:** Complete Bio-Pyramids for self-selected biographies. Share these in Stage Three.
- **Art Center:** Create portraits of subjects of biographies read.
- **Writing Center:** Write Autobio-Pyramids.

Teacher-Facilitated Whole-Group Reflection and Goal Setting

- **Share** completed Bio-Pyramids from Stage Two.
- **Reflect** on how good summaries from informational texts include the most essential information and how the pyramid helped to guide that.
- **Set new goals** or extend existing ones.

Reflect: I reminded the students that a good summary includes the most essential information and that the Bio-Pyramid was one way to structure that. They responded that they thought this was fun and liked it better than writing a paragraph. They agreed that it was neat to hear the many different ways that students were able write the information in the pyramid format. They also liked that the pyramid guided them in knowing what was the most important information.

STAGE TWO: Teacher-Guided Small-Group Instruction

Text: *A Picture Book of Frederick Douglas* (Adler, 1993) (Texts varied according to students' abilities.)

Review: I reviewed the comprehension strategies readers use and then focused on summarizing and Bio-Pyramids.

Guide: The students had finished the biography *A Picture Book of Frederick Douglas* by David Adler. I asked them to summarize the key points in a Bio-Pyramid. We completed the first four lines together. This is how we started the pyramid:

Frederick Douglas

Freedom fighter

Born a slave

Lost his mother early

I had students revisit the text to help them find specific information to write the statements.

Practice: The students completed the rest of the pyramid in pairs. I supported when needed, but they did not need much help. We then shared the ideas. Here is a sample of the last four lines:

Taught black children to read

Made a plan to escape slavery

Gave speeches about the horrors of slavery

Spent his life helping free the black people

Reflect: We talked about what makes a good summary, especially for biographies. The students enjoyed completing the pyramids and shared that it helped them know what information to include. They also commented on the challenge of making the ideas fit in the pyramid format.

Student-Facilitated Comprehension Centers

Biography Center: I had blank Bio-Pyramids at the center and asked the students to complete them after reading about a person. They shared these in Stage Three.

Art Center: I had directions and samples for drawing portraits at the center. Students used chalk to draw a portrait of the person they had read about at the biography center.

Writing Center: Students completed Autobio-Pyramids. Then they worked with a partner and used the Autobio-Pyramids to create oral summaries of their lives.

Student-Facilitated Comprehension Routines

Literature Circles: Students each read a different biography and created a Bio-Pyramid based on that person's life. Then they met as a group and used the completed Bio-Pyramids to prompt discussion. Students shared their ideas and compared and contrasted the accomplishments of the people they had read about.

Reciprocal Teaching: Students read the same biography and engaged in Reciprocal Teaching. They then completed Bio-Pyramids about the person as a way to summarize the information they learned.

STAGE THREE: Teacher-Facilitated Whole-Group Reflection and Goal Setting

Share: Students shared their pyramid applications from Stage Two in small groups. Then each group shared with the class.

Reflect: We talked about the importance of identifying the essential information in the texts that we read. We reflected on the difference between essential and nonessential information and how the Bio-Pyramid helped to guide the students' choices.

Set New Goals: Everyone felt confident using Bio-Pyramids while reading biographies, so we decided to extend our use to other genres.

Assessment Options

I reviewed the Bio-Pyramids and Autobio-Pyramids the students completed during Stage Two. This helped me know that they could determine the essential information in the biographies. I also observed students' contributions during all stages of Guided Comprehension.

THEME RESOURCES

Texts

Adler, D. (1989). *A picture book of Abraham Lincoln*. New York: Scholastic.

Adler, D. (1989). *A picture book of George Washington*. New York: Scholastic.

Adler, D. (1989). *A picture book of Martin Luther King, Jr.* New York: Scholastic.

Adler, D. (1993). *A picture book of Frederick Douglas*. New York: Scholastic.

Anderson, W. (1998). *Pioneer girl: The story of Laura Ingalls Wilder*. New York: HarperCollins.

Anholt, L. (1994). *Camille and the sunflowers: A story about Vincent Van Gogh*. New York: Barrons Juveniles.

Anholt, L. (1998). *Picasso and the girl with a ponytail: A story about Pablo Picasso*. New York: Barrons Juvenile.

Bedard, M. (1992). *Emily*. New York: Bantam Doubleday Dell.

Bradby, M. (1995). *More than anything else*. New York: Orchard Books.

Bray, R.L. (1995). *Martin Luther King*. New York: Greenwillow.

Burleigh, R. (1998). *Home run*. Orlando, FL: Harcourt Brace.

Cline-Ransome, L. (2000). *Satchel Paige*. New York: Simon & Schuster.

Coburn, B. (2000). *Triumph on Everest: A photobiography of Sir Edmund Hillary*. Washington, DC: National Geographic Society.

Coles, R. (1995). *The story of Ruby Bridges*. New York: Scholastic.

Cooney, B. (1996). *Eleanor*. New York: Scholastic.

Davidson, M. (1969). *Helen Keller*. New York: Scholastic.

Demi. (2001). *Gandhi*. New York: Margaret K. McElderry.

Durrant, L. (1998). *The beaded moccasins: The story of Mary Campbell*. New York: Dell Yearling.

Feris, J. (1991). *Native American doctor: The story of Susan LaFlesche Picotte*. Minneapolis, MN: Carolrhoda Books.

Forbes, E. (1946). *America's Paul Revere*. Boston: Houghton Mifflin.

Freedman, R. (1987). *Lincoln: A photobiography*. New York: Clarion Books.

Freedman, R. (1993). *Eleanor Roosevelt: A life of discovery*. New York: Clarion Books.

Freedman, R. (1997). *Out of darkness: The story of Louis Braille*. New York: Clarion Books.

Freedman, R. (1998). *Martha Graham: A dancer's life*. New York: Clarion Books.

Freedman, R. (1999). *Babe Didrikson Zaharias: The making of a champion*. New York: Clarion Books.

Fritz, J. (1969). *George Washington's breakfast*. New York: Coward-McCann.

Fritz, J. (1973). *And then what happened Paul Revere?* New York: Coward-McCann.

Fritz, J. (1975). *What's the big idea Ben Franklin?* New York: Coward-McCann.

Fritz, J. (1975). *Where was Patrick Henry on the 29th of May?* New York: Coward-McCann.

Fritz, J. (1976). *Will you sign here, John Hancock?* New York: Coward-McCann.

Fritz, J. (1977). *Can't you make them behave, King George?* New York: Coward-McCann.

Fritz, J. (1983). *The double life of Pocahontas*. New York: The Trumpet Club.

Fritz, J. (1987). *Shh! We're writing the Constitution*. New York: G.P. Putnam's Sons.

Fritz, J. (1992). *George Washington's mother*. New York: Grosset & Dunlap.

Giblin, J.C. (2000). *The amazing life of Benjamin Franklin*. New York: Scholastic.

Hart, T. (1994). *Leonardo da Vinci*. Hauppauge, NY: Barron's Educational Series.

Haskins, J., & Benson, B. (1984). *Space challenger: The story of Guion Bluford*. Boston: Houghton Mifflin.

King, C. (1997). *I have a dream, Dr. Martin Luther King, Jr*. New York: Scholastic.

Martin, J. (1998). *Snowflake Bentley*. New York: Scholastic.

Marzollo, J. (1991). *In 1492*. New York: Scholastic.

McDonough, Y.Z. (1997). *Anne Frank*. New York: Henry Holt and Company.

McGovern, A. (1962). *Christopher Columbus*. New York: Scholastic.

Myers, W. (1964). *Malcom X: By any means necessary: A biography*. New York: Scholastic.

Naden, C., & Blue, R. (1991). *Christa McAuliff: Teacher in space*. Brookfield, CT: Millbrook Press.

Nichol, B. (1993). *Beethoven lives upstairs*. New York: Orchard Books.

Peet, B. (1989). *Bill Peet: An autobiography*. Boston: Houghton Mifflin.

Pinkney, A. (1994). *Dear Benjamin Banneker*. Orlando, FL. Harcourt Brace.

Pinkney, A. (1998). *Duke Ellington*. New York: Scholastic.

Rappaport, D. (2001). *Martin's big words*. New York: Hyperion.

Ringgold, F. (1995). *My dream of Martin Luther King*. New York: Alfred A. Knopf.

Roop, P., & Roop, C. (1985). *Keep the lights burning, Abbie*. Minneapolis, MN: Carolrhoda Books.

Roop, P., & Roop, C. (1990). *I, Columbus: My journal 1492–1493*. New York: International Marine/ Tab Books.

Ryan, P. (1999). *Amelia and Eleanor go for a ride*. New York: Scholastic

Sabin, F. (1982). *The courage of Helen Keller*. Mahwah, NJ: Troll.

Sis, P. (1991). *Follow the dream: The story of Christopher Columbus*. New York: Alfred A. Knopf.

Sis, P. (1996). *Starry messenger*. New York: Farrar Straus Giroux.

Spedden, D. (1994). *Polar, the Titanic bear*. Boston: Little, Brown.

Spencer, E. (1993). *A flag for our country*. New York: Steck-Vaughn.

Stanley, D. (1986). *Peter the great*. New York: Aladdin Books.

Sullivan, G. (1999). *In their own words: Lewis and Clark*. New York: Scholastic.

Sweeney, J. (2000). *Suzette and the puppy: A story about Mary Cassatt*. New York: Barrons Juveniles.

Venezia, M. (1990). *Monet*. Chicago: Children's Press.

Wallner, A. (1994). *Betsy Ross*. New York: Scholastic.

Walner, A. (1997). *Laura Ingalls Wilder*. New York: Scholastic.

Websites

Arts and Entertainment's Biography
www.biography.com

Biography Maker: Page 2
www.bham.wednet.edu/bio/biomak2.htm

Biography Writing With Patricia and Fredrick McKissack
teacher.scholastic.com/writewit/biograph/index.htm

Education Planet: Columbus Day Resources
www.educationplanet.com/articles/columbusday.html

Home of the American Civil War
www.civilwarhome.com

Lives: The Biography Resource
www.amillionlives.com

Performance Extensions Across the Curriculum

Social Studies
- Explore biographies of people in a specific time period in history.
- Write biographies of grandparents or other relatives, focusing on changing lives and times.
- Tape-record oral histories of community members.

Science
- Use biographies to explore contributions of famous scientists, including women and racial and cultural minorities.

Math
- Research contributions of famous mathematicians and use the information to create math problems incorporating the math concepts they developed.

Art
- Investigate the lives of famous artists and create document panels presenting key events, artwork, and styles.
- Explore art styles, topics, and techniques of artists and create original works using that style.

Music
- Write original songs based on biographies or autobiographies.

Culminating Activity

Celebrating Our Lives, Celebrating Others: Display students' performances from across the curriculum. Invite parents and community members to participate in the celebration. Students can either serve as tour guides for their projects or become the subject of a biography they have read and tell participants about that person's life. Students' autobiographies, as well as biographies they have written about a family or community member, will be posted as a volume on the school's website. A PowerPoint slide show of the volume will be featured during the celebration, and the students will give special printed copies to the subjects of the biographies they wrote. All these presentations will include the portraits students created of themselves and the subjects of their biographies.

CHAPTER 7

Fantasy: Flights of Imagination

Fantasy is the level of imagination that allows us to think beyond the usual. Traditional tales, stories about imaginary creatures and worlds, and time travel characterize this genre. Titles representative of each of these are included in this theme. In the Theme Resources section of this chapter, we extend our interpretation of fantasy to include historical, scientific, and artistic flights of imagination. That broadens the scope of related readings to include expository text.

The Sample Theme-Based Plan for Guided Comprehension: Fantasy (see Figure 27) presents a sampling of goals, state standards, assessments, texts, technology resources, comprehension strategies, teaching ideas, comprehension centers, and comprehension routines. The plan begins by delineating examples of student goals and related state standards. The student goals for this theme include the following:

- using appropriate comprehension strategies
- describing and discussing the characteristics of the fantasy genre
- writing stories in the fantasy genre
- communicating effectively

These goals support the following state standards:

- learning to read independently
- reading, analyzing, and interpreting literature
- types and quality of writing
- speaking and listening

Observation, strategy application, student writing, and student self-assessments are among the measures used during Guided Comprehension. The following are the comprehension strategies and corresponding teaching ideas on which the lessons are based:

- Previewing: Story Impressions
- Self-Questioning: "I Wonder" Statements

Figure 27. Sample Theme-Based Plan for Guided Comprehension: Fantasy

Goals and Connections to State Standards

Students will

- use appropriate comprehension strategies. Standard: learning to read independently
- describe and discuss characteristics of fantasy. Standard: reading, analyzing, and interpreting literature
- write stories for the fantasy genre. Standard: types and quality of writing
- communicate effectively. Standards: speaking and listening

Assessment

The following measures can be used for a variety of purposes, including diagnostic, formative, and summative assessment:

Drawing Visualizations Observation
Fantasy Book Reviews Story Impressions
I Wonder Statements Student Self-Assessments
Narrative Pyramids Summaries

Text	Title	Theme	Level
1.	Weslandia	F	4
2.	The Mouse and the Motorcycle	F	3
3.	The Rainbabies	F	2
4.	Tuesday	F	3

Technology Resources

Scholastic: Fantasy and the Imagination
  teacher.scholastic.com/lessonrepro/lessonplans/fantasy.htm
Scholastic Kids Fun Online: Harry Potter
  www.scholastic.com/harrypotter/home.asp
The Harry Potter Lexicon: The Ultimate Harry Potter Reference
  www.i2k.com/~svderark/lexicon

Comprehension Strategies

1. Previewing
2. Self-Questioning
3. Visualizing
4. Summarizing

Teaching Ideas

Story Impressions
"I Wonder" Statements
Drawing Visualizations
Narrative Pyramids

Comprehension Centers

Students will apply the comprehension strategies and related teaching ideas in the following comprehension centers:

Art Center
Fantasy Genre Center
Poetry Center
Writing Center

Comprehension Routines

Students will apply the comprehension strategies and related teaching ideas in the following comprehension routines:

Literature Circles
Questioning the Author
Reciprocal Teaching

- Visualizing: Drawing Visualizations
- Summarizing: Narrative Pyramids

Weslandia, *The Mouse and the Motorcycle*, *The Rainbabies*, and *Tuesday* are the texts used in teacher-directed whole-group instruction. Numerous additional texts, including those employed in teacher-guided small-group instruction and the student-facilitated comprehension centers and routines, are included in the Theme Resources at the end of the chapter.

Art, fantasy genre, poetry, and writing are examples of centers students use in comprehension centers; Literature Circles, Reciprocal Teaching, and Questioning the Author are examples of comprehension routines.

GUIDED COMPREHENSION LESSONS

Guided Comprehension Strategy: Previewing
Teaching Idea: Story Impressions

STAGE ONE: Teacher-Directed Whole-Group Instruction

Text: *Weslandia* (Fleischman, 1999)

Explain: I explained to the students that we were going to try Story Impressions (McGinley & Denner, 1987; see Appendix A, *Guided Comprehension: A Teaching Model for Grades 3–8*, and Appendix, page 182), a new activity that would help them to preview the story by making predictions. I reviewed previewing and explained that we were going to write a story together to help us make a prediction about what the book would be about. I introduced the list of words that I had prepared in advance of the lesson: *Wesley, outcast, no friends, summer project, new civilization, plant, spinning wheel and loom, new counting system, happy, new language, friends.* I was careful to note that, when I was deciding which words to include on the list, I chose words that related to the narrative elements: characters, setting, problem, and resolution. I reviewed the elements with the students through discussion. Then I explained that because the story related to these elements, it would be important for us to use the words in the exact order in which they appeared on the list. I shared the title of the book and reviewed each of the words on the list. I had the students predict which element of the story each word might relate to (character, setting, problem, resolution). Then I noted that after we had written our story, we would read the original story to verify our predictions.

Demonstrate: I looked at the first word and said, "The main character in this story must be Wesley so I am going to start the story 'One day a boy named Wesley was walking home from school.'" Then I said, "I think Wesley must be an outcast," so I wrote, "He really didn't like school because he was an outcast and had no friends."

Guide: Next, I encouraged the students to look at the next few words and think about how the story could continue. I reminded them that we needed to create a problem, and I prompted them with a few questions. Together we came up with "It was almost time for summer vacation, and Wesley was thinking about what to do for his summer project."

Practice: As we continued, students worked in pairs to develop sentences to complete Story Impressions. They seemed to enjoy the process of writing the story, and they were eager to read the real story to see how their impression compared to the author's original story. The following is the Story Impression we wrote together:

> One day a boy named Wesley was walking home from school. He really didn't like school because he was an outcast and had no friends. It was almost time for summer vacation and Wesley was thinking about what to do for his summer project. He decided to research a new civilization. He investigated their plants and how they made clothes. He found out they used a spinning wheel and loom. He also discovered they used a new counting system and he thought this was cool. It made him happy. He spent time learning the new language of this civilization and it helped him make new friends. He finally didn't feel like an outcast anymore.

GUIDED COMPREHENSION: FANTASY PREVIEWING: STORY IMPRESSIONS

Teacher-Directed Whole-Group Instruction

- **Explain** the importance of previewing and introduce the Story Impression.
- **Demonstrate** how to start a predictive story, using the first few words on the list. Think aloud about the process.
- **Guide** the students to continue the predictive story, including problem and events.
- **Practice** by having pairs of students create a solution to the story using the remaining words.
- **Reflect** on how the Story Impression helped them preview by predicting and setting a purpose for reading.

Student-Facilitated Comprehension Routines

- **Literature Circles:** Write Story Impressions from lists of words related to the circle story. Compare and contrast before reading. Revise predictions throughout the reading.
- **Reciprocal Teaching:** Create individual Story Impressions and share with group. Engage in Reciprocal Teaching while reading.

Teacher-Guided Small-Group Instruction

- **Review** all strategies and focus on previewing and Story Impressions.
- **Guide** students to write Story Impressions for the new book they will read. Share and start reading. Revise or modify predictions.
- **Practice** by having students continue to read the story, documenting new predictions in Guided Comprehension Journals.
- **Reflect** on how previewing helped them prepare to read and enhanced their engagement with the text.

Student-Facilitated Comprehension Centers

- **Writing Center:** Write Story Impressions from lists of words connected to selected books.
- **Poetry Center:** Write Poetry Impressions from word lists connected to poems.

Teacher-Facilitated Whole-Group Reflection and Goal Setting

- **Share** Story Impressions created in Stage Two. Discuss how original predictions were confirmed or revised from author's clues.
- **Reflect** on the importance of predicting and setting purposes before reading.
- **Set new goals** by having students decide how they can preview texts in other settings.

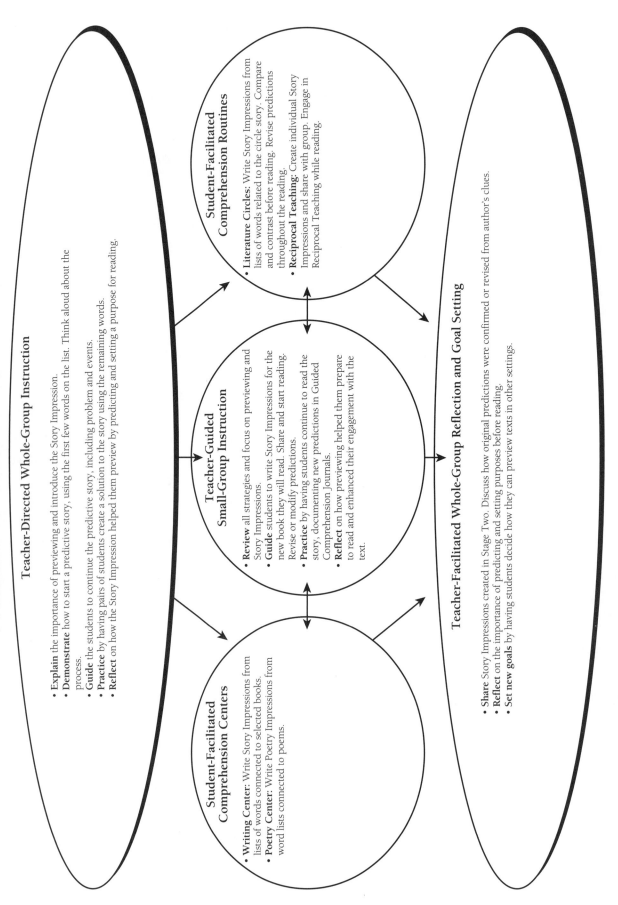

After we completed the predictive story, I read the book aloud to the students. I stopped at several places and had them compare their predictions with what was really happening. When I finished, we used the original wordlist to write a summary of the story. We compared the summary with our original predictions.

Reflect: I encouraged the students to reflect on the Story Impressions process and how it helped them get ready to read the story. They said that it really got them excited to know how the story might turn out and that it helped them learn some of the words in the story. We talked about the importance of previewing before reading and how we could use Story Impressions in the future.

STAGE TWO: Teacher-Guided Small-Group Instruction

Text: *James and the Giant Peach* (Dahl, 1961) (Texts varied according to students' abilities.)

Review: I reviewed the comprehension strategies readers use and then focused on previewing and Story Impressions.

Guide: I showed the students the cover of the new book they were going to read, *James and the Giant Peach*. I had prepared a list of words and encouraged the students to look at the first few words and start the story. I reminded them that we needed to introduce a character and setting. The students created this beginning: "This is a story about a boy named James who lives with his aunts." I then guided them to use the next few words to create a problem. They came up with "One day, James went walking and was attacked by large insects." Next, I reminded the students that we needed to use the rest of the words to finish our predictive story. I encouraged them to include more ideas about the problem, attempts to resolve the problem, and resolution.

Practice: The students finished their stories in pairs. I prompted them when they were stuck, but they really didn't have too much difficulty. Then I had them share their stories with the group. Afterward, we revisited the title and cover and reviewed predictions. Next, I had the students read the first three pages silently. We revisited our predictions, made new ones, and the students read three more pages. We continued this process until they finished reading the chapter. We then compared the students' original stories with what had happened so far, and then we made new predictions based on the author's clues and the clue words from the Story Impression.

Reflect: We reflected on how prediction is important to comprehension and how the Story Impression helped them make predictions. The students talked about using previewing before reading and continuing to make predictions as they read.

Student-Facilitated Comprehension Centers

Writing Center: I had made Story Impressions word lists for some of the fantasy genre books at the reading center. I put them at the writing center and I asked the students to write predictive stories, either alone or in pairs, before they began to read the books. I also encouraged them to keep reflections in their Guided Comprehension Journals about how their predictive stories compared to the real story.

Poetry Center: Students wrote and illustrated Poetry Impressions from word lists taken from poems related to the fantasy genre.

Student-Facilitated Comprehension Routines

Literature Circles: I provided each group with a list of words to write Story Impressions. The students wrote group impressions with markers on large sheets of paper and posted them. I had them put a blank sheet next to each predictive story, and students briefly summarized the book after each reading. They used these sheets to compare and contrast their group impression and the actual book and used this information to spark discussion. The following is one group's impression of *Tuck Everlasting*:

> One day Winnie Foster was walking by a lake near the village of Treegap. She met her best friend Mae Tuck as she was walking along the lake. They decided to go swimming in the lake and then a stranger drove up in a boat. The stranger asked the girls to gather the wood for him to help him make a fire. Mae's little brother Jesse Tuck came walking nearby and noticed a spurt of water coming out of the boat. He wondered if the boat was sinking. The girls walked around the boat to see Jesse and as they did the stranger reached out and grabbed them. The girls started screaming and Jesse heard them. He was worried the stranger would kidnap Winnie and Mae. The girls were hoping that they would live forever and the stranger would not murder them. Before the man could get away with the girls, they jumped out of the boat and Jesse grabbed them. They felt like it was a jailbreak. After that they make a decision not to go back to the lake and to move away for good.

Reciprocal Teaching: I made Story Impression word lists for students working in Reciprocal Teaching groups. The students completed their predictive stories independently and then shared them with the students in their group. As the students read their book, they participated in Reciprocal Teaching. They also kept notes in their Guided Comprehension Journals about their thinking during reading and how their initial predictions changed while reading the story.

STAGE THREE: Teacher-Facilitated Whole-Group Reflection and Goal Setting

Share: Students shared their Story and Poem Impressions in small groups.

Reflect: I engaged the students in conversation about the importance of previewing texts and in particular prediction. We talked about how the cover and title provide us with some information but that the author gives us other clues as we read.

Set New Goals: The students were enthusiastic about using Story Impressions again and set goals for using previewing in other settings.

Assessment Options

I observed the students as they created stories with me and in pairs. This helped me understand how well they understood the structure of stories and how well they could use clue words to create predictive stories. I also read the reflections they made in their Guided Comprehension Journals to determine their ability to use additional clues in the story to refine or modify predictions.

Guided Comprehension Strategy: Self-Questioning
Teaching Idea: "I Wonder" Statements

STAGE ONE: Teacher-Directed Whole-Group Instruction

Text: *The Mouse and the Motorcycle* (Cleary, 1965)

Explain: I began by explaining self-questioning and focusing on "I Wonder" Statements (Harvey & Goudvis, 2000; see Appendix A, *Guided Comprehension: A Teaching Model for Grades 3–8*) as a way to generate questions to guide reading. Then I asked the students to wonder why *The Mouse and the Motorcycle* is classified as a fantasy.

Demonstrate: I demonstrated "I Wonder" Statements by reading aloud "The New Guests" (Chapter 1 of *The Mouse and the Motorcycle*) and using an overhead projector. I stopped periodically to wonder aloud and share the reasoning that prompted my wonderings. For example, before I began I said, "After reading the title and seeing the cover of the book, I wonder if a mouse really is going to ride a motorcycle in this book."

When I had finished reading, I said, "During Chapter 1, the author introduces several characters, including Mr. and Mrs. Gridley, their son Keith, and Matt the bellboy, and Keith does unpack a toy that is a red motorcycle. There is no mouse in the story yet, but there are illustrations of mice. So, I still don't know if a mouse will really ride a motorcycle."

Guide: I guided the students' use of "I Wonder" Statements by reading the beginning of Chapter 2 and stopping occasionally to guide students to wonder aloud and explain reasoning. For example, shortly after the start of the chapter, I stopped and a student noted that Ralph the mouse was in the story and now she wondered if he would ride the motorcycle. Later in the chapter, we observed that Ralph did, indeed, ride the motorcycle and it crashed. At that point, another student wondered if the motorcycle would be able to be fixed.

Practice: Pairs of students practiced creating "I Wonder" Statements as I read aloud Chapter 3, stopping periodically to hear their wonderings and related thoughts. The students enjoyed the story line and creating their wonderings, which prompted discussion.

Reflect: We reflected by reacting to the earlier "wonderings" about what makes this book a fantasy. We decided it was a fantasy from the talking animals category because the mouse could talk and do human things like ride a motorcycle. Then we discussed how "I Wonder" Statements help us to understand what we read, and how we can use "I Wonder" Statements with other texts in other settings.

STAGE TWO: Teacher-Guided Small-Group Instruction

Text: *The BFG* (Big Friendly Giant) (Dahl, 1997) (Texts varied according to students' abilities.)

Review: I reminded the students about the comprehension strategies that good readers use and focused on self-questioning using "I Wonder" Statements.

Guide: I guided the students' reading of a chapter of a fantasy book, *The BFG* (Big Friendly Giant). They stopped at least twice to wonder and explain their reasoning. I provided support as needed. Then we discussed the wonderings and reasoning.

Practice: The students practiced by reading the next chapter, stopping at least twice to wonder and explain their thinking. The students used sticky notes to record their wonderings and reasoning. Then we discussed their ideas.

GUIDED COMPREHENSION: FANTASY
SELF-QUESTIONING: "I WONDER" STATEMENTS

Teacher-Directed Whole-Group Instruction

- **Explain** self-questioning and focus on "I Wonder" Statements as a way to generate questions to guide reading. Wonder why *The Mouse and the Motorcycle* is classified as a fantasy.
- **Demonstrate** "I Wonder" Statements by reading Chapter 1 of *The Mouse and the Motorcycle*. Stop periodically to wonder aloud. Share the reasoning that prompts the wonderings. Discuss.
- **Guide** the students' use of "I Wonder" Statements by reading the beginning of Chapter 2 and stopping to wonder aloud and explain reasoning. Continue to read Chapter 2, stopping periodically to encourage students to share their wonderings and explain their reasoning.
- **Practice** by reading Chapter 3 and stopping periodically to have students share their wonderings and their thinking.
- **Reflect** by responding to the earlier "wondering" about what makes this book a fantasy. Discuss how "I Wonder" Statements help us to understand what we read and how we can use "I Wonder" Statements in other settings.

Student-Facilitated Comprehension Routines

- **Literature Circles:** Use your wonderings and your reasoning as the basis of discussion as you continue to read *The Lion, the Witch, and the Wardrobe*.
- **Reciprocal Teaching:** Use "I Wonder" Statements to facilitate the portion of the routine that focuses on questioning as you continue reading *A Wrinkle in Time*.
- **Questioning the Author:** Use "I Wonder" as the format for queries about and discussion of *Dinotopia: The World Beneath*.

Teacher-Guided Small-Group Instruction

- **Review** the comprehension strategies that good readers use and focus on self-questioning using "I Wonder" Statements.
- **Guide** students to partner-read a chapter of a fantasy *BFG (Big Friendly Giant)* and stop at least twice to wonder and explain their reasoning. Provide support as needed. Discuss.
- **Practice** by having students read the next chapter, stopping at least twice to wonder and explain their thinking. Have students use sticky notes to record their wonderings and reasoning. Discuss.
- **Reflect** on how self-questioning and "I Wonder" Statements help us to guide our reading of text.

Student-Facilitated Comprehension Centers

- **Fantasy Genre Center:** Work with a partner. Use the fantasy books you created last week. Wonder about what might happen next if both stories continued. Sketch what you think might happen. Share your sketches and discuss your reasoning.
- **Writing Center:** Work with a partner to create a fantasy genre story about an animal.

Teacher-Facilitated Whole-Group Reflection and Goal Setting

- **Share** applications of "I Wonder" Statements from Stage Two and assess ability to use them.
- **Reflect** on how self-questioning promotes engagement and guides our reading.
- **Set new goals** or extend existing ones.

Reflect: The students and I reflected on how self-questioning and "I Wonder" Statements help guide our reading of text.

Student-Facilitated Comprehension Centers

Fantasy Genre Center: The students visited this center and used the fantasy books they had created last week. They introduced their stories and then read one another's books, stopping frequently to wonder. The students recorded their wonderings and reasoning on the "I Wonder" bookmarks (see Appendix, page 183) provided at the center and inserted them in a book. Then the students shared their wonderings about one another's books. Figure 28 shows part of Maria's "I Wonder" Bookmark for Ralph the Mouse's Hawaiian Motorcycle Adventure, which had been written by her classmate Matt.

Figure 28. Maria's "I Wonder" Bookmark

> **"I Wonder" Bookmark**
>
> Cover
>
> I wonder…
> if Ralph the Mouse is going to ride his motorcycle on the beach
>
> because…
> the cover shows Ralph and his motorcycle near a beach.
>
> Page 1
>
> I wonder…
> how Ralph will get his motorcycle out of the deep sand
>
> because…
> when he rode on the beach, his motorcycle got stuck on the sand and there was no one there to help.
>
> Page 2
>
> I wonder…
> if Ralph will ride his motorcycle up to the top of the volcano
>
> because…
> there was a volcano in the drawing on page 2 and Ralph needs somewhere to go now that his bike isn't stuck anymore.

Next the students wondered about what might happen if both stories continued. They wrote their wonderings in their Guided Comprehension Journals and sketched and labeled what they thought what might happen next. Then the students shared their sketches and discussed their reasoning.

Writing Center: Students worked in pairs to write fantasy stories about animals taking on human roles. They created a series of "I Wonder" Statements to serve as the basis for writing their story and had the character wonder during the stories. For example, Steve and Malia wrote a story about Nittany, a shaggy dog who was a racecar driver. At one point in the story, Nittany wondered how he would repair his car before the next big race. Stewart and Ian used the Harley-Davidson slogan "The road begins here. It never ends" to start their story about a new adventure for Ralph the mouse. At various points in the story, Ralph wonders where the never-ending road will take him and his motorcycle next.

Student-Facilitated Comprehension Routines

Literature Circles: The students continued to read *The Lion, the Witch, and the Wardrobe*, using their Guided Comprehension Journals to record their wonderings and reasoning. Then they used these entries as a basis of their group discussion.

Reciprocal Teaching: As the students continued to read *A Wrinkle in Time*, they used "I Wonder" Statements to facilitate the portion of the routine that focused on questioning. They used their Guided Comprehension Journals to record their thinking.

Questioning the Author: The students used "I Wonder" Statements as a format for querying the author as the basis for discussing *Dinotopia: The World Beneath*. They wrote their queries and their predicted responses in their Guided Comprehension Journals.

STAGE THREE: Teacher-Facilitated Whole-Group Reflection and Goal Setting

Share: We shared applications of "I Wonder" Statements from Stage Two and assessed our ability to use them.

Reflect: We reflected on how self-questioning promoted engagement and guided our reading.

Set New Goals: Feeling confident with our ability to use "I Wonder" Statements to engage in self-questioning when reading narrative text, we extended our goal to using this technique with expository text.

Assessment Options

I observed students in all stages of the process, listening carefully to their wonderings and reasoning. I also reviewed their bookmarks and stories, as well as their sketches and wonderings in their Guided Comprehension Journals.

Guided Comprehension Strategy: Visualizing
Teaching Idea: Drawing Visualizations

STAGE ONE: Teacher-Directed Whole-Group Instruction

Text: *The Rainbabies* (Melmed, 1992)

Explain: I explained to the students that today we were going to work on visualizing while we read. I reminded them that visualizing was making pictures in their minds based on what the text made them think about. I introduced the teaching idea called Drawing Visualizations (see Appendix, page 163).

Demonstrate: I chose to use the book *The Rainbabies* because it is short enough for demonstration but has enough descriptive language to evoke good visualizations. Although it is a picture book, I chose not to show the pictures on the first read because I wanted the students to work on making pictures in their minds. I read the first two pages aloud and then thought aloud about the picture I was making in my mind from the descriptions the author gave. I then drew that visualization on an overhead transparency using the Drawing Visualizations form (see Appendix, page 184). Underneath the drawing, I wrote a sentence describing it. I demonstrated how to return to the book to help with vocabulary choice and spelling. I repeated this process with the next two pages.

Guide: I then read the next two pages aloud and engaged the students in a discussion about what they were "seeing" in their minds. I had them draw those ideas on their papers and write a sentence to go with it. I did the same on the overhead. We talked about why our drawings were not all the same, and I reinforced to them that it was good that we all did not make the exact same visualizations. I explained to them that the pictures we make in our minds are influenced by the text and by our own prior experiences. They thought this was an interesting concept and were eager to do more. I read the next two pages aloud and had the students talk about and then draw their visualizations. They also wrote a sentence about their drawings.

Practice: I then finished the story by reading it aloud in small sections. After each section, I gave the students a few minutes to draw and write about their visualization. They shared the drawings in small groups.

Reflect: I focused the students' reflection on how visualizing is so important for understanding and how Drawing Visualizations and sharing their work helped them. They liked drawing and expressed that it really did help them to make a point of making the pictures in their minds so they could then have something to draw. They found that sharing drawings helped them broaden their understanding of the story and gave them ideas for drawing.

STAGE TWO: Teacher-Guided Small-Group Instruction

Text: *Harry Potter and the Sorcerer's Stone* (Rowling, 1997) (Texts varied according to students' abilities.)

Review: I reviewed the comprehension strategies good readers use and then focused on visualizing and Drawing Visualizations.

Guide: I showed the students the cover of the new book they were going to read, *Harry Potter and the Sorcerer's Stone*. I asked them to make predictions based on the cover and what they already knew about Harry Potter. Then they read the first four pages and talked about the pictures

GUIDED COMPREHENSION: FANTASY
VISUALIZING: DRAWING VISUALIZATIONS

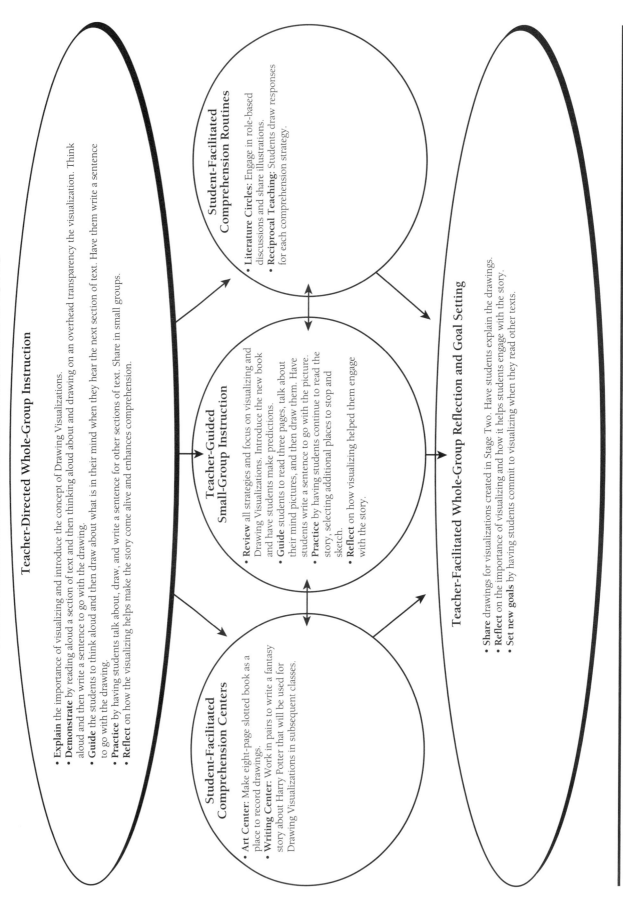

Teacher-Directed Whole-Group Instruction

- **Explain** the importance of visualizing and introduce the concept of Drawing Visualizations.
- **Demonstrate** by reading aloud a section of text and then thinking aloud about and drawing on an overhead transparency the visualization. Think aloud and then write a sentence to go with the drawing.
- **Guide** the students to think aloud and then draw about what is in their mind when they hear the next section of text. Have them write a sentence to go with the drawing.
- **Practice** by having students talk about, draw, and write a sentence for other sections of text. Share in small groups.
- **Reflect** on how the visualizing helps make the story come alive and enhances comprehension.

Student-Facilitated Comprehension Centers

- **Art Center:** Make eight-page slotted book as a place to record drawings.
- **Writing Center:** Work in pairs to write a fantasy story about Harry Potter that will be used for Drawing Visualizations in subsequent classes.

Teacher-Guided Small-Group Instruction

- **Review** all strategies and focus on visualizing and Drawing Visualizations. Introduce the new book and have students make predictions.
- **Guide** students to read three pages, talk about their mind pictures, and then draw them. Have students write a sentence to go with the picture.
- **Practice** by having students continue to read the story, selecting additional places to stop and sketch.
- **Reflect** on how visualizing helped them engage with the story.

Student-Facilitated Comprehension Routines

- **Literature Circles:** Engage in role-based discussions and share illustrations.
- **Reciprocal Teaching:** Students draw responses for each comprehension strategy.

Teacher-Facilitated Whole-Group Reflection and Goal Setting

- **Share** drawings for visualizations created in Stage Two. Have students explain the drawings.
- **Reflect** on the importance of visualizing and how it helps students engage with the story.
- **Set new goals** by having students commit to visualizing when they read other texts.

they were making in their minds. I prompted them with guiding questions, and I encouraged them to be specific and find text support for their images. Next, I gave them a few minutes to sketch the visualizations they had and write a sentence about them.

Practice: The students finished reading the chapter, stopping to sketch and write about their visualizations two more times. We used these drawings to spark discussion about the story. It was interesting to compare what the students drew and what they focused on in their sentences. It provided an excellent process for discussing the text.

Reflect: We reflected on how important visualizing is and in what ways it helped us understand text.

Student-Facilitated Comprehension Centers

Art Center: Students made eight-page slotted books and drew their visualizations at least eight times while independently reading a fantasy book. Then they shared these with a peer and placed them on display in our Flights of Imagination Gallery.

Writing Center: Students worked in pairs to write a fantasy story about Harry Potter. In subsequent classes, other students used these books to engage in Drawing Visualizations. Their drawings and sentences were then included at the end of the book.

Student-Facilitated Comprehension Routines

Literature Circles: Students all took on the role of "artful artist" in addition to their other role. They drew their visualizations as their illustrations. After engaging in role-based discussion, students shared their illustrations with the group.

Reciprocal Teaching: Students drew their visualizations to record ideas for the comprehension strategy they were focusing on: predicting, clarifying, questioning, and summarizing. They kept the illustrations in their Guided Comprehension Journals.

STAGE THREE: Teacher-Facilitated Whole-Group Reflection and Goal Setting

Share: Students shared their drawings in small groups and with the class. Then we discussed how well we could engage in Drawing Visualizations. The students felt that they were able to use the technique, and their applications confirmed their thinking.

Reflect: Sharing students' applications brought up a discussion about how seeing a movie after reading a book is often different and not as good. We talked about how the pictures in their minds are based on their own understandings and interpretations, whereas the movie is based on the director's interpretation. Most agreed that although they enjoyed seeing movies, they liked the "movies in their minds" better. We also reflected on how visualization helped us understand what we read.

Set New Goals: Students noted that they enjoyed using visualization to relate to text. Then we decided to extend our goal to using visualizing in other settings.

Assessment Options

I observed the students in all stages of Guided Comprehension. I was able to observe their contributions to discussions and their willingness and ability to draw their visualizations. Work completed at centers also provided valuable information about their strength in visualizing.

Guided Comprehension Strategy: Summarizing
Teaching Idea: Narrative Pyramids

STAGE ONE: Teacher-Directed Whole-Group Instruction

Text: *Tuesday* (Wiesner, 1991)

Explain: I began by clarifying the components of summarizing, focusing on the components of narrative summaries. Then I introduced the Narrative Pyramids (see Appendix A, *Guided Comprehension: A Teaching Model for Grades 3–8*) for the fantasy genre.

Demonstrate: I explained that in *Tuesday*, the book we would be using, the author used his illustrations to tell the story. I used a think-aloud to ponder the narrative elements before sharing the book with the students. While sharing the book, I thought aloud about a story line that supported the pictures and about why this book is included in the fantasy genre. After sharing the book, I used an overhead projector and a think-aloud activity to record the narrative elements and the fantasy genre connection on a Narrative Pyramid. We orally summarized the book using the information from the Narrative Pyramid. Then we discussed the summary and why the book is a fantasy. We decided that it was a fantasy because frogs do not fly and they do not operate the remote controls.

Guide: I guided students by sharing a section of *Sector 7*, another wordless picture book authored by David Weisner, and prompting them as they completed the first three lines of the Narrative Pyramid.

Practice: The students practiced by listening to the rest of the story as I thought aloud about a story line. They worked in pairs to complete the Narrative Pyramids, which they shared with another pair. Then they used the pyramids to complete oral summaries.

Reflect: We reflected on how Narrative Pyramids help us summarize stories even when there are no words. We also reflected on how we can use Narrative Pyramids in other settings. Our group Narrative Pyramid appears in Figure 29.

STAGE TWO: Teacher-Guided Small-Group Instruction

Text: *Stranger in the Woods* (Sams & Stoick, 2000) (Texts varied according to students' abilities.)

Review: I reminded the students about the comprehension strategies that good readers use and focused on summarizing using Narrative Pyramids.

Guide: The students and I previewed a photographic fantasy titled *Stranger in the Woods*. As they began reading the first part of the book (14 pages), I encouraged them to think about why the book is considered a fantasy. When they finished reading that section, we discussed why the book may be a fantasy. They noted that the animals talked and that the placement of the photos and print seemed to support their thinking. Then I guided them in completing the first two lines of the Narrative Pyramid.

Practice: The students practiced by reading to the end of the book and completing the Narrative Pyramid for the fantasy genre. We used the pyramid to generate an oral summary of the story. Most of the students were surprised to learn the identity of the stranger in the woods. All agreed that Carl Sams is a great photographer. They noted again how the structure of the book contributed to the fantasy.

Reflect: The students reflected on summarizing and how Narrative Pyramids can help us to summarize any story-based genre. They noted the pyramid was more fun than just writing a summary, and they liked that they had to manipulate language to use just the right number of words for each line.

GUIDED COMPREHENSION: FANTASY
SUMMARIZING: NARRATIVE PYRAMIDS

Teacher-Directed Whole-Group Instruction

- **Explain** summarizing, focusing on the components of narrative summaries, and introduce Narrative Pyramids for the fantasy genre.
- **Demonstrate** using *Tuesday*, a wordless picture book. Think aloud about the narrative elements before sharing the book with students. When sharing the book, think aloud about a story line supported by the pictures and why this book is included in the fantasy genre. After sharing, use the overhead projector and a think-aloud to record the narrative elements and the fantasy genre connection on a Narrative Pyramid. Then summarize the book using the information from the Narrative Pyramid. Discuss the summary and why the book is a fantasy.
- **Guide** students to complete a Narrative Pyramid by sharing *Sector 7*, another wordless picture book, and inviting students to think aloud about a story line supported by the pictures and why this book is considered a fantasy. Then guide them to complete the first three lines of the pyramid.
- **Practice** by having students work in pairs to complete the Narrative Pyramids. Share. Have students write summaries based on their pyramids. Share and discuss the summaries and what makes this book a fantasy.
- **Reflect** on how Narrative Pyramids help us summarize stories even when there are no words and how we can use Narrative Pyramids in other settings.

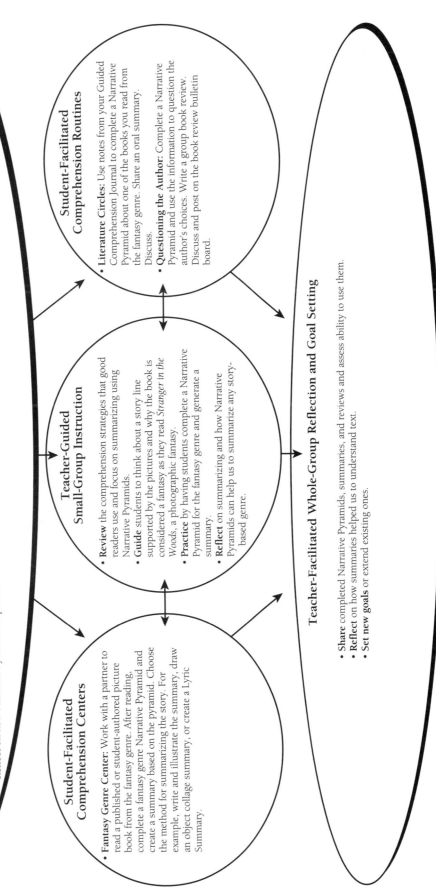

Student-Facilitated Comprehension Routines

- **Literature Circles:** Use notes from your Guided Comprehension Journal to complete a Narrative Pyramid about one of the books you read from the fantasy genre. Share an oral summary. Discuss.
- **Questioning the Author:** Complete a Narrative Pyramid and use the information to question the author's choices. Write a group book review. Discuss and post on the book review bulletin board.

Teacher-Guided Small-Group Instruction

- **Review** the comprehension strategies that good readers use and focus on summarizing using Narrative Pyramids.
- **Guide** students to think about a story line supported by the pictures and why the book is considered a fantasy as they read *Stranger in the Woods*, a photographic fantasy.
- **Practice** by having students complete a Narrative Pyramid for the fantasy genre and generate a summary.
- **Reflect** on summarizing and how Narrative Pyramids can help us to summarize any story-based genre.

Student-Facilitated Comprehension Centers

- **Fantasy Genre Center:** Work with a partner to read a published or student-authored picture book from the fantasy genre. After reading, complete a fantasy genre Narrative Pyramid and create a summary based on the pyramid. Choose the method for summarizing the story. For example, write and illustrate the summary, draw an object collage summary, or create a Lyric Summary.

Teacher-Facilitated Whole-Group Reflection and Goal Setting

- **Share** completed Narrative Pyramids, summaries, and reviews and assess ability to use them.
- **Reflect** on how summaries helped us to understand text.
- **Set new goals** or extend existing ones.

Guided Comprehension in Action: Lessons for Grades 3–8 by Maureen McLaughlin and Mary Beth Allen ©2002. Newark, DE: International Reading Association. May be copied for classroom use.

Figure 29. Group Narrative Pyramid

Boy
Character's name

School student
Two words describing the character

Empire State Building
Three words describing the setting

He meets a cloud.
Four words stating the problem

They fly to Sector 7.
Five words describing one event

Boy turns clouds into sea animals.
Six words describing another event

Boy is banished but cloud finds him.
Seven words describing a third event

Boy and cloud live together at boy's house.
Eight words describing a solution to the problem

Sector 7 is a fantasy because in this story a boy is able to fly, clouds change into sea animals, and a cloud becomes a boy's friend and follows his school bus home.

Student-Facilitated Comprehension Centers

Fantasy Genre Center: The students worked with a partner to read a published or student-authored picture book from the fantasy genre. After reading their choice of book, the students completed a fantasy genre Narrative Pyramid and created a summary in the mode of their choice. For example, they could write and illustrate the summary, draw an object collage summary, use clip art, or create a Lyric Summary. The clip art summary in Figure 30 was created by Tom and Caitlin.

Student-Facilitated Comprehension Routines

Literature Circles: Students used notes from Guided Comprehension Journal entries to complete Narrative Pyramids about the books they had read from the fantasy genre. Then they used the completed Pyramids to share oral summaries with their group members and engage in further discussion.

Questioning the Author: Students used the information from the completed Narrative Pyramids to question the author. Then the students wrote a group review of the book, using the Book Review Planner (see Appendix, page 174) to structure their writing. Finally, the students discussed their reviews and posted them in our Critics Corner.

Figure 30. Clip Art Summary

STAGE THREE: Teacher-Facilitated Whole-Group Reflection and Goal Setting

Share: We began by sharing the completed pyramids, summaries, and reviews. We also assessed our ability to use them.

Reflect: The students reflected on how summarizing helped us comprehend what we had read and how Narrative Pyramids helped us by providing the information needed to create a good story summary. One of the students noted that a good summary includes all the information on the pyramid.

Set New Goals: Because we were feeling confident with our ability to use Narrative Pyramids for summarizing works in the fantasy genre, we decided to extend our goal and apply Narrative Pyramids to other types of literature.

Assessment Options

I used a variety of sources to assess students including the following: observation, students' multiple applications of summarizing, and their self-assessments.

THEME RESOURCES

Texts

Babbitt, N. (1996). *Tuck everlasting*. New York: Farrar, Straus, Giroux.

Cleary, B. (1965). *The mouse and the motorcycle*. New York: Harper Trophy.

Dahl, R. (1961). *James and the giant peach*. New York: Knopf.

Dahl, R. (1964). *Charlie and the chocolate factory*. New York: Knopf.

Dahl, R. (1970). *Fantastic Mr. Fox*. New York: Viking.

Dahl, R. (1997). *The BFG (big friendly giant)*. New York: Puffin.

Dixon, R. (1994). *The witch's ring*. New York: Hyperion.

Doyle, D., & Macdonald, J.D. (1990). *Circle of magic*. Mahwah, NJ: Troll.

Eager, E. (1956). *Knights castle*. Orlando, FL: Harcourt Brace Jovanovich.

Ende, M. (1983). *The neverending story*. New York: Doubleday.

Fleischman, P. (1999). *Weslandia*. New York: Scholastic.

Gormley, B. (1996). *Back to the day Lincoln was shot*. New York: Scholastic.

Gurney, J. (1995). *Dinotopia: The world beneath*. Atlanta, GA: Turner Publishing.

Irving, W. (1990). *Legend of Sleepy Hollow*. New York: HarperCollins.

Kimmel, A.E. (1994). *Anansi and the talking melon*. New York: Holiday House.

L'Engle, M. (1962). *A wrinkle in time*. New York: Dell.

Lewis, C.S. (1950). *The lion, the witch, and the wardrobe*. New York: Macmillan.

Melmed, L.K. (1992). *The rainbabies*. New York: Scholastic.

Rowling, J.K. (1997). *Harry Potter and the sorcerer's stone*. New York: Scholastic.

Rowling, J.K. (1998). *Harry Potter and the chamber of secrets*. New York: Scholastic.

Rowling, J.K. (1999). *Harry Potter and the prisoner of Azkaban*. New York: Scholastic.

Rowling, J.K. (2000). *Harry Potter and the goblet of fire*. New York: Scholastic.

Rowling, J.K. (2001). *Fantastic beasts and where to find them*. New York: Scholastic.

Rowling, J.K. (2001). *Quidditch through the ages*. New York: Scholastic.

Rowling, J.K. (2002). *Harry Potter and the order of the Phoenix*. New York: Scholastic.

Sams, C.R., & Stoick, J. (2000). *Stranger in the woods: A photographic fantasy*. Milford, MI: Carl Sams II Photography.

Scieszka, J. (1989). *The true story of the 3 little pigs!* New York: Penguin Books.

Scieszka, J. (1991). *The frog prince continued*. New York: Viking.

Scieszka, J. (1992). *The Stinky Cheese Man and other fairly stupid tales*. New York: Penguin Books.

Scieszka, J. (2001). *Baloney (Henry P.)*. New York: Viking.

Scieszka, J. The Time Warp Trio series. New York: Puffin.

Scieszka, J., & Lane, S. (1998). *Squids will be squids: Fresh morals for beastly fables*. New York: Viking.

Tolkien, J.R.R. (2001). *The lord of the rings* (Paperback box set). Boston: Houghton Mifflin.

White, E.B. (1952). *Charlotte's web*. New York: HarperCollins.

Wiesner, D. (1991). *Tuesday*. New York: Clarion.

Wiesner, D. (1999). *Sector 7*. New York: Clarion.

Websites

Beams's Doorway: Fantasy
    beamsdoorway.bizland.com/fantasy.htm

Be More Creative.com
    bemorecreative.com/p-scien.htm

Discovery Channel
  dsc.discovery.com

Harry Potter Homepage
  harrypotter.warnerbros.com

The Harry Potter Lexicon: The Ultimate Harry Potter Reference
  www.i2k.com/~svderark/lexicon

Orbital Trading Post: Fantasy Top 50
  www.computercrowsnest.com/shopbooks/amz7.htm

Scholastic: Fantasy and the Imagination
  teacher.scholastic.com/lessonrepro/lessonplans/fantasy.htm

Scholastic Kids Fun Online: Harry Potter
  www.scholastic.com/harrypotter/home.asp

Performance Extensions Across the Curriculum

Social Studies

- Investigate the Seven Wonders of the World and create the Eighth Wonder. Work in cooperative groups to create a multimedia exhibition to share such information as what it is, where it is, and why you chose it as the Eighth Wonder of the World. Use technological resources for research and presentation.
- Research "Flights of Imagination" from different time periods (da Vinci, the Wright Brothers, Clara Barton, Amelia Earhart, Jonas Salk) and share what you have learned through dramatization or song.

Science

- Use your imagination to describe and create a model of an invention for the 22nd century. Explain its function and how you think it will benefit life in that time.

Math

- Use geometric shapes to create imaginative artwork in the style of Picasso or Gris.
- Create a journal of geometry in everyday life. Share and discuss in class.

Art

- Study the works of cubist artists such as Picasso or Gris and interpret the paintings or collages. Create an original artwork in response to the work you have studied.
- Explore the art of M.C. Escher (*Waterfall*, *Three Worlds*, *Another World*) and create oral imaginative stories of what they represent. Write original fantasies based on these artworks.

Culminating Activity

Celebrating Flights of Imagination Past, Present, and Future: Provide theme-related background music ("I Believe I Can Fly," "Imagine," "Up, Up, and Away," "Fly Me to the Moon") for a celebration of imagination and creativity. Display students' performances and invite families and community members. The students will turn the multipurpose room into an imagination museum to display their theme-based performances. Students will create, display, and explain an invention for the future. (They will make a detailed drawing or three-dimensional model and develop an infomercial, brochure, or website to market it.) Students will engage in musical and dramatic presentations related to the theme and offer an exhibit of their artistic responses to imaginative ideas of the past and present.

CHAPTER 8

Situating Guided Comprehension in Other Themes

I
n Chapters 2 through 7, we situated Guided Comprehension in a variety of themes and provided planning ideas, lessons, examples of student work, and a variety of resources. We addressed the themes of multiple perspectives, mysteries, favorite authors, poetry, biography and autobiography, and fantasy. Now we invite you to situate Guided Comprehension in other themes.

In this chapter, we provide the resources necessary to plan theme-based Guided Comprehension lessons on the following topics:

- Alternative Fairy Tales (*Cinderella*, *The Three Little Pigs*, others)
- Turning Points in U.S. History: The American Revolution, The Civil War, World War II, Vietnam
- Historical Fiction
- More Favorite Authors (Judy Blume, Beverly Cleary, Patricia Polacco, Jerry Spinelli)

We have included blank forms for theme planning and developing Guided Comprehension lessons (see pages 144 and 145). To facilitate your planning process, we also have included booklists, websites, performance extensions across the curriculum, and a culminating activity for each theme. Simply set the goals for your lessons, select the comprehension strategies and teaching ideas you want to teach, and use the resources we have provided to complete your plans. Remember that detailed explanations of several of the teaching ideas used in this volume and a variety of blackline masters are included in the Appendix. (For a more extensive resource on comprehension strategies and teaching ideas, see *Guided Comprehension: A Teaching Model for Grades 3–8*.)

SAMPLE THEME-BASED PLAN FOR GUIDED COMPREHENSION

Goals and Connections to State Standards	Students will

• • •

Assessment

The following measures can be used for a variety of purposes, including diagnostic, formative, and summative assessment:

Comprehension Strategies		Teaching Ideas
1.		
2.		
3.		
4.		

Text	Title	Theme	Level
1.			
2.			
3.			
4.			

Comprehension Centers

Students will apply the comprehension strategies and related teaching ideas in the following comprehension centers:

Technology Resources

Comprehension Routines

Students will apply the comprehension strategies and related teaching ideas in the following comprehension routines:

Guided Comprehension in Action: Lessons for Grades 3–8 by Maureen McLaughlin and Mary Beth Allen ©2002. Newark, DE: International Reading Association. May be copied for classroom use.

GUIDED COMPREHENSION PLANNING FORM

Strategy: _____

Teaching Idea: _____

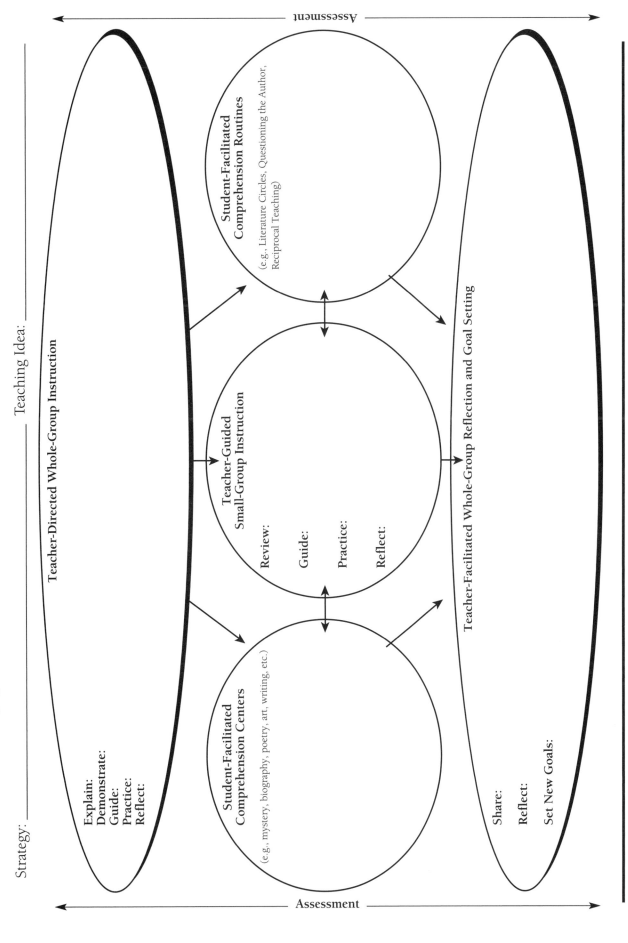

Teacher-Directed Whole-Group Instruction

Explain:
Demonstrate:
Guide:
Practice:
Reflect:

Student-Facilitated Comprehension Routines

(e.g., Literature Circles, Questioning the Author, Reciprocal Teaching)

Teacher-Guided Small-Group Instruction

Review:
Guide:
Practice:
Reflect:

Student-Facilitated Comprehension Centers

(e.g., mystery, biography, poetry, art, writing, etc.)

Teacher-Facilitated Whole-Group Reflection and Goal Setting

Share:
Reflect:
Set New Goals:

Assessment

Assessment

THEME RESOURCES

Alternative Fairy Tales

Booklists

Cinderella

Climo, S. (1993). *The Korean Cinderella*. New York: HarperCollins.

Climo, S. (1996). *The Irish Cinderlad*. New York: HarperCollins.

Cochrane, O. (1988). *Cinderella chant*. Winnipeg, MB: Whole Language Consultants.

Cole, B. (1987). *Prince Cinders*. New York: G.P. Putnam's Sons.

Edward, P. (1997). *Dinorella: A prehistoric fairy tale*. New York: Scholastic.

Huck, C. (1989). *Princess Furball*. New York: Scholastic.

Jackson, E. (1994). *Cinder Edna*. New York: Lee and Shepard Books.

Lowell, S. (2000). *Cindy Ellen: A wild western Cinderella*. New York: HarperCollins.

Martin, R. (1992). *The rough-face girl*. New York: G.P. Putnam's Sons.

Meddaugh, S. (1997). *Cinderella's rat*. New York: Houghton Mifflin.

Minters, F. (1994). *Cinder-Elly*. New York: Penguin.

Myers, B. (1985). *Sidney Rella and the glass sneaker*. New York: Macmillan.

Perlman, J. (1992). *Cinderella penguin or the little glass flipper*. New York: Scholastic.

San Souci, R. (1989). *The talking eggs*. New York: Dial.

San Souci, R. (1994). *Sootface: An Ojibwa Cinderella story*. New York: Bantam Doubleday Dell.

San Souci, R. (1998). *Cendrillon: A Caribbean Cinderella*. New York: Simon & Schuster.

San Souci, R. (2000). *Cinderella skeleton*. Orlando, FL: Silver Whistle Harcourt.

Shorto, R. (1990). *Cinderella: The untold story*. New York: Carol.

Wegman, W. (1993). *Cinderella*. New York: Lookout Books.

Winthhrop, E. (1991). *Vasilissa the beautiful*. New York: HarperCollins.

Yen Mah, A. (2001). *The Chinese Cinderella*. New York: Delacorte.

The Three Little Pigs

Adams, D. (1994). *Three little pigs go to greasy Pete's*. Ottawa, KS: Flatland Tales.

Celsi, T. (1990). *The fourth little pig*. Austin, TX: Steck Vaughn.

Hooks, W. (1989). *The three little pigs and the fox*. New York: Macmillian.

Laird, D. (1990). *Three little Hawaiian pigs and the magic shark*. Nantucket, MA: Barnaby Books.

Laverde, A. (2000). *Alaska's three pigs*. Seattle, WA: Sasquatch Books.

Lowell, S. (1992). *The three little javelinas*. Maple City, MI: Rising Moon Books.

McNaughton, C. (1996). *Oops!* Orlando, FL: Harcourt Brace.

Scieszka, J. (1989). *The true story of the 3 little pigs!* New York: Penguin.

Trivizas, E. (1993). *The three little wolves and the big bad pig*. New York: Macmillan.

Tuyosi, M. (1986). *Socrates and the three little pigs*. New York: Philomel Books.

Other Alternative Fairy Tales

Auch, M. (1993). *Peeping beauty*. New York: Holiday House.

Ernest, L.C. (1995). *Little Red Riding Hood: A newfangled prairie tale*. New York: Scholastic.

French, F. (1986). *Snow White in New York*. Oxford, UK: Oxford University Press.

Grimm, B. (1979). *Snow White and Rose Red*. Mahwah, NJ: Troll.

Perlman, J. (1994). *The emperor penguin's new clothes*. New York: Scholastic.

Scieszka, J. (1991). *The frog prince continued*. New York: The Trumpet Club.

Scieszka, J. (1992). *The Stinky Cheese Man and other fairly stupid tales*. New York: Scholastic.

Smith, D. (1999). *Hogsel and Gruntel*. New York: Scholastic.

Tolhurst, M. (1990). *Somebody and the three Blairs*. New York: Orchard Books.

Wildsmith, B., & Wildsmith, R. (1994). *Jack and the mean stock*. New York: Alfred A. Knopf.

Yep, L. (1999). *The Dragon Prince: A Chinese beauty & the beast tale*. New York: HarperCollins.

Yolen, J. (1981). *Sleeping Ugly*. New York: Coward-McCann.

Websites

Childrenstory.com

    www.childrenstory.com/tales

The Cinderella Project

    www-dept.usm.edu/~engdept/cinderella/cinderella.html

The Little Red Riding Hood Project

    www-dept.usm.edu/~engdept/lrrh/lrrhhome.htm

Stories, Folklore, and Fairy Tales Theme Page

    www.cln.org/themes/fairytales.html

University of Maryland Fairy Tale Site

    www.inform.umd.edu/EdRes/ReadingRoom/Fiction/FairyTales

Performance Extensions Across the Curriculum

Social Studies

• Explore fairy tales and folk tales across cultures. Compare and contrast story elements and examine cultural influences in each.

Science

• Read tales and legends about animals (see http://www.planetozkids.com/oban/legends.htm for a variety of animal legends). Research the evolutionary development of animals and compare with legends. Identify aspects included in the legends that represent authentic traits of the animals.

• Explore legends and folklore related to astronomy and the constellations at http://nuevaschool.org/~debbie/library/cur/sci/sky.html. Compare and contrast with authentic information from research.

Art

• Investigate the art techniques highlighted in folk tales and fairy tales (weaving, sculpture, painting, drawing). Examine the storytelling aspects of the art and create original stories using that art technique.

Culminating Activity

    Once Upon a Time: A Celebration of Fairy Tales: Display students' performances from across the curriculum and invite parents and community members to attend an evening of dramatic interpretation. Students will write and perform original fairy tales using costumes, scenery, and props they have designed.

Turning Points in U.S. History

The American Revolution

Booklist

Collier, J., & Collier, C. (1989). *My brother Sam is dead*. New York: Scholastic.

Griffin, J. (1977). *Phoebe the spy*. New York: Scholastic.

Moore, K. (1997). *If you lived at the time of the American Revolution*. New York: Scholastic.

Peacock, L. (1998). *Crossing the Delaware: A history in many voices*. New York: Scholastic.

Quakenbush, R. (1999). *Daughter of liberty: A true story of the American Revolution*. New York: Scholastic.

Turner, A. (1992). *Katie's trunk*. New York: Aladdin.

Websites

Carol Hurst's Children's Literature Site: Revolutionary War
    www.carolhurst.com/subjects/ushistory/revolution.html

The History Place: American Revolution
    www.historyplace.com/unitedstates/revolution/index.html

Kid Info
    www.kidinfo.com/american_history/american_revolution.html

The Civil War

Booklist

Ackerman, K. (1990). *Tin heart*. New York: Atheneum.

Bunting, E. (1996). *The blue and the gray*. New York: Scholastic.

Fritz, J. (1993). *Just a few words: Mr. Lincoln: The story of the Gettysburg Address*. New York: Putnam.

Gauch, P. (1975). *Thunder at Gettysburg*. New York: G.P. Putnam's Sons.

Levine, E. (1988). *If you traveled on the Underground Railroad*. New York: Scholastic.

Lyon, G. (1991). *Cecil's story*. New York: Orchard Books.

Moore, K. (1994). *If you lived at the time of the Civil War*. New York: Scholastic.

Murphy, J. (1990). *The boy's war*. New York: Clarion Books.

Polacco, P. (1994). *Pink and Say*. New York: Philomel Books.

Turner, A. (1987). *Nettie's trip south*. New York: Simon & Schuster.

Winter, J. (1988). *Follow the drinking gourd*. New York: Dragonfly Books.

Websites

Home of the American Civil War
    www.civilwarhome.com

Small Planet Communications: The Civil War
    www.smplanet.com/civilwar/civilwar.html

The United States Civil War Center: Ask an Expert
    www.lib.lsu.edu/cwc/question2.htm

World War II

Booklists

American-Japanese Internment Camps

Bunting E. (1998). *So far from the sea*. New York: Clarion Books.

Mochizuki, K. (1996). *Baseball saved us*. New York: Lee & Low Books.

Tunnell, M. (1996). *The Children of Topaz: The story of a Japanese-American internment camp based on a classroom diary*. New York: Holiday House.

Uchida, Y. (1992). *Journey home*. Glenview, IL: Scott Foresman.

Uchida. Y. (1993). *The bracelet*. New York: Philomel Books.

Uchida, Y. (1995). *The invisible thread: An autobiography*. New York: Beech Tree Books.

The Holocaust

Bunting, E. (1980). *Terrible things*. Philadelphia: The Jewish Publication Society.

Garner, E. (1999). *Eleanor's story: An American girl in Hitler's Germany*. Atlanta, GA: Peachtree.

Greene, B. (1973). *Summer of my German soldier*. New York: Bantam Doubleday Dell.

Kerr, J. (1971). *When Hitler stole pink rabbit*. New York: Scholastic.

Lowry, L. (1989). *Number the stars*. Boston: Houghton Mifflin

Peril, L., & Lazan, M. (1996). *Four perfect pebbles: A Holocaust story*. New York: Scholastic.

Yolen, J. (1988). *The devil's arithmetic*. New York: Scholastic.

Hiroshima

Coerr, E. (1997). *Sadako*. New York: Putnam.

Coerr, E. (1999). *Sadako and the thousand paper cranes*. New York: Puffin.

Ishii, T. (2001). *One thousand paper cranes: The story of Sadako and the children's peace statue*. New York: Laureleaf.

Kodama, T., & Ando, N. (1995). *Shin's tricycle*. New York: Walker.

Maruki, T. (1980). *Hiroshima no pika*. New York: Lothrop, Lee & Shepard Books.

Morimoto, J. (1987). *My Hiroshima*. New York: Penguin.

Tames, R. (2001). *Hiroshima: The shadow of the bomb (Point of Impact)*. Portsmouth, NH: Heinemann.

Yep, L. (1996). *Hiroshima*. New York: Scholastic.

Websites

Carol Hurst's Children's Literature Site
www.carolhurst.com/newsletters/22bnewsletters.html

Holocaust Links
history1900s.about.com/library/holocaust/blholocaust.htm

A Listing of World War II Websites
www.ih.k12.oh.us/eshonesty/world_war_ii_web_sites.htm

Masumi Hayashi Photographs and Information about Japanese Internment Camps
www.csuohio.edu/art_photos

Pictures of World War II
www.nara.gov/nara/nn/nns/ww2photo.html

World War II Resource Lists
www.awesomelibrary.org/Classroom/Social_Studies/History/World_War_II.html

Vietnam

Booklist

Ashabranner, B. (1988). *Always remember: The story of the Vietnam memorial*. New York: Scholastic.

Bunting, E. (1990). *The wall*. New York: Clarion Books.

Donnelly, J. (1991). *The wall of names*. New York: Random House.

Nelson, T. (1991). *And one for all*. New York: Yearling Books.

Paterson, K. (1988). *Park's quest*. New York: Puffin.

Pevsner, S., & Tang, F. (1997). *Sing for your father, Su Phan*. New York: Clarion Books.

Porter, F. (1996). *A place called heartbreak: A story of Vietnam (Stories of America)*. Austin, TX: Raintree/Steck-Vaughn.

Websites

Vietnam Echoes From the Wall
    www.teachvietnam.org

Vietnam Yesterday and Today
    servercc.oakton.edu/~wittman

The Virtual Wall
    www.thevirtualwall.org

Performance Extensions Across the Curriculum

Social Studies

• Investigate the social and cultural factors that influenced the start of each war. For example, research the religious, economic, political, and geographic causes of each war. Compare and contrast the causes among the wars. Record results and infer how each cause contributed to the outcome. Use original sources as well as reference materials.

Science

• Explore the impact of war on environments and people.
• Explore the evolution and ethical issues of nuclear and biological warfare.

Math

• Examine the economic impact of each war. Estimate costs in today's values. Compare and contrast with the cost of more recent wars, such as the Persian Gulf War or the War on Terrorism.

Art

• Investigate the forms of visual representations used to document each war—from paintings and drawings to photography and film to video to digital. Examine the perspectives and emotions conveyed in samples of each form. Select a form and a war or particular battle. Create an original work of art that represents your perspective.

Culminating Activity

Turning Points in U.S. History: Students create and maintain a website titled *Turning Points in U.S. History*. As they study each major subtopic, students prepare information—such as related slide shows, literature, links, projects, and timelines—to post on the site. Invite parents and community members to the premiere of the completed website. Students can serve as commentators on different aspects of the site and community members (for example, soldiers from the more recent wars or Holocaust survivors) can serve as living resources for a variety of turning points.

Historical Fiction

Booklist

Avi. (1987). *The fighting ground*. New York: Harper Trophy.

Bennett, C., & Gottesfeld, J. (2001). *Anne Frank and me*. New York: G.P. Putnam's Sons.

Bunting, E. (1996). *The blue and the gray*. New York: Scholastic.

Cherry, L. (1992). *A river ran wild*. Orlando, FL: Harcourt Brace Jovanovich.

Collier, J.L., & Collier, C. (1984). *My brother Sam is dead*. New York: Simon & Schuster.

Collier, J.L., & Collier, C. (1987). *Jump ship to freedom*. Yearling Books.

Collier, J.L., & Collier, C. (1987). *War comes to Willy Freeman*. Yearling Books.

Collier, J.L., & Collier, C. (1989). *The bloody country*. New York: Scholastic.

Gauch, P.L. (1975). *Thunder at Gettysburg*. New York: G.P. Putnam's Sons.

Hamilton, V. (1993). *Many thousands gone: African Americans from slavery to freedom*. New York: Knopf.

Harness, C. (2001). *Remember the ladies: 100 great American women*. New York: HarperCollins.

Hesse, K. (1997). *Out of the dust*. New York: Scholastic.

Hest, A. (1997). *When Jessie came across the sea*. Cambridge, MA: Candlewick.

Lowry, L. (1989). *Number the stars*. New York: Houghton Mifflin.

Morimoto, J. (1987). *My Hiroshima*. New York: Penguin.

O'Dell, S. (1980). *Sarah Bishop*. New York: Houghton Mifflin.

Reeder, C. (1989). *Shades of gray*. New York: Avon Books.

Say, A. (1993). *Grandfather's journey*. New York: Houghton Mifflin.

Tsuchiya, Y. (1988). *Faithful elephants*. Boston: Houghton Mifflin.

Wild, M., & Vivas, J. (1991). *Let the celebration begin*. New York: Orchard Press.

Woodruff, E. (1999). *The memory coat*. New York: Scholastic.

Yolen, J. (1992). *Encounter*. Orlando, FL: Harcourt Brace Jovanovich.

Websites

Carol Hurst's Children's Literature Site: U.S. History and Children's Literature
www.carolhurst.com/subjects/ushistory/ushistory.html

Historical Fiction Guide Picks
childrensbooks.about.com/cs/historicalfiction/index.htm

Internet School Library Media Center Historical Fiction Page
falcon.jmu.edu/~ramseyil/historical.htm

Why and How I Teach with Historical Fiction by Tarry Lindquist
teacher.scholastic.com/lessonrepro/lessonplans/instructor/social1.htm

Performance Extensions Across the Curriculum

Social Studies
• Students read historical fiction related to the topic of study. Use research to document authentic events mentioned in the novels.

Science

• Read historical fiction about scientists or inventors. Determine the plausibility of the inventions and support with facts.

Art

• Examine mosaics or tapestries from various time periods. Discuss the story that is represented in the mosaic. Tell or write the story that is presented.

Culminating Activity

Celebration of the Past: Students write a work of historical fiction, and research the historical facts. Students use a variety of creative methods to present their work: dramatic play, musical performance, or art exhibit. Parents and community members attend this Celebration of the Past, which also features displays of students' performances from throughout the theme.

More Favorite Authors

Judy Blume

Booklist

Blume, J. (1970). *Are you there God? It's me Margaret*. New York: Bantam Doubleday Dell.

Blume, J. (1970). *Iggie's house*. New York: Bantam Doubleday Dell.

Blume, J. (1971). *Freckle juice*. New York: Bantam Doubleday Dell.

Blume, J. (1971). *Then again, maybe I won't*. New York: Bantam Doubleday Dell.

Blume, J. (1972). *It's not the end of the world*. New York: Bantam Doubleday Dell.

Blume, J. (1972). *Otherwise known as Sheila the great*. New York: Bantam Doubleday Dell.

Blume, J. (1972). *Tales of the fourth grade nothing*. New York: Bantam Doubleday Dell.

Blume, J. (1973). *Deenie*. New York: Dell Laurel-Leaf Books.

Blume, J. (1974). *Blubber*. New York: Bantam Doubleday Dell.

Blume, J. (1974). *The pain and the great one*. New York: Bantam Doubleday Dell.

Blume, J. (1975). *Forever*. Scarsdale, NY: Bradbury Press.

Blume, J. (1977). *Starring Sally J. Freedman as herself*. New York: Bantam Doubleday Dell.

Blume, J. (1980). *Superfudge*. New York: Bantam Doubleday Dell.

Blume, J. (1981). *The one in the middle is the green kangaroo*. New York: Bantam Doubleday Dell.

Blume, J. (1981). *Tiger eyes*. Scarsdale, NY: Bradbury Press.

Blume, J. (1986). *Letters to Judy: What your kids wish they could tell you*. New York: G.P. Putnam's Sons.

Blume, J. (1987). *Just as long as we're together*. New York: Bantam Doubleday Dell.

Blume, J. (1990). *Fudge-a-mania*. New York: Bantam Doubleday Dell.

Blume, J. (1993). *Here's to you Rachel Robinson*. New York: Bantam Doubleday Dell.

Websites

Judy Blume: Official Website
   www.judyblume.com

Judy Blume: Teacher Resource File
   falcon.jmu.edu/~ramseyil/blume.htm

Scholastic Authors Online: Judy Blume
   teacher.scholastic.com/authorsandbooks/authors/blume/bio.htm

Teachers@Random: Judy Blume
   www.randomhouse.com/teachers/authors/blum.html

Beverly Cleary

Booklist

Cleary, B. (1950). *Henry Huggins*. New York: William Morrow.

Cleary, B. (1951). *Ellen Tebbits*. New York: William Morrow.

Cleary, B. (1952). *Henry and Beezus*. New York: William Morrow.

Cleary, B. (1953). *Otis Spofford*. New York: William Morrow.

Cleary, B. (1954). *Henry and Ribsy*. New York: William Morrow.

Cleary, B. (1955). *Beezus and Ramona*. New York: William Morrow.

Cleary, B. (1957). *Henry and the paper route*. New York: William Morrow.

Cleary, B. (1961). *Emily's runaway imagination*. New York: William Morrow.

Cleary, B. (1965). *The mouse and the motorcycle*. New York: William Morrow.

Cleary, B. (1968). *Ramona the pest*. New York: Scholastic.

Cleary, B. (1970). *Runaway Ralph*. New York: William Morrow.

Cleary, B. (1975). *Ramona the brave*. New York: William Morrow.

Cleary, B. (1981). *Ramona Quimbly, age 8*. New York: William Morrow.

Cleary, B. (1982). *Ralph S. Mouse*. New York: William Morrow.

Cleary, B. (1983). *Dear Mr. Henshaw*. New York: Dell.

Websites

Author Profile: Beverly Cleary
   www.trelease-on-reading.com/cleary.html

Beverly Cleary: Teacher Resource File
   falcon.jmu.edu/~ramseyil/cleary.htm

Bibliographies, Lessons, and Internet Sites: Beverly Cleary
   www.indiana.edu/~eric_rec/ieo/bibs/cleary.html

Scholastic Authors Online: Meet Beverly Cleary
   teacher.scholastic.com/authorsandbooks/authors/cleary/bio.htm

The World of Beverly Cleary
   www.beverlycleary.com/

Patricia Polacco

Booklist

Polacco, P. (1988). *Rechenka's eggs*. New York: Putnam.

Polacco, P. (1989). *Boat ride with Lillian Two Blossom*. New York: Philomel.

Polacco, P. (1991). *Applemando's dreams*. New York: Philomel.

Polacco, P. (1992). *Chicken Sunday*. New York: Philomel.

Polacco, P. (1993). *The bee tree*. New York: Philomel.

Polacco, P. (1994). *Firetalking (meet the author)*. Katonah, NY: Richard C. Owen.

Polacco, P. (1994). *My rotten redheaded older brother*. New York: Simon & Schuster.

Polacco, P. (1994). *Pink & Say*. New York: Philomel.

Polacco, P. (1994). *Some birthday!* Glenview, IL: Scott Foresman.

Polacco, P. (1996). *I can hear the sun*. New York: Philomel.

Polacco, P. (1996). *The trees of the dancing goats*. New York: Simon & Schuster.

Polacco, P. (1997). *In Enzo's splendid gardens*. New York: Philomel.

Polacco, P. (1998). *Thank you, Mr. Falker*. New York: Philomel.

Polacco, P. (1999). *I can hear the sun: A modern myth*. New York: Puffin.

Polacco, P. (1999). *Meteor*. New York: Philomel.

Polacco, P. (2001). *Betty doll*. New York: Penguin.

Polacco, P. (2001). *The keeping quilt*. New York: Aladdin.

Polacco, P. (2001). *Mr. Lincoln's way*. New York: Philomel.

Websites

Patricia Polacco: Biography and Lesson Plans
  falcon.jmu.edu/~ramseyil/polacco.htm

Patricia Polacco Official Website
  www.patriciapolacco.com

Scholastic Authors Online: Patricia Polacco
  teacher.scholastic.com/authorsandbooks/authors/polacco/bio.htm

Jerry Spinelli

Booklist

Spinelli, J. (1990). *Maniac Magee*. Boston: Little, Brown.

Spinelli, J. (1992). *The bathwatergang*. Boston: Little, Brown.

Spinelli, J. (1993). *There's a girl in my hammerlock*. New York: Aladdin.

Spinelli, J. (1995). *Do the funky pickle*. New York: Apple.

Spinelli, J. (1996). *Fourth grade rats*. New York: Apple.

Spinelli, J. (1997). *Crash*. New York: Random House.

Spinelli, J. (1998). *The library card*. New York: Apple.

Spinelli, J. (1998). *Wringer*. New York: Harper Trophy.

Spinelli, J. (2000). *Jason and Marceline*. Boston: Little, Brown.

Spinelli, J. (2000). *Space station 7th grade*. Boston: Little, Brown.

Spinelli, J. (2000). *Stargirl*. New York: Knopf.

Spinelli, J. (2000). *Who put that hair in my toothbrush?* Boston: Little, Brown.

Websites

Bibliographies, Lessons, and Websites
  www.indiana.edu/~eric_rec/ieo/bibs/spinel.html

Carol Hurst's Children's Literature Site: Teaching Ideas for *Maniac Magee*
    www.carolhurst.com/titles/maniacmagee.html
In the Spotlight: Jerry Spinelli
    www.carr.lib.md.us/authco/spinelli-j.htm
Jerry Spinelli: Teacher Resource File
    falcon.jmu.edu/~ramseyil/spinelli.htm
Scholastic Authors Online: Jerry Spinelli
    teacher.scholastic.com/authorsandbooks/events/spinelli/index.htm

Performance Extensions Across the Curriculum

Social Studies

• Examine family relationships presented in the books. Discuss what makes a family and the many ways they are represented in stories and in the students' lives. Students investigate their cultural backgrounds or heritages and create a family history and a family website.

Math/Science

• Create a survey for the class or school to find out each student's favorite author, favorite book, and favorite genre. Tally all results and use the computer to present findings in charts and graphs. Write an analysis of the results and share with appropriate audiences (librarians, teachers, students).

Art

• Examine the artwork in Patricia Polacco books. Have students notice how the author used color, shape, texture, and line to create the images. Pay special attention to the horizon line, foreground and background, and development of characters. Have students use similar techniques to create paintings to accompany books they write in the style of their favorite author and illustrator.

Culminating Activity

Authors' Day: Students conduct a celebration of works written by their favorite authors and themselves. The works are exhibited and each student (or pair of students) shares information about the lives and writing careers of his or her favorite authors and himself or herself. Students can share books that link learning across the curriculum and that they have authored in reading, social studies, science, mathematics, music, or art.

Teaching Ideas and Blackline Masters

TEACHING IDEAS AT A GLANCE

Teaching Idea	When to Use	Comprehension Strategy	Text
Mind and Alternative Mind Portraits	After	Evaluating	Narrative Expository
Contrast Charts	After	Evaluating	Narrative Expository
Thinking Hats	After	Making Connections Evaluating	Narrative Expository
Mystery Cubes	After	Summarizing	Narrative Expository
Comic Strip Summaries	After	Summarizing	Narrative Expository
That Was Then... This Is Now	Before After	Previewing Visualizing Summarizing	Narrative Expository
Photographs of the Mind	During	Making Connections Visualizing	Narrative Expository
Text Transformations	After	Knowing How Words Work	Narrative Expository
Bio-Cubes	After	Summarizing	Expository
Drawing Visualizations	During After	Visualizing	Narrative Expository

TEACHING IDEAS

Mind and Alternative Mind Portraits

(See blackline, page 165.)

Purpose: To examine a topic or issue from two perspectives.

Comprehension Strategy: Evaluating

Text: Narrative, Expository   **Use:** After Reading

Procedure: (Begin by explaining and modeling Mind and Alternative Mind Portraits.)

1. Discuss the text and examine which perspective is prevalent. Then contemplate a perspective that is not presented equally or is silenced or missing from the text.

    Mind Portrait: Draw the outline of a head to represent the perspective of one person or character. Label the portrait. Inside the portrait, write, draw, or collage ideas and experiences that delineate that person's perspective.

    Alternative Mind Portrait: Draw the outline of a head that represents a different perspective. Label the portrait. Inside the portrait, write, draw, or collage ideas and experiences that delineate another person's perspective on the same issue.

2. Share and discuss portraits to compare and contrast perspectives.

3. Display completed portraits for others to view.

Ideas for using:

> Narrative Text: Perspectives — two characters from a story
>
> Expository Text: Perspectives — two viewpoints on a topic

Adaptations:

> Narratives and Alternative Narratives
>
> Photographs and Alternative Photographs
>
> Videos and Alternative Videos

Example: See Chapter 2.

Source: McLaughlin, M. (2001, December). *Sociocultural influences on content literacy teachers' beliefs and innovative practices.* Paper presented at the 51st Annual Meeting of the National Reading Conference, San Antonio, TX.

Contrast Charts

(See blackline, page 166.)

Purposes: To contrast two views of an issue; to analyze authors' and illustrators' choices and how they affect perspective.

Comprehension Strategy: Evaluating

Text: Narrative, Expository   **Use:** After Reading

Procedure: (Begin by explaining and modeling Contrast Charts.)

1. After reading, determine a perspective of the story or issue expressed in the text. Write ideas that characterize that perspective in the left-hand column of the chart. Use specific words, phrases, or events from the text to support ideas.

2. Determine another view of the story or issue that contrasts the first perspective and write contrasts in the right-hand column of the chart. Be sure to record the contrasts directly opposite original perspective.

3. Share and discuss contrasts with a partner, small group, or whole class.

Ideas for using:

• To contrast and discuss information presented in texts.

• To chart two perspectives on decision making.

• To contrast different versions of a story or different perspectives of expository text.

Example: See Chapter 2.

Source: Adapted from Tompkins, G. (2001). *Literacy for the 21st century: A balanced approach* (2nd ed.). Saddlebrook, NJ: Prentice Hall.

TEACHING IDEAS

Thinking Hats

(See blacklines, pages 167–168.)

Purposes: To examine a topic from a variety of perspectives; to think critically and creatively.

Comprehension Strategy: Evaluating

Text: Narrative, Expository   **Use:** After Reading

Procedure: (Begin by explaining and modeling Thinking Hats.)

1. After reading, organize groups of four, five, or six. Each participant takes on a different perspective or role to discuss the story or issue.

2. Participants reflect on roles and make notes in Guided Comprehension Journals to prompt discussion.

3. Participants engage in discussion of a topic from a variety of perspectives. Everyone can engage in small-group discussions, or one group can discuss and the other students can observe.

Ideas for using:

    Narrative Example: **Text:** *Cinderella*

    Perspectives: Cinderella, stepmother, fairy godmother, prince

    Expository Example: **Text:** *Columbus' Exploration*

    Perspectives: Columbus, Queen Isabella, the leader of the Tainos, a crew member from the Santa Maria

Example: See Chapter 2.

Source: Adapted from DeBono, E. (1985). *Six thinking hats.* Boston: Little, Brown.

Mystery Cubes

(See blackline, page 170.)

Purpose: To structure key points for summarizing a mystery or other texts.

Comprehension Strategy: Summarizing

Text: Expository, Narrative   **Use:** After Reading

Procedure: (Begin by explaining and modeling the Mystery Cube.)

1. Explain the idea of the Mystery Cube to students. Describe the information that goes on each of the six sides of the cube.

2. Demonstrate the process of writing key ideas on the cube. Use a read-aloud and a think-aloud. Show the students how to assemble the cube.

3. In small groups, guide the students to read a mystery and create a Mystery Cube.

4. Share ideas with the class.

5. Encourage students to create their own cubes as follow-ups to reading mysteries at the mystery center.

Information for Mystery Cubes:

Side	Option 1	Option 2
1	Setting	Setting
2	Detective	Archeologist/Scientist/Historian/Explorer
3	Crime or Mystery	Mystery (Natural, Historical, Scientific)
4	Victim	Clues
5	Three Clues	Solution/Hypothesis
6	Solution	Illustration

Source: Adapted from McLaughlin, M., & Allen, M.B. (2002). *Guided comprehension: A teaching model for grades 3–8.* Newark, DE: International Reading Association.

TEACHING IDEAS

Comic Strip Summaries

Purpose: To structure summarizing of key points in a narrative or expository text.

Comprehension Strategy: Summarizing

Text: Narrative, Expository   **Use:** During and After Reading

Procedure: (Begin by explaining and modeling Comic Strip Summaries.)

1. Fold a paper into four, six, or eight sections.

2. Use colorful drawings to retell the story or event. Put one drawing in each cell, following a particular sequence. Write a statement describing each cell.

3. Share comic strips in small groups and display for all to read.

Example: See Chapter 4.

Source: McLaughlin, M., & Allen, M.B. (2002). *Guided comprehension in action: Lessons for grades 3–8.* Newark, DE: International Reading Association.

That Was Then...This Is Now

(See blackline, page 175.)

Purposes: To compare and contrast ideas and beliefs before and after reading; to create mental images while reading; to write summary statements.

Comprehension Strategies: Previewing, Visualizing, Summarizing

Text: Narrative, Expository   **Use:** Before and After Reading

Procedure: (Begin by explaining and modeling That Was Then...This Is Now.)

1. Sketch thoughts about a specific topic prior to reading and write a summary statement.

2. Create mental images while reading.

3. Sketch thoughts about the topic after reading and write a summary statement.

4. Compare and contrast pre- and post-thinking.

Example: See Chapter 5.

Source: McLaughlin, M., & Allen, M.B. (2002). *Guided comprehension in action: Lessons for grades 3–8.* Newark, DE: International Reading Association.

TEACHING IDEAS

Photographs of the Mind

(See blackline, page 176.)

Purposes: To visualize while reading text; to make connections to the ideas presented in the text.

Comprehension Strategies: Visualizing, Making Connections

Text: Narrative, Expository   **Use:** During Reading

Procedure: (Begin by explaining and modeling Photographs of the Mind.)

1. Preview text to be read.

2. Read text. At designated or self-selected points in the text, stop and sketch a visualization related to the reading.

3. Share sketches in small groups.

Example: See Chapter 5.

Source: Keene, E., & Zimmerman, S. (1997). *Mosaic of thought*. Portsmouth, NH: Heinemann.

Text Transformations

(See blackline, page 178.)

Purposes: To write alternative versions of rhymes and poems; to develop vocabulary in engaging ways.

Comprehension Strategy: Knowing How Words Work

Text: Expository, Narrative   **Use:** After Reading

Procedure: (Begin by explaining and modeling Text Transformations: Silly Rhymes, Silly Poems.)

1. Share original rhymes or poems. Discuss and use these as the models for transformations.

2. Share the rhyme or poem with specific words left out.

3. Have students brainstorm words (synonyms, antonyms, same part of speech) to replace the left-out words. Use dictionaries and thesauruses to help find new words.

4. Share new rhymes and poems.

Adaptations:

• Use the structure of the original poem to create new poems.

• Rewrite nursery rhymes with new characters or events.

Example: See Chapter 5.

Source: McLaughlin, M., & Allen, M.B. (2002). *Guided comprehension in action: Lessons for grades 3–8*. Newark, DE: International Reading Association.

TEACHING IDEAS

Bio-Cubes

(See blackline, page 170.)

Purpose: To structure key points for summarizing a person's life.

Comprehension Strategy: Summarizing

Text: Expository   **Use:** After Reading

Procedure: (Begin by explaining and modeling the Bio-Cube.)

1. Describe the information that goes on each side of the cube.

2. Demonstrate by using a read-aloud and a think-aloud based on a biography. Think aloud while writing key ideas on the cube. Show the students how to assemble the cube.

3. In small groups, guide the students to read a biography and create a Bio-Cube.

4. Share ideas with the class.

5. Encourage students to create Bio-Cubes as follow-ups to reading biographies of their choice at the biography center.

Information for Bio-Cubes:

Side	Information
1	Person's name, birth date, and birthplace
2	Personal background
3	Issue the person struggled to overcome
4	Why this person should be remembered
5	Epitaph
6	Illustration

Example: See Chapter 6.

Source: Adapted from McLaughlin, M., & Allen, M.B. (2002). *Guided comprehension: A teaching model for grades 3–8.* Newark, DE: International Reading Association.

Drawing Visualizations

(See blackline, page 184.)

Purposes: To convey mental images created while reading; to visually represent important information about text.

Comprehension Strategy: Visualizing

Text: Narrative, Expository   **Use:** During and After Reading

Procedure: (Begin by explaining and modeling Drawing Visualizations.)

1. Demonstrate how to use visual representations (pictures, shapes, lines) to communicate pictures created in the mind while reading.

2. Think aloud about the visualizations, represent them on the overhead, and then model writing a sentence or paragraph about them.

3. Have students listen to a selection and then ask them to create a visual representation of their mind pictures. Have them share their drawings in small groups, explaining why they drew what they did.

Ideas for using:

• Use as prompts for literature discussions.

• Use as a literacy center activity.

Source: Adapted from McLaughlin, M., & Allen, M.B. (2002). *Guided comprehension: A teaching model for grades 3–8.* Newark, DE: International Reading Association.

QUESTIONING THE AUTHOR: TRIPLE-ENTRY JOURNAL

My Author Queries:	My Reasoning:	Group's Author Responses:

MIND AND ALTERNATIVE MIND PORTRAITS

Mind Portrait

Alternative Mind Portrait

CONTRAST CHART

1.	1.
2.	2.
3.	3.
4.	4.
5.	5.

THINKING HATS

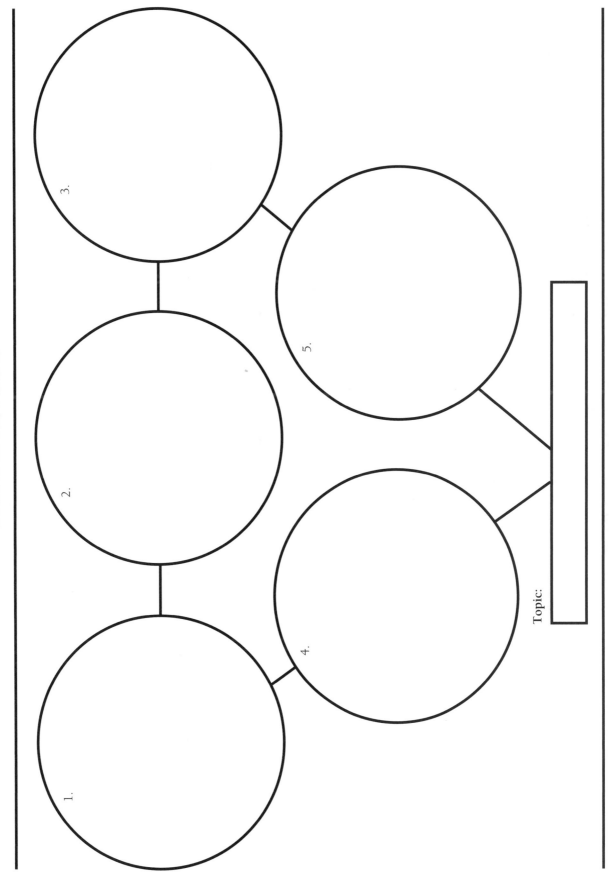

1.

2.

3.

4.

5.

Topic:

ILLUSTRATED THINKING HATS

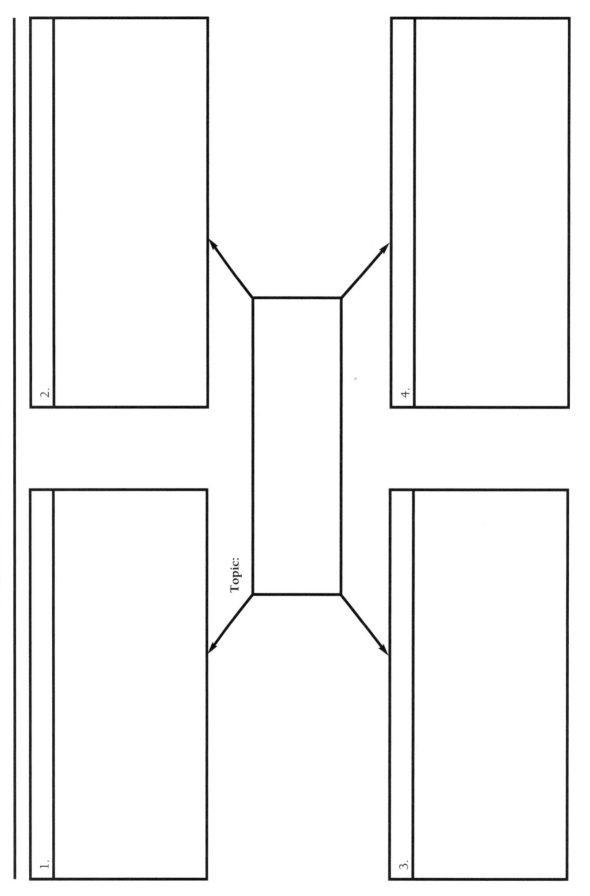

1.

2.

3.

4.

Topic:

THE ELEVENTH HOUR CLUE ORGANIZER

Page	Clues	Suspect	Reason

CUBE

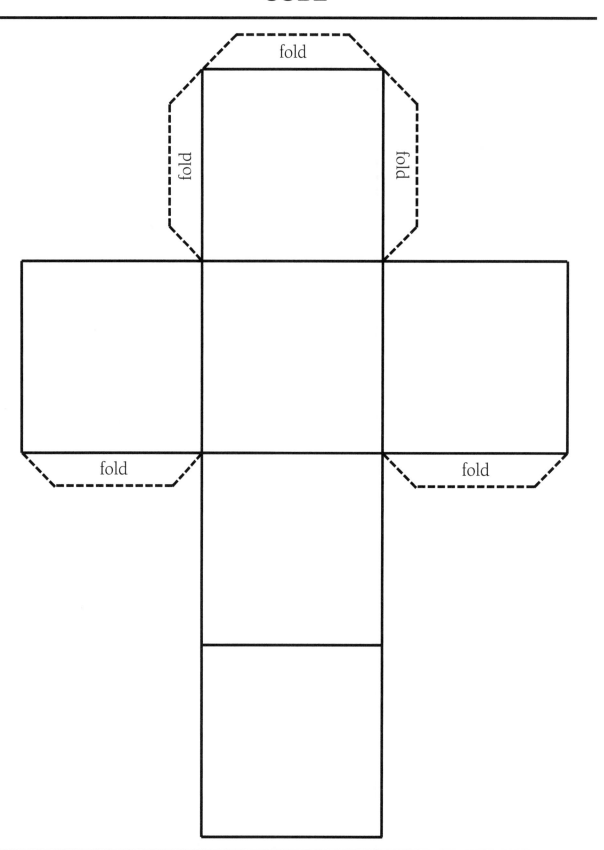

fold

fold

fold

fold

fold

SAVE THE LAST WORD FOR ME

Side 1: Choose an idea, phrase, quote, concept, word, or fact from the text that interests or intrigues you and write it below.

Side 2: Explain why you chose what you wrote on Side 1, or share your reaction to it.

CONTEXT CLUE ORGANIZER

Unknown Word	Page	Possible Meaning	Verification

CHAPTER WORD MAP

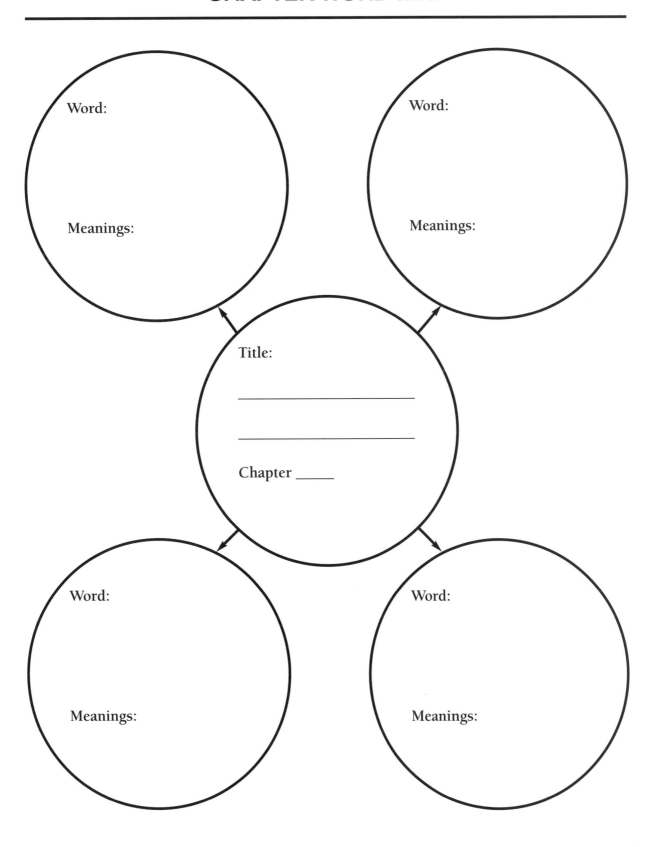

Word:

Meanings:

Word:

Meanings:

Title:

_____

_____

Chapter _____

Word:

Meanings:

Word:

Meanings:

BOOK REVIEW PLANNER

Name: _____

Title: _____

Author: _____

Part One:

• What is your overall impression of the book?

• On a scale of 1–10, how would you rate this book? Justify your thinking.

Part Two:

• What was the best part of the book? Explain your reasoning.

• What was the worst part of the book? Explain your choice.

• What word would you use to describe the effectiveness of the book format? The illustrations?

• What two comments or suggestions would you offer to the author? To the illustrator?

Part Three:

• Why would you (or would you not) recommend this book to other readers?

• If friends told you they wanted to read this book, what advice would you give them?

THAT WAS THEN...THIS IS NOW

That Was Then...	This Is Now...

Sketch:

Sketch:

Label: _____
_____
_____
_____

Label: _____
_____
_____
_____

PHOTOGRAPHS OF THE MIND

1	2
3	4

DIAMANTE: A FORM POEM

_____
Subject—One noun

_____ _____
Two adjectives describing the subject

_____ _____ _____
Three participles ("ing" words) telling about the subject

_____ _____ _____ _____
Four Nouns—First two relate to the first noun, last two to opposite

_____ _____ _____
Three participles ("ing" words) telling about the opposite

_____ _____
Two adjectives describing the opposite

_____
Opposite of subject—One noun

TEXT TRANSFORMATIONS

Part One: Replace each missing word with a synonym.

Jack and Jill _____ up the hill

To _____ a pail of water.

Jack fell down and broke his _____

And Jill came _____ after.

Part Two: Write a silly rhyme using the same structure.

_____

_____

_____

_____

THICK AND THIN QUESTIONS

Text: _____

Page	Thin Questions	Thick Questions

BIOGRAPHY/AUTOBIOGRAPHY ORGANIZER

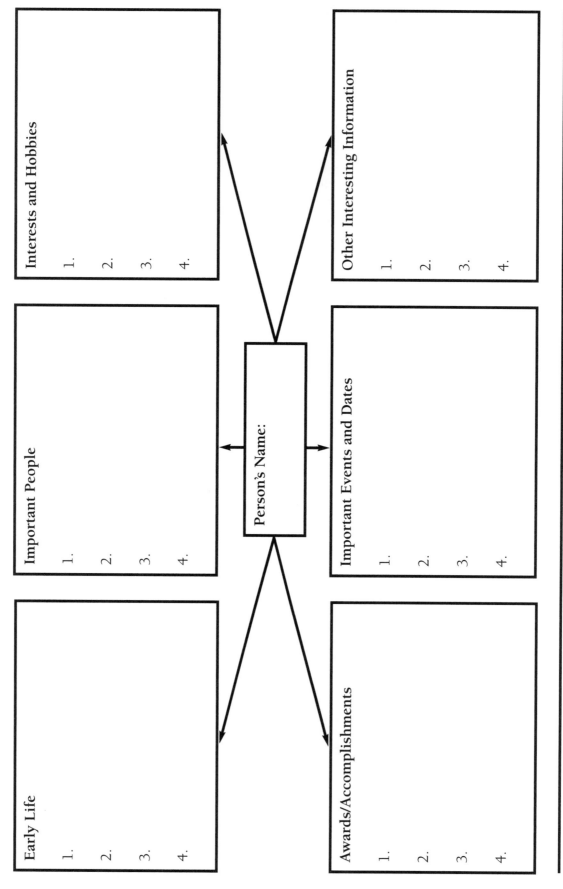

Early Life

1.

2.

3.

4.

Important People

1.

2.

3.

4.

Interests and Hobbies

1.

2.

3.

4.

Person's Name:

Awards/Accomplishments

1.

2.

3.

4.

Important Events and Dates

1.

2.

3.

4.

Other Interesting Information

1.

2.

3.

4.

AUTOBIOGRAPHY QUILT SQUARE PATTERN

Directions: Work with the fabric of your choice to complete your square. Be sure to include the information listed in the square below. Remember that you can use words or art to communicate the information about your life.

- Your name

- Important people in your life

- Your hobbies and interests

- Your accomplishments

- Important events and dates

- Your favorite book and favorite song

STORY IMPRESSION

Title: _____

Words

Prediction

"I Wonder" Bookmark

Page _____

I wonder…

_____

_____

_____

because…

_____

_____

_____

Page _____

I wonder…

_____

_____

_____

because…

_____

_____

_____

Page _____

I wonder…

_____

_____

_____

because…

_____

_____

_____

DRAWING VISUALIZATIONS

1.

Drawing:

Sentence:

2.

Drawing:

Sentence:

3.

Drawing:

Sentence:

REFERENCES

Alvermann, D.F. (1991). The discussion web: A graphic aid for learning across the curriculum. *The Reading Teacher, 45,* 92–99.

Bean, T.W. (1997). ReWrite: A music strategy for exploring content area concepts. *Reading Online* [Online]. Available: http://www.readingonline.org/literacy/bats/index.html.

Beane, J.A. (1995). Curriculum integration and the disciplines of knowledge. *Phi Delta Kappan, 76,* 616–622.

DeBono, E. (1985). *Six thinking hats.* Boston: Little, Brown.

Duffy, G.G. (2001, December). *The case for direct explanation of strategies.* Paper presented at the 51st Annual Meeting of the National Reading Conference, San Antonio, TX.

Duke, N. (2001, December). *A new generation of researchers looks at comprehension.* Paper presented at the 51st Annual Meeting of the National Reading Conference, San Antonio, TX.

Harvey, S., & Goudvis, A. (2000). *Strategies that work: Teaching comprehension to enhance understanding.* York, ME: Stenhouse.

Hobbs, R. (1996). Expanding the concept of literacy. In R.W. Kubey (Ed.), *Media literacy in the information age: Current perspectives* (pp. 163–183). New York: Transition Press.

Keene, E., & Zimmerman, S. (1997). *Mosaic of thought.* Portsmouth, NH: Heinemann.

Lipson, M.Y., Valencia, S.W., Wixson, K.K., & Peters, C.W. (1993). Integration and thematic teaching: Integration to improve teaching and learning. *Language Arts, 70,* 252–263.

Lipson, M.Y., & Wixson, K. (1997). *Assessment and instruction of reading and writing disability: An interactive approach* (2nd ed.). New York: Longman.

McGinley, W., & Denner, P. (1987). Story impressions: A prereading/prewriting activity. *Journal of Reading, 31,* 248–253.

McLaughlin, M. (2000). Inquiry: Key to critical and creative thinking in the content areas. In M. McLaughlin & M.E. Vogt (Eds.), *Creativity and innovation in content area teaching* (pp. 31–54). Norwood, MA: Christopher-Gordon.

McLaughlin, M. (2001, December). *Sociocultural influences on content literacy teaching.* Paper presented at the 51st Annual Meeting of the National Reading Conference, San Antonio, TX.

McLaughlin, M., & Allen, M.B. (2002). *Guided comprehension: A teaching model for grades 3–8.* Newark, DE: International Reading Association.

McLaughlin, M., & Bean, T. (2001, December). *Sociocultural influences on content literacy teachers' innovative practices.* Paper presented at the 51st Annual Meeting of the National Reading Conference, San Antonio, TX.

Meinbach, A.M., Rothlein, L., & Fredericks, A.D. (2000). *The complete guide to thematic units: Creating the integrated curriculum* (2nd ed.). Norwood, MA: Christopher-Gordon.

Paugh, B., McLaughlin, M., Call, B., & Vandever-Horvath, A. (2000). Poetry: A creative resource for teaching and learning in the content areas. In M. McLaughlin & M.E. Vogt (Eds.), *Creativity and innovation in content area teaching* (pp. 135–155). Norwood, MA: Christopher-Gordon.

Pearson, P.D. (2001, December). *What we have learned in 30 years.* Paper presented at the 51st Annual Meeting of the National Reading Conference, San Antonio, TX.

Readence, J.E., Bean, T.W., & Baldwin, R.S. (2000). *Content area reading: An integrated approach* (7th ed.). Dubuque, IA: Kendall Hunt.

Rosenblatt, L. (1980). What facts does this poem teach you? *Language Arts, 57*(4), 386–394.

Shanahan, T. (1997). Reading-writing relationships, thematic units, inquiry-learning...in pursuit of effective integrated literacy instruction. *The Reading Teacher, 51,* 12–19.

Shanahan, T., Robinson, B., & Schneider, M. (1995). Avoiding some of the pitfalls of thematic units. *The Reading Teacher, 48,* 718–719.

Short, K.G., Harste, J.C., & Burke, C.L. (1996). *Creating classrooms for authors and inquirers.* Portsmouth, NH: Heinemann.

Tompkins, G. (2001). *Literacy for the 21st century: A balanced approach* (2nd ed.). Saddlebrook, NJ: Prentice Hall.

Vacca, R.T., & Vacca, J.L. (2002). *Content area reading: Literacy and learning across the curriculum* (7th ed.). New York: Longman.

Wiggins, G., & McTighe, J. (1998). *Understanding by design*. Alexandria, VA: Association for Supervision and Curriculum Development.

Wood, K. (1984). Probable passages: A writing strategy. *The Reading Teacher, 37,* 496–499.